*Cruising in British
and Irish Waters*

# CRUISING IN BRITISH AND IRISH WATERS

## What to Do and See Afloat and Ashore

John Watney

120 black and white photographs
10 maps

DAVID & CHARLES
Newton Abbot   London   North Pomfret Vt

**British Library Cataloguing in Publication Data**

Watney, John
    Cruising in British and Irish waters.
    1. Coasts—Great Britain
    2. Boats and boating—Great Britain—Handbooks,
    manuals, etc.
    I. Title
    797.1′ 24     GV811.6

    ISBN 0-7153-8402-3

Typeset by Typesetters (Birmingham) Ltd,
and printed in Great Britain
by R. J. Acford Ltd, Chichester, Sussex
for David & Charles (Publishers) Limited
Brunel House     Newton Abbot     Devon

Published in the United States of America
by David & Charles Inc
North Pomfret     Vermont 05053     USA

# Contents

# Introduction

Some yachtsmen are happiest when they are making long passages out of sight of land for days at a time. The open sea is their playground, seamanship their creed, and an accurate landfall the reward for their navigational skill. For them the land itself is of secondary interest; time spent ashore is sailing time lost.

But the majority of boat owners and their families normally only make open-sea passages of necessity, to get from one coast to another. Much of their pleasure comes from watching the changing panorama of the coastline, exploring estuaries, creeks and lochs, finding picturesque anchorages, going ashore in strange places and renewing acquaintances in familiar havens.

Although few of them would admit it in the yacht club, they are tourists who travel by boat. What they will admit to is that they have more freedom, fun and companionship with far less aggravation than those tourists who have to keep to the roads. Certainly they get coastal views which people ashore never see and, when they arrive, it is usually to a far warmer welcome.

Unfortunately, because charts do not show more than the barest details of conspicuous landmarks and contours on their land areas, and because pilot guides and cruising directions are concerned almost exclusively with matters nautical, the average skipper and his crew often have little idea of what they are looking at as a strange coastline slips by. So much of interest is missed for lack of knowledge of the geography, history, flora, fauna and way of life of the land which they are passing.

When it comes to going ashore they often do not know which way to turn to make the best use of their time. Local information is usually available, but it needs searching out and they may not be ashore long enough to discover the points of interest, be they historic buildings, fine views or congenial pubs and restaurants. They may arrive late in the evening or on a Sunday when everything is closed – the Sabbath is a particularly bleak day for visitors in some parts of the British Isles.

All too often crews play safe and make for the local sailing club or go into the first pub they find, and when they leave they have really seen nothing and know nothing of the place they put in to. If they had known to walk a little further, or in a different direction, they might have found more interesting things to see and people to talk to. Their stay, however short, could have been memorable instead of just pleasant.

Many hundreds of books have been written by cruising authors and between them they cover almost every mile of the British coasts. But, with rare exceptions, they are written by people for whom sailing is a sufficient end in itself; they write at length about how to get there, but little about why it is worth going.

I have a different view. To me a boat is a vehicle which is best used for its original purpose of travelling from one place to another. The actual sailing I find challenging, exciting or relaxing and nearly always therapeutic, but it is only part of the pleasure of cruising. The other part is arriving. In some twenty years and a few thousand miles of travelling by boat I have more memories of places and people than I have of sea distances covered.

If those remarks raise a few eyebrows among my yachting friends, so be it; but I believe that there is a large minority – perhaps a small majority – of sailing families, if not always their skippers, who would agree with me. This book is written with them in mind. It is for people who travel or would wish to travel by boat, who are curious about what they see, have exploring minds, are interested in other people and how they live, and who like to use their legs. It is also for those who enjoy taking a tender up a creek or landing on a bird island as much as thrashing to windward surrounded by nothing but sea and sky.

This book is not an attempt to produce a cruising-man's gazetteer. It is largely a subjective account of some of my own coastal explorations by boat and on foot with a leavening of guidebook facts and figures. For the most part I have only described places inland which can be reached within an hour's walk of the nearest harbour or anchorage.

Those who know nothing about sailing but feel they might like cruising as a way of travelling should not be deterred by ignorance or the lack of a boat. There are many sailing schools which run cruising courses, charter boats with experienced skippers who are happy to take novices on board, and flotilla fleets which offer cruising in the company of others of modest experience. There are also several excellent sail-training organisations such as the Ocean Youth Club and the Island Cruising Club which take completely novice crews on quite adventurous cruises in large boats. Whether one remains a passenger or learns to become a useful crew member is up to the individual. The cost, even on the more expensive charter yachts, compares very favourably with the price of an hotel holiday.

Cruising is the only way left to travel free of the crowds. The world is an altogether nicer place seen from a boat with a little water between you and them.

South Stack Lighthouse on its 'pear-shaped islet'
some 100ft high and over 300yd long. The 380
steps up from it are a small nature trail

# 1 Holyhead and the West of Anglesey

When making for the North Wales coast by sea there are six proper harbours to choose from, and the shelter of the Menai Strait. Coming up from the south Aberdovey and Barmouth are the first available, but they are not easy for strangers and lie too far off the beaten track to be bases for cruising the area. Porthmadog is an excellent place once you are in, but it has a sometimes nasty bar and a tedious 3-mile channel from the bar buoy to the harbour. Small boats drawing no more than 3ft can, in fine weather, get in and out comfortably at half flood, but larger boats may have no more than an hour either side of high water. Strong onshore winds can cause very heavy seas on the bar and make entry frightening, if not dangerous. It is, therefore, not a wise choice as a first port of call when coming from a distance, but there are many reasons why it is well worth visiting when you have the time and when conditions are right.

Pwllheli, 10 miles westwards, is a much easier proposition and a favourite destination of crews sailing over from Ireland. The town is a seaside resort of little charm, but there are ample services and facilities for the visitor and it is a port of refuge in all conditions once there is sufficient water over the bar at the entrance. There will never be less than 5ft at half tide, and it never sets up anything more disconcerting than a good chop. In reasonable weather or offshore winds a mooring can be picked up in the anchorage just outside the bar while waiting for water. From there a tender can be sent ashore at any time. Pwllheli station is the western terminus of the Cambrian Coast Railway, one of BR's most scenic routes, but there are constant rumours of it being closed.

After Pwllheli the choice is either Caernarfon and Menai Strait or all the way to Holyhead. The Strait is without doubt the most fascinating water in this area, a cruising ground in its own right and an ideal base from which to set out to explore the rest of the coast. Deserving of a chapter of its own, I will first go on to Holyhead. If the weather is in any way unsettled with a chance of strong winds then, from whatever direction you are coming, Holyhead will always give you a very easy port to enter, and from there you can go out in any direction round the coast once you know what the weather is going to do.

From the south there are no very strong tides until Bardsey Island, after which they become far more crucial because round the coast of Anglesey both ebb and flood tides are quite strong – at springs in some parts a good 5 knots. If possible, time your arrival off Bardsey to take the whole of the flood the 30 miles up to Holyhead. Only those coming from Porthmadog, Pwllheli or Abersoch would use the inshore route through Bardsey Sound. It is best to lay a course which passes 1 mile west of Bardsey and 3 miles west of South and North Stacks on Holy Island. South Stack is a lighthouse, but North Stack is only a fog-signal station. In good visibility it may be possible to see Holyhead Mountain all the way, but in poor visibility you will be sailing out of sight of land for some time and even the North Wales mountains will disappear from view.

Between South and North Stacks there is a tidal race which, although not often dangerous, can be frightening; it is at its strongest at half ebb and half

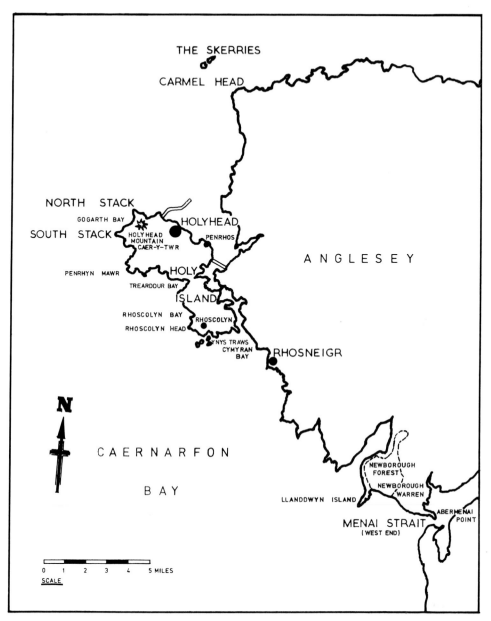

THE SKERRIES

CARMEL HEAD

NORTH STACK
GOGARTH BAY
SOUTH STACK
HOLYHEAD
HOLY HEAD
PENRHOS
MOUNTAIN
CAER-Y-TWR

ANGLESEY

PENRHYN MAWR
HOLY
TREARDDUR BAY

ISLAND

RHOSCOLYN BAY
RHOSCOLYN
RHOSCOLYN HEAD
YNYS TRAWS
CYMYRAN
BAY
RHOSNEIGR

N

CAERNARFON

BAY

NEWBOROUGH
FOREST
NEWBOROUGH
WARREN
LLANDDWYN ISLAND
ABERMENAI
POINT
MENAI STRAIT
(WEST END)

0   1   2   3   4   5 MILES
SCALE

flood. It is feasible to cut the corner and go close in to the two Stacks at slack water and then into Holyhead harbour, but if arrival cannot be timed right then anything less than 3 miles out could be a bit rough and, in gale winds, dangerous. If arriving before slack water you can sail through close in with the tide in light winds although there will still be overfalls because of the contours of the bottom. But coming from the south there will often be a following wind and the overfalls will make it extremely difficult not to jibe. If sailing in very light winds you may lose steerage way coming into an overfall, the violent motion will spill the wind out of the sails, and your boat will rock and the boom crash from side to side. If caught in that situation get the engine started and motor through it as quickly as possible. Boats have broken their masts rolling and jerking around there.

Once past North Stack, whether standing out or sailing close in, it is perfectly safe to turn directly towards the end of the Holyhead breakwater. It is 1¼ miles long, shaped like a dog leg, pointing north-east with a lighthouse (top half black, bottom half white) at its end. Allowing for the tide, steer a course to enter the harbour by passing close to the end of the breakwater but, having passed it, do not turn too quickly to starboard as there is a shingle spit running southwards from near the end of the breakwater. Holyhead Sailing Club has put a tiny conical buoy there which is almost too small to see. Stand on towards the aluminium-ore jetty until halfway there, and then turn to starboard and make for the yacht moorings on the south side of the harbour. Do not go round to the east side of the jetty. The yacht moorings are very obvious between Mackenzie Pier to the east and Trinity House flagstaff to the west.

There are normally a few vacant moorings to go on to. Go ashore to the Holyhead Sailing Club which has a slipway at the western end of the beach. The club administers the moorings and will usually be able to arrange one for a temporary stay. Facilities include a good bar, showers and hot meals during summer weekends (tel 0407 2526). The Coastguard Station is a prominent building on the sea front (tel 0407 2051), and they are always pleased to see visitors. The Holyhead Boatyard (tel 0407 2568) is beside Mackenzie Pier. It has a fuelling service, a runner lift, and can undertake repairs. Beside the landward end of the breakwater at Soldiers' Point there is a clean sandy beach where you can dry out between tides to work on your bottom.

The average depth in the area of the yacht moorings is between 25 and 30ft and there is perfect shelter except when the wind is from the east. It then has a fetch of about two miles right across the harbour and can build up an uncomfortable sea. April is the only month when such winds are at all frequent. Safe as the harbour is, I have seen the water pouring green over the great breakwater in a westerly gale, but that deluge was a long way from the club moorings and the anchorage in the armpit of the breakwater off Soldiers' Point. However, on the same day boats were blown upside down in the sailing-club dinghy park. I have had to stand anchor watch in the harbour during an early summer cyclonic storm which came in from the north-east. A most important local telephone number is the Met Office at RAF Valley (0407 2288) which is operational Monday to Friday, 9am to 5pm. They are very helpful and accurate. Otherwise telephone Cardiff Weather Centre (0222 397020) or Manchester Weather Centre (061 8326701).

The most direct approach to Holyhead is from Ireland. It is due east straight across from Dun Laoghaire until you see Holyhead Mountain and then alter course, if necessary, to come in between the tidal race off South and North Stacks and the tidal race off the Skerries, a 7-mile-wide gate. At night you pick up the South Stack Light and the Skerries Light. Make a course roughly between the two, but giving the Skerries a berth of at least 1 mile. Then pick up the breakwater light at the harbour entrance. The only possible danger coming into Holyhead is the group of Cliperau rocks off the mainland shore. They are marked by the Cliperau bell buoy 5 cables north-east of the end of the breakwater. It is a good rule if arriving from Ireland during the start of the ebb to aim for the Skerries, and if during the start of the flood to aim for the Stacks. Then any small error in landfall should put you up-tide of the breakwater; getting down-tide can cost you 6 hours.

Coming from the north and west a course should be set to stand 2–3 miles out round the Skerries then line up as if coming from Ireland. From Point Lynas on the north-east of Anglesey to the Skerries there is an increasing number of overfalls culminating in the Skerries overfalls which are quite severe. Although there is a gap of 2 miles, no attempt should be made to come in between the Skerries and Carmel Head in bad weather where there can be very steep seas and the area is thick with platters. A safe inshore passage close in under Carmel Head is only for those with local knowledge.

During the season Holyhead is normally a placid enough place to lie, and is also the obvious jumping off point for Ireland, the Isle of Man or a passage round Galloway to the Clyde and the Highlands and Islands beyond. The town itself has a rather grey aspect, and when I first sailed in there in the 1960s I thought little of it. There was no entertainment for the visitor and certainly no nightlife. A town of hotels, boarding houses and nondescript shops with no good eating to be had and dry on Sundays, I felt depressed at the thought of being stuck there for five days – as did George IV in 1821 waiting with unseemly impatience to hear if his queen had died. However, the place improves on closer acquaintance and has, in fact, picked up a lot in the last few years.

The harbour won new work when Southampton went on strike, and the sailing has grown immensely. The Holyhead Boatyard was a shambles when I first saw it, but is now a thoroughly modern complex with facilities to lift out yachts up to 80ft, moorings and winter storage. In 1975 they got the Shell pipeline-servicing contract for Amlwch and, for a time, rather forgot about yachtsmen. Now they are wooing them again. There are some 200 boats on the Holyhead Sailing Club trots, and the club itself is the best organised on the North Wales coast with a good launch service. It is the only one where you can get a three-course dinner at weekends; it has two bars, one for oilies and another upstairs for after you have used their superb showers. Holyhead is now the start point for several ocean races and, during the season, there is plenty of activity with boats coming from and going to the Isle of Man and Ireland and calling in from all round the coast. At weekends the harbour is alive with club racing, sailing-school dinghies and the ubiquitous sailboards.

Apart from boating, Holyhead and its environs have enough geographical and historical features to occupy a couple of days ashore. And Dublin is only 3½ hours away by the Holyhead–Dun Laoghaire ferry if the weather is a bit off-putting to do it in your own boat. Holy Island, which is joined to Anglesey by a causeway, has a long history of invasion by the ancient Irish and the Vikings who looted the monastery of St Cybi in AD 961. The walls round St Cybi (now the local church) between the High Street and the sea are the remains of an earlier Roman outpost. Elizabeth I authorised the first regular ferry service to Ireland, and in the time of James II and after the accession of William of Orange in 1689 Holyhead was a restricted area with sea patrols and a garrison on shore to prevent contact between disaffected persons of the Realm and the rebels in Ireland. The intractable 'Troubles' were old news even then.

The town began to grow in size and importance after the opening of Telford's iron suspension bridge over the Menai Strait in January 1826 completing the great London–Holyhead Road scheme, now the A5. In 1848 George Stephenson's tubular Britannia railway bridge, a mile south of the suspension bridge, heralded the night-sleeper service from London to Dublin. The railway station, with its curving canopy and heavily decorated cast-iron clock, was a classic example of Victorian industrial architecture. It was designed by Rennie and opened by Edward, Prince of Wales, on 17 June 1880. The train-ferry steamers actually berth inside the station alongside the platform. The Station Hotel has recently been demolished and the whole complex has undergone a major refit, so sadly there is now little remaining of the original Victoriana.

The breakwater, nearly 1½ miles long (7,860ft to be exact) and giving shelter to 667 acres of water, was for its time a mammoth civil-engineering feat. It was designed by James Meadows Rendal in 1845, work started on it in 1847, and it took 26 years of hard labour to finish it. Stone quarried from Holyhead Mountain was carried by railway trucks along an elevated timber staging and deposited in the sea at a rate of up to 24,000 tons a week. Rendal died in 1856, and the work was taken over by John Hawkshaw until its completion in 1873. He built himself a large white square castellated house on Soldiers' Point, a rocky outcrop on the shore, from which he could watch the work from his front windows. It is now an hotel, and the rock on which it stands and those around are Holyhead quartz-ite, the oldest rock in Britain and often visited by geology students with their little hammers. The top of the breakwater, 39ft above the low-water mark, is a promenade as good as any seaside pier, and longer too.

There is a walk which everybody with the time should find the energy to make – to the 722ft summit of Holyhead Mountain. The easiest way up is by a path on the way to South Stack lighthouse. Follow the coast footpath along the clifftop to the North Stack fog-signal station which is built on a spur of the mountain 150ft above the water. It overlooks the North Stack, a 60ft-high steep rock separated from the land by a gully, about 40ft wide, through which the sea often boils. But in fine weather when there is no swell running it can be navigated near high water by a good-size boat. The only purpose in doing so, except for the fun of it, would be to get a close view of the sea birds which inhabit the cliffs and the stack. The north-west side of Holy Island is renowned for its sea birds, but they are more clearly and safely observed from above than by sailing close inshore even in calm conditions – the high cliffs cause fluky winds, from the just disconcerting to fierce squalls.

After North Stack the path tends to go inland round Gogarth Bay towards South Stack, a mile further on. About halfway along there is a track up to the top of the mountain. Apart from a precipitous section on the west face, the summit is encircled by a dry-stone wall which is nearly 10ft high. It is thought to be the remains of an Iron Age fortress known as Caer-y-Twr. Whatever its purpose, it was supplied with water from a spring at the top of a gully which cuts down the north-west side of the mountain. The remains of a hermit's cell by the spring are now visible only to the trained eye.

Given a very clear day the top of the mountain provides an all-round panoramic view taking in the peaks of the Lake District, the Isle of Man, the mountains of County Down and the Wicklow Hills in Ireland, the Cambrian range and the length of the Snowdon range. Such days are rare in the season, but on all but the haziest it is possible to make a detailed study of the coastline below, the whole of Holyhead town and harbour and out to sea to Carmel Head and the Skerries.

Coming off the mountain take the path which leads south-west to South Stack. On the lower slope near a farm called Ty Mawr are some very good remains of a second- to fourth-century village of circular and rectangular huts, Cytiau'r Gwyddelod (212820). The remains of twenty huts out of an estimated fifty can still be seen, and some have central hearths and upright cut stones marking the positions of benches or beds. The line of protective earthworks can be traced running down to near the edge of the cliffs above the pinnacle Pen-Las stack in the bay called Abraham's Bosom. The stack separates two coves, Hen Borth and Porth-y-Gwyddel, which provided landing places for the inhabitants of the village and almost certainly also for the Irish invaders who attacked them.

The village is only 2½ miles from the outskirts of Holyhead, an easy walk keeping to the base of the mountain, but for the more idle and those with small children, there is a bus service from the town which turns round at the South Stack car park a few hundred yards beyond the signpost to the prehistoric village. The lighthouse, which is open from 1400hrs until sunset, is a popular tourist site. It was built in 1808 by Daniel Alexander, who also built Dartmoor Prison.

South Stack itself is a flat-topped pear-shaped islet about 100ft high and over 300yd long. The tall white tower of the lighthouse and the white lightkeepers' houses are surrounded by white stone walls. On the end of the Stack is the foghorn which, from seawards, looks a bit like a large section of honeycomb. The 'stalk' of the islet is a chain suspension bridge spanning the gap between the Stack and the cliff face. Below the bridge the sea flows fast through a rock-strewn gorge just over 160ft wide. The level of the bridge, nearly 100ft above low water, makes a grandstand from which to view the cliffs marching away to the north and south with more often than not a white frill of breaking water at their feet. From the bridge 380 steps zig-zag up to the road above.

The steps ascending over 160ft constitute a small nature trail with observation points marked by numbers on the wall which correspond to the numbers in a descriptive leaflet issued by the North Wales Nature Trust. At the top the heath vegetation – gorse, heather and tormentil – takes over from the cliff plants: thrift, scurvy grass and wild thyme, squill (a relative of the bluebell), English stonecrop, sea campion, kidney vetch, wild carrot and golden samphire. The bare rockfaces support a variety of green and yellow lichens, the abundance of which indicates the pollution-free atmosphere. Those noisy scavengers, herring gulls, take up most of the air space and foul the cliffs, but puffin, razorbill and guillemot also breed on South Stack, as do fulmar which a century ago were confined to St Kilda out in the Atlantic off the Outer Hebrides. They then started spreading and arrived to nest on Anglesey in 1948.

The rocks are formed of deposits of sand and mud laid down under the sea 800 million years ago. Under the weight of subsequent sediments they were compacted into sandstones and shales. While still under the sea they were metamorphosed by pressures generated by earthquakes and volcanic activity of the earth's crust producing the curvy folds which can be seen today. They were thrust up from the sea by later crust movements some 400 million years ago and have since been worn and sculpted by rain, wind, frost, glaciation and marine erosion. The original sandstones are much harder than the shales, which have eroded more, leaving convenient ledges for the nesting sea birds. That note on the South Stack nature trail can largely be applied to the whole cliff coastline of north and west Anglesey.

From the top of the steps leading from the lighthouse, if the sun is shining and the sky blue, the scene below with its geometric pattern of white buildings and walls, is suggestive of a Greek island monastery. If your intention is to climb up inside the lighthouse and look at the lantern and its beautifully polished brass clockwork try and time your arrival outside school holidays when there is likely to be a patient queue at the door. At those times the lantern room will be too full of people to get a long close look at everything, and the keepers must perforce keep their lecture short. Also be ready for a big surprise if there is sea mist about. One clear August afternoon in 1981 I walked all the way from Holyhead to the top of the steps above the lighthouse, arriving just in time to see the stack and the lighthouse vanish in seconds as a thick damp fog rolled in from the sea. It was while waiting for the fog to lift that I found the South Stack Kitchen 200 yards from the car park. Outwardly it looks like yet another trippers' cafe and souvenir shop, but inside the cafeteria is way above average, serving homemade bread, cakes, pies, soups and pâtés. In another part, separated from the sight and sound of coach parties, is a pleasant restaurant which is open for luncheon every day and for dinner on Fridays and Saturdays only. The wine list was surprisingly good.

Back in Holyhead there is another less spectacular nature trail to the east of the town at Penrhos at the end of the Stanley Embankment, which carries the road and railway on to Holy Island. It is the concept of a local ex-policeman, Ken

Williams, and has thirteen viewing stations illustrating rocky and sandy coast, woodland, lakes and some archaeological remains. Two miles from the town centre along the A5, it is an effortless walk along the flat, but the trail itself wanders for 5 miles so it is a half-day expedition to see it all. Entry is free and there is a canteen and shop.

A first day sail from Holyhead might be south to Trearddur Bay, a very pretty group of coves and islets with a big sandy beach. It has its own special sailing community which races 20ft Seabird half-raters (a local class started in 1900, and some of the boats are actually that old) which were imported from Lancashire. They were probably brought in by the new affluent merchants and industrialists who have been colonising Trearddur Bay with holiday homes since the turn of the century. Ashore it is regarded as a 'posh' place and is still expanding further and further inland with mushroom growths of boxey holiday homes for letting. It has several hotels and boarding houses. Sailing there past North and South Stacks and round Penrhyn Mawr the scenery is wonderful, and when you arrive the coves are ideal for swimming, skin diving or snorkelling – you can see your anchor in 12ft of water. Most summer days dinghy sails flutter in and out between the rocks like butterflies, and the many sandy-bottomed pools echo with the sound of children. This pretty, animated postcard scene can be enjoyed from an anchored boat without getting involved in the crowds ashore. Out of season you will have a choice of pools and coves all to yourself and can go ashore for a drink and a meal in peace.

The trip should be planned for a day when Holyhead high water is in the morning and leaving an hour before to arrive off South Stack at slack water. A course can then be taken close to the lighthouse, and from there on it is a clear passage due south with the ebb down to the headland, Penrhyn Mawr. Once that is cleared Trearddur Bay is in sight to the east. It is best to anchor in the main bay off Towyn-y-Capel beach in an area about 150 yards north of the flagstaff on the south side of the bay. It is the most obvious bay with the big sandy beach, and there will be 1½ fathoms at low-water springs. Then visit the coves by tender. Trearddur Bay Boatyard (tel 0407 860501) is in Porth Diana, the cove south of the anchorage suggested above. It has a small chandlery and can supply diesel, calor gas and water. If you draw more than 3ft you can only get into this cove within 2 hours either side of high water. If returning to Holyhead leave on the last of the ebb, which will be weak up to South Stack which can then be rounded at slack water and you will have the early flood up to Holyhead.

Approaching Trearddur Bay from the south there is plenty of water off Ravens Point; round it, head into the middle of the bay and then go in. A small, uncharted overfall off the point may surprise, but is of no consequence. There is ample room in the bay to tack the average-size family cruiser against an onshore wind, providing it is not too strong. Except in the most settled weather, it is not a good place to anchor overnight. Better than Trearddur Bay in north winds, and one of the most picturesque anchorages in Anglesey, is off Porth Dafarch where there is about 16ft at low water. If continuing south Rhoscolyn Bay is a suitable night stop. South-west of Rhoscolyn Bay there is a small tide race off the end of the Beacon Rocks so most people give them a fair berth but, if conditions allow, it is interesting to sail close by to look at their colony of Atlantic and grey seals. On the west shore of Rhoscolyn Bay there is an old lifeboat house, and in front of it an island, Ynys Traws, with a cairn on top. The water in between looks like the entrance, but it is not. Keep a good 100 yards away from the island until you are well east of it, and then go in on a heading for Rhoscolyn church on a hill about one mile inland. Do not go too far into the bay as there are rocks near the shore, which dries 200 yards. Maen Piscar is a very dangerous rock which dries 5½ft but is usually just below the surface. It is almost exactly on a direct line between Rhoscolyn Head and Penrhyn Mawr – clearly marked on all charts at about seven cables north-west of Rhoscolyn Head. It has sunk two yachts in the past few years. To avoid it keep a half-mile seaward of the direct line between Rhoscolyn Head and Penrhyn Mawr when approaching from the south until Trearddur Bay beach is open and then go straight in. Alternatively, keep within 2 cables of the cliffs after rounding Rhoscolyn Head and go inside the rock. The echo sounder is not much help as it is an isolated pinnacle.

The bay gives access to good cliff walks in both directions, and if you go west to Rhoscolyn Point you may find St Gwenfaen's Well whose water was reputed to cure mental disorders. A mile walk the other way around Silver Bay takes you to the shore of the inland sea which divides Holy Island from Anglesey. It dries to a trickle at low tide and is the haunt of waders and wild fowl. There was once a very good reason for visiting Rhoscolyn, and that was to eat at the White Eagle, one of the best restaurants in Wales. Situated on the cliff top it commanded a fine view. It is now a pub which does bar snacks.

I would suggest giving Rhosneigr and the next ten miles of coast a good offing after which I highly recommend a stop in Pilot's Cove and a visit to Llanddwyn Island (3862), one of the most delightful places to go ashore for a walk while cruising hereabouts. As the Michelin Guide would say: 'It is well worth a journey'. The island is about a mile long and a mere 600 yards at its widest. It is a knobbly, grass- and sand-covered terrain rising to only about 50ft with rocky coves all round it. The rocks are awesome and amongst the oldest in the country – not less than 600 million years old. An old tower built in 1873 (once the lighthouse with its lantern projecting from the ground floor), an 1800 'pepper pot' with a flashing light now atop it, the remains of a priory, a row of pilots' cottages recently restored for the wardens and to house a Nature Conservancy exhibition, a Celtic cross and a magic wishing well are the man-made offerings. But most of all it is a nature reserve. Of all the places that I have visited around the North Wales coast, Llanddwyn Island is one of the most memorable. It is a natural garden of wild flowers, and a small sanctuary of animal and bird life.

The west side is a miniature 'Côte Sauvage', open to the prevailing winds with the sea rushing in and out between the rocks and, on windy days or when there is a heavy swell, sending spouts of water and spumes of spray into the air. The east side is sheltered and tranquil, except in exceptional easterlies, with sandy coves. A causeway leads to Newborough Forest, again full of animal and plant life with several Forestry paths for the public. Running west from the causeway is a superb beach of firm but silky-white sand 3½ miles long backed by Newborough Warren – an expanse of mobile dunes held in check by marram grass. Near the beach can be found a great variety of dune plants and flowers which are extinct in most other parts of Britain. The dunes are also the home of many mammals and a large assortment of birds. There is a very well thought-out Forestry information hut by the car park just off the beach where everything is illustrated and explained and leaflets are available to help the novice naturalist. For children the beach is bliss. And what finer 'sand castle' than the family bilge keeler halfway up it. These sands are so extensive that even the hundreds of trippers (in high season) are no deterrent, but many of them make the walk over to Llanddwyn Island where they do crowd the few public paths. Then the island is best visited before 10am, but that is no problem if you have anchored in Pilot's Cove overnight.

The south-western extremity of Llanddwyn Island breaks up into three prongs of islets and rocks, the furthest out being South West Rock 3½ cables offshore. To the west of the prongs are Bird Rocks (which are true to their name). All these rocks need to be cleared if coming from the west as there is no anchorage or shelter of any kind on the western side of the island. There are several well-used inshore passages between the rocks known to local people. The visitor, however, should take the outer course around the South West Rock buoy, which is half a cable south of the rock. Then head north-north-east towards the buoy marking South East Rock, which lies opposite Pilot's Cove. The anchorage is just off the mouth of the cove on a line between the 'pepper pot' on the end of the island and the seaward end of the Well Rocks, which form the north-east arm of the cove. With the wind in the west there is good shelter in about three fathoms. When there are south-westerly gales, a bad swell and a breaking sea at low water run into the cove. Strong winds from the south and south-east could also be most uncomfortable. In fine weather and for a stay of only a few hours it is possible to anchor inside the cove nearer the beach soon after the early flood until near the end of the ebb, when almost the whole of it dries out.

There are two other possible anchorages: Mermaid Cove, about two cables further along the shore, and Porth Dafydd Owen in the north-east corner of the island. Apart from its charm and interest, Llanddwyn Island is a very useful 'lay by' for boats waiting for water to go over the Caernarfon bar. For example, if, after leaving Holyhead, you want to go into Caernarfon or further up the Menai Strait and you have kept sailing with the tide all the way, there will probably be from one to two hours of ebb still to flow and little water over the bar. There will also be the ebb coming out of the Strait against you. You will then need a further two hours of flood to give you enough water over the bar – a wait of up to four hours. In reasonable weather Pilot's Cove is the place in which to wait.

Porth Dinllaen, a boat-building place last
century, now a cluster of holiday cottages. The
public can approach its Ty Coch Inn only by
foot along the clifftop, along the beach or by
boat

*2 The Lleyn Peninsula*

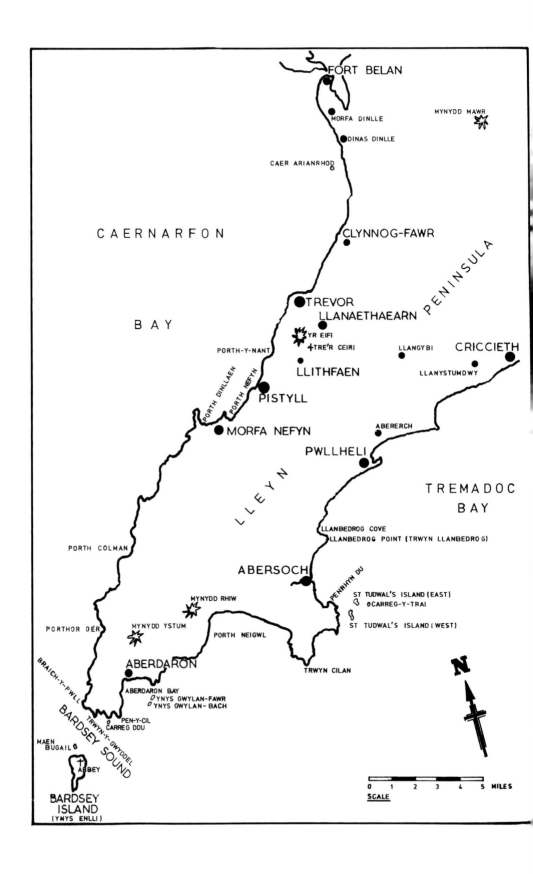

FORT BELAN

MYNYDD MAWR

MORFA DINLLE

DINAS DINLLE

CAER ARIANRHOD

CAERNARFON

CLYNNOG-FAWR

PENINSULA

BAY

TREVOR
LLANAETHAEARN

YR EIFI

PORTH-Y-NANT

TRE'R CEIRI

LLANGYBI

CRICCIETH

LLITHFAEN

LLANYSTUMDWY

PORTH DINLLAEN

PORTH NEFYN

PISTYLL

ABERERCH

MORFA NEFYN

PWLLHELI

LLEYN

TREMADOC
BAY

PORTH COLMAN

LLANBEDROG COVE
LLANBEDROG POINT (TRWYN LLANBEDROG)

ABERSOCH

PENRHYN DU

ST TUDWAL'S ISLAND (EAST)

MYNYDD RHIW

CARREG-Y-TRAI

MYNYDD YSTUM

PORTH NEIGWL

ST TUDWAL'S ISLAND (WEST)

PORTHOR OÉR

ABERDARON

TRWYN CILAN

BRAICH-Y-PWLL

ABERDARON BAY
YNYS GWYLAN-FAWR
YNYS GWYLAN-BACH

TRWYN-Y-GWYDDEL

PEN-Y-CIL
CARREG DDU

BARDSEY SOUND

MAEN
BUGAIL

ABBEY

N

BARDSEY
ISLAND
(YNYS ENLLI)

0 1 2 3 4 5 MILES
SCALE

The Lleyn Peninsula (OS 123) points south-west from Morfa Dinlle – a sand-duned spit tipped by Fort Belan at the entrance to the Menai Strait – to Braich-y-Pwll, the most westerly point of Wales at the entrance to Bardsey Sound, a distance of 30 miles and presenting some of the most dramatic coastal scenery in North Wales. At the start of a passage from either Llanddwyn or the Strait, the Snowdon range and Snowdon itself can be seen on the port hand. Then the hills of the peninsula keep you company. High and rounded with emerald-green skirts dotted with sheep, and purple and brown tops, they march all the way down to Bardsey Sound, some creeping a little way inland, others dropping precipitously to the sea. Between them are cliff-girt sandy coves, most of them tempting anchorages but only to be trusted in settled weather. The final drama is passing under the 400ft almost-sheer wall of Mynydd Mawr going through the Sound.

The route is exposed to the prevailing winds, south-westerlies in summer and north-easterlies in spring, which blow along its length and the only reasonable shelter is Porth Dinllaen, and that is wide open to the north. A cruise, as opposed to a straight passage, should therefore be planned for a day or two of fine settled weather. A day or two for 30 miles? Yes indeed, because for the curious and energetic there is something for them ashore nearly all the way.

The Lleyn Peninsula was well inhabited during the late Bronze and Iron Ages, and the remains of stone-hut villages can be found on many hill tops, and on the flat bits of coast are the traces of fortifications built by the Irish and Scandinavian invaders during their many efforts at colonisation which went on into the tenth century. There is scant evidence of any Roman occupation of what was then a stronghold of Celtic tribes. After the Romans had left Britain another 'invasion' started which has left its mark on Lleyn to this day. It was the arrival of the early Christian missionaries from Ireland, and the founding of a Celtic monastery on Bardsey Island in the sixth century by one Einion Frenhin. The monastic community was soon increased by the survivors of the massacre of the monks at Bangor-is-Coed by the Saxon King Ethelfrid in 615 at a time when the Roman church was beginning to establish itself in England.

In the thirteenth century an Augustine abbey was built on the island dedicated to St Mary, and its ruins can be seen today. St Mary's fame grew as a place of such great sanctity that a couple of pilgrimages to Bardsey became worth, in indulgences, a single trip to Rome. But North Wales to the rest of the Christian world was then a most remote place and the Lleyn Peninsula the remotest part of it, added to which there was the crossing of the Sound with its wicked tidal stream and often turbulent water in a boat probably no more robust than a coracle. There are said to be 20,000 saints buried on the island – surely a romantic exaggeration!

The pilgrim route to Bardsey lay along both coastlines of the peninsula and converged on Aberdaron, from where the sea crossing had to be made. A chain of churches, hospices and holy wells was established along both routes, and the more or less intact remains of many of them can still be found within a short walk of the sea. But none can be seen from offshore as they were invariably sited in hollows to hide them from the greedy eyes of coastal marauders. The people of the Lleyn Peninsula have always resisted outsiders whether Romans, seaborne invaders or the English, and today are mostly staunch Welsh Nationalists. But because of its insular position they have been spared involvement in the battles and conflicts which have plagued other parts of Wales.

The terrain is a mixture of high moorland with a few craggy peaks, and fertile farmland in the valleys and along the coastal slopes. Until quite recently quarrying was an important industry with the stone being shipped out by sea. The shoreline is dotted with abandoned quarry ports and jetties which, with one exception, can no longer be used by boats but do provide some landing place for tenders. By far the best way to explore the Lleyn Peninsula is by car on the roads which approximately follow the pilgrim route, with frequent sallies on foot to hilltop and coast sites. However, in calm weather and with time to spare, most of the places worth visiting can be reached within a one hour's walk of an anchorage.

With an inshore tidal stream of less than 2 knots and the prevailing south-westerlies, it is impractical to sail down the coast and make the distance from Caernarfon to Bardsey Sound in one ebb tide in order to get through the Sound on the last of the ebb or just on slack water. If time dictates getting to the Sound on one tide you will have to be satisfied with a more distant view of the coastline and set a course out into Caernarfon Bay to pick up the main stream flowing across its chord – a line from South Stack to the west of Bardsey Island – when you will have 3½ knots or more under you. But short tacking down the coast is well worthwhile if you are in no hurry. A full day stop-over at Porth Dinllaen would allow for a good expedition ashore, an evening in the pub (try not to make it a Sunday) and a night at anchor before picking up the ebb the next day.

The first 12 miles is across a very shallow bay between the sand dunes of Morfa Dinlle and the cliffs at Trevor at the foot of the seaward peak of Yr Eifl; the shoreline is flat with pebble beaches. At Dinas Dinlle the silhouette of a high mound with a trig point on top is the site of a coastal fort of c100 BC. There is nothing else to see and it is flanked by a shanty-town holiday development. It is not a good stopping place, being exposed and drying far out. A few super optimists search the low-tide mark with metal detectors in the hope of finding gold coins from the wreck of a full-rigged Spanish ship which foundered there at the end of the eighteenth century. A mile south is the small hazard of Caer Arianrhod, a rock which dries at low-water springs. It is 1,000 yards offshore and is, in fact, the remaining stonework of the Castle of Arianrhod believed to have stood there before the sixth century AD. Arianrhod features in the Welsh Triads as one of the three most beautiful women in Britain.

Further down the coast Clynnog-fawr should be visited, either by anchoring off the beach and using the tender if it is a calm day, or by putting into Trevor 3 miles further on and walking back. For so small a village it has a surprisingly large church, looking more like a scaled-down cathedral. It stands on ground hallowed since AD 630 when it was given to St Beuno, the most famous of the Celtic saints, for a sanctuary which became richly endowed by pilgrims on their way to Bardsey. Its holy well is found behind a gate beside the road 200 yards away and still has water in it. The pilgrims believed that the water had great healing powers, but it was a kill-or-cure treatment. After bathing in the well the patient had to lie all night on the cold slab of St Beuno's tomb. Belief in the efficacy of this treatment lasted for many centuries. Thomas Pennant who toured Wales in 1170 wrote:

> In the midst [of the church] is the tomb of the saint plain and altar shaped. It was customary to cover it with rushes and leave on it till morning sick children, after making them first undergo ablutions in the neighbouring holy well; and I myself once saw on it a poor paralytic from Merionethshire who had laid the whole night after undergoing the same ceremony.

A monastery of Cistercian monks was established round the original sanctuary, then in the thirteenth century it became a collegiate church and continued as such until the time of Henry VIII. The present church dating from 1530, with parts of earlier buildings, is late perpendicular in style and cruciform in shape. Inside there is a restored rood screen, Tudor stalls and misericord. Among the antiquities is a pair of iron dog tongs used to deal with unruly animals during services, a stone incised with a cross and said to have been made by the saint himself when he was given the grant of land, and a 4ft-long strong chest made from a single piece of timber with three locks. Until a little over a hundred years ago the custom persisted of offering to the church animals with the mark of St Beuno on them – a slit sometimes found on the ears of Welsh cattle at birth. These animals were sold by the church wardens on Trinity Sunday and the proceeds placed in the chest. In the churchyard there is an ancient Saxon sundial marking the times of the canonical hours. Between the church and the sea stands a fine cromlech, Bach Wen Penarth, 8ft long, 5ft wide and 6ft high. It can be reached by a farm road beside the church leading to Bach Wen farm.

Going south-west from Clynnog-fawr along the A499 the ground rises steeply inshore to heights of 1,500ft and ahead is the distinctive line of the three peaks of Yr Eifl and the old quarry port of Trevor. A pier points north from the disused quay in the west end of a small cove. There is about 8ft of water alongside the quay at high-water neaps, but the whole cove dries out at low water. If you get in in time and take the ground or lie against the quay you will be sheltered from all but northerly winds. But it is a desolate and unattractive place dominated by quarry workings high up the hillside which, incidentally, produce high-quality curling stones. The cove is 'paved' with flat rocks with a sand bottom only near the quay. Also beware of strong gusts off the land in easterly winds, and a surge alongside the quay when gales are blowing in the Irish Sea from any direction.

Trevor is a poor alternative to Porth Dinllaen, the next shelter 9 miles on, but it gives the nearest access to the most fascinating stretch of this seaboard. It is a good 30-minute uphill walk from Trevor inland to Llanaelhaearn, nearly 300ft above sea level. Here there is a church dating back to the sixth century with curious inscriptions attributed to pilgrims, and also St Aelhaearn's well, once used by pilgrims and now part of the village water supply. From the village it is nearly a mile up the B4417 to the signpost to the Iron Age fort Tre'r Ceiri which crowns the most easterly peak of Yr Eifl.

The climb up the well-marked path is worth the effort both for the views from the top of the whole peninsula and for the archaeological interest of Tre'r Ceiri (Town of the Giants) arguably the most dramatic Iron Age fortification in Britain, certainly in Wales. It covers an area of 5 acres surrounded by large dry-stone walls enclosing several groups of huts, each facing into a common courtyard. Traces remain of a defensive stone parapet and walkway inside the wall, and also parts of two outer walls. It was probably first built in the late Bronze Age by the Goidels and remained occupied through the Iron Age and into the time of the Roman occupation. Time and the feet of thousands of careless visitors have reduced many of the stone walls to shapeless piles, but some still stand as high as 15ft.

The topography of the Lleyn Peninsula was first revealed to me from above the fort before I ever saw it from the sea. A friend who keeps his boat at Caernarfon took me there instead of going for a day sail because, he said, it would be more instructive. It was. I have been back three times since, but have never been lucky enough to have clear visibility. On the last occasion the rain came down as I reached the summit, and the wind drove me wet and shivering into the remaining shelter of a Goidel's hut. Life must have been very hard up there 2,000 years ago with a 1,000ft walk up and down to farm the lower slopes. At least the climate was warmer then.

On the west side of Yr Eifl where the seaward peak slopes steeply down to the sea is a deep cwm known as Vortigern's Ravine and marked on the OS map as Nant Gwrtheyrn (350448). A rocky rutted path drops by hairpin bends nearly 900ft in half a mile to a deserted village on a grassy ledge above the sea. The steep sides have been planted with trees by the Forestry Commission – one wonders how – and it is not until the last moment that one sees the village and the sea beyond. In places the gradient is about 1 in 3, and the walk back is a taxing exercise for all but the fittest. It was in this brooding place that the outcast King Vortigern sought refuge in his castle after betraying the British to the Jutes under Hengist and Horsa in AD 499. Nature avenged his people; he died a violent death in his burning castle after it was struck by lightning.

In more recent times a community of farmers scraped a living off the small amount of fertile land there. With the coming of the Industrial Revolution the face of Yr Eifl was quarried for granite, and a completely self-contained model village was built for the workforce with a chapel, school and a row of two-storey houses round two sides of a green, enclosed by a stone wall. Outside the wall a grander house was built for the quarry manager with a pretentious little drive. Everything needed for the village and its quarry had to come by sea, except for what could be brought by foot or by horse-drawn sled down the ravine. The quarry closed in the 1950s, and the broken lumps of the quay and twisted skeleton of the loading pier lie awash on the beach. The houses now stand empty with the wind whistling and moaning through the sightless windows, and the manager's drive is overgrown. At one time it became a hippy commune, but that did not last long. The climb out of the ravine and the mile walk to the nearest shop must have been too much for them.

On my last visit in 1981 desultory work was going on to renovate some of the houses by the Welsh Language Society with a view to establishing a summer language school. I did not meet the brave man who brought in the building materials by Land-Rover. Even with a short-wheel-base model most of the bends need a three-point turn to negotiate with a sheer drop on one side. The top of the ravine is reached by taking the minor road north out of the village of Llithfaen soon after leaving the track down from Tre'r Ceiri, or in calm weather by anchoring in Porth-y-Nant Bay and landing on the beach. It is then a steep walk up to the village and thence up the ravine. But if you have the energy you will return on board having seen something quite unusual.

To visit the next pilgrim church and the most charming of them all – St Beuno's at Pistyll (328420) – it would be better to put into Porth Dinllaen and walk from there. In light airs or with the wind in the south or east it would be reasonable to anchor in Porth Nefyn Bay and walk along the beach to the path which leads up to the road near Pistyll. St Beuno's Church lies in a hollow beside the road well hidden from the sea, and so tiny that it might at first be mistaken for a small farm building. It is of certain Celtic origin, although the date 1050 is carved in stone above the altar window. The arch above the little doorway is Romanesque, and the stone font Celtic. The symbols carved round it depict life without beginning or end somewhat in the manner of the symbols on Buddhist prayer wheels. A feature of great interest is the leper's window on the north side through which they watched the raising of the Host. Before being slated about a hundred years ago, the church was thatched and must have looked very much like a byre and is equally dark inside. Apart from the aperture of the leper's window, there are only two small windows in the chancel, but the congregations being illiterate had no need of light in their part of the church. Beneath the altar is buried a tall saint, or at least a tall person, one of three such remains with claims to being those of St Beuno himself.

When I first visited this little single-cell sanctuary some years ago it was Harvest Festival time and the dim interior was a profusion of autumn flowers, grasses and farm produce lit by dozens of little candles in foil cake cups. The whole place was a pot-pourri of country scents. On another occasion I was there on the Saturday before Easter and saw the pretty sight of a procession of village children carrying bunches of flowers and greenery down the path to the church.

St Beuno's is no dead monument, but a living place of worship with a service being held at 3pm every Sunday throughout the year. In the oval churchyard is the grave of Rupert Davies of Maigret fame. I will always remember it as it was when I first came across it in its little hollow, hiding from marauders from the sea and, more recently, from the road. Now its peace and quiet have been rudely disturbed by a rash of roadside signs advertising a camp site, gift shop and pony-trekking centre which have been developed around it. Nothing is sacred to the tourist industry.

Porth Dinllaen is a beach-side village tucked into the west corner of Dinllaen Bay and protected by a north-pointing headland, on top of which are nine of the eighteen holes of the local golf course. In the eighteenth and early nineteenth centuries it was a shipbuilding and coastal trading port – it was visited by no less than 700 ships in 1804 – and there were great hopes at one time that it would become the railhead for Ireland, but Holyhead was chosen instead. The shipbuilding slipways have long since vanished and the pier, built in anticipation of the packet boats which never came, is in ruins. The cluster of cottages between the cliff and the beach is brightly painted and, when the sun shines, gives the place the look of a Mediterranean fishing village. But it is no longer a real village for they are all holiday homes. The Ty Coch Inn is still in business and very much a yachtsman's pub. Boats which can take the ground can anchor within a stone's throw of the bar door, and their crews walk to the pub dry shod in their wellies. Otherwise boats can anchor in about three fathoms just south of the lifeboat slip within a short row of the beach.

The 90ft-high headland gives this anchorage good shelter in all but north and north-easterly winds, and many local boats have moorings there throughout the summer. Running eastwards is the 2-mile-long crescent of Dinllaen beach, which is ideal for children. There is no public road across the golf course to Porth Dinllaen, but a steep lane runs from the village of Morfa Nefyn down to the centre of the beach and is much used for launching trailed boats. There is a Coastguard Station next door to the golf club on the clifftop overlooking the bay, and a footpath leads to a Coastguard lookout and traces of a prehistoric fort on the end of the headland. The best approach to Porth Dinllaen is to the east of the beacon on Careg y Chwislen, then head south until the pub comes into view and make towards it. There is a way in between the beacon and the headland, but there are off lying rocks to be avoided.

The shortest walk to the local village, Morfa Nefyn, is along the beach to the steep lane. It is a bungalow development of no interest apart from shops, but Nefyn, the small town a mile further along the road, is worth visiting. Take an empty bottle with you and fill it with water from St Mary's Well. I have never tasted water like it before; it is as enjoyable as anything you can get in the pub across the road. The original well covered 20sq yd with benches for pilgrims to sit on and recesses in a 10ft-high wall in which they stowed their belongings while they rested. In 1868 the corporation rebuilt it in the form of a typical

Porth Dinllaen provides reasonable shelter except in northerlies. In fair weather it is a good port for exploring the Lleyn Peninsula and its rich archaeological sites. There is a golf course on the top of the headland

Victorian monument, and the water now comes out of a pipe near the ground and runs away down a drain. The water may not look good, but it certainly tastes good. St Mary's church, which dates back to the fifth century, is a plain rectangular building with a square tower, topped by a weather vane in the shape of a brigantine of the type which used to be built at Porth Dinllaen. When I visited the church some years ago it was derelict, vandalised and locked. The tower had been taken over by a large flock of pigeons, and the caretaker was making himself some pocket money selling their droppings for garden fertiliser. The place has since been repaired and turned into a local museum.

Pistyll and St Beuno's church are 2 miles further up the road. For some hill walking there is Garn Boduan, a conical mountain 918ft high half-a-mile south of Nefyn. On the summit are the remains of the ramparts and hut circles of a fortified village similar to Tre'r Ceiri, but not so extensive. Nearby there is a large flat stone known as Bwrdd-y-Brenin (the King's Table) under which – legend has it – a hoard of gold is buried. The coast onwards from Porth Dinllaen to Braich-y-Pwll is a succession of rocky coves and sandy bays with three distinct headlands. There is a sub-aqua centre on Traeth Penllech in Colmon Bay, a popular fair-weather anchorage. Another place to go ashore is Porth Oer for a walk on the Whistling Sands, so called because they make a squeaking or whistling sound underfoot.

Altogether there are twelve porths, or bays, to choose from on this 12-mile length of coast, all of which are safe in fine weather with little wind and no swell, but there are times when they become good surfing beaches. Some are popular, with road signs directing people to clifftop car parks, others have no access and are likely to be deserted even in the summer holidays. The seaboard is very rural and probably not much changed since the days when pilgrims walked along the shore on their way to Bardsey. For the last 2 miles the ground rises over 500ft to the summit of Mynydd Mawr overlooking Bardsey Sound. Before reaching that end of the peninsula it may be necessary to make about 1½ miles out to sea to avoid the overfalls of the Tripods, three miniature mountains rising from the sea bed, which at times cause a very confused sea; nothing dangerous in moderate weather, but uncomfortable. Although there are at least 5½ fathoms over them, they are best avoided in strong winds and when the full flood or ebb is running.

In light winds the passage can be made through Bardsey Sound during the last of the ebb, but if there is a strong wind blowing, especially from the south-west across the tide, then it would be far wiser to wait for slack water. That may mean waiting for about 2 hours heading the flood coming up the west side of Bardsey Island at about 3½ knots. It would then be better to stand out and make the detour round the south of the island. In the Sound there is a minimum depth of 13 fathoms everywhere and only two rocks to be avoided. One is Carreg Ddu, lying about a cable off the mainland shore below the cliffs at Trwyn Bychestyn. Depending on the state of the tide, there can be turbulent overfalls immediately to the east or west of that rock. The other rock is Maen Bugail off the northern tip of Bardsey Island, but there should be no need to go anywhere near it. The tidal stream through the Sound runs at up to 6 knots in normal conditions, and it would be senseless to try and force a passage against the tide either way.

The Sound should never be attempted in winds over force 5; anything greater would be treacherous. If circumstances demand that a detour is made round Bardsey Island, it should be made well to the west of it to clear some off-lying overfalls and then follow an easterly track to clear the south-western tip of the island close inshore between Ship Ledge and the island. A more circuitous route is to proceed further south and then turn east keeping clear of the Bostram Shoals.

Then an easterly or northerly course, depending on the route taken, can be set for the shelter of Aberdaron Bay. The anchor should be dropped inside the bay somewhere on a line between the twin islands of Ynys Gwylan Bach and Ynys Gwylan Fawr and the village, and well inside the shelter of the westerly point of Pen-y-Cil. Small boats can anchor within a cable of the beach opposite the church to seaward of the line of orange buoys marking the limits of the water-skiing area. This anchorage is only tenable in settled weather or offshore winds. It is vital that the anchor is holding. At most states of the tide the stream makes an anti-clockwise sweep of the bay. It could sweep a boat out of the bay and into the Sound; an anchor watch is wise here. When going ashore in the tender pick your landing place with care as there are a number of rocks just off the beach. In the village are two pubs and some small shops. It was from Aberdaron that all those saints and pilgrims set off for Bardsey Island in ancient times.

On the site of the original communal kitchen for the pilgrims there is a seventeenth-century building whose kitchen now provides cafe meals for holidaymakers. The dark austere church stands a little above and only a few feet from the beach, but a few hundred years ago it was well inland. It was saved from being washed into the sea by the building of a sea wall around 1860. The Post Office which fits in well with the white plastered stone cottages was designed by Clough Williams-Ellis of Portmeirion fame. It is a decidedly pretty village which would be at home in Cornwall. Unhappily the two pubs which, a few years ago, were snug and smokey have been 'improved' inside and lost all their character.

For walkers there are three hills. Mynydd Carreg, 2 miles to the north, is only a couple of hundred feet high but is of pre-Cambrian rock with deep-red jasper and rose dolomite. Mynydd Ystum is 2 miles north-east with small remains of an early British fortress on its 480ft summit. Four miles to the east Mynydd Rhiw rises to 999ft with a commanding view of the whole sweep of Porth Neigwl (Hell's Mouth). Then there are the clifftops overlooking the Sound, with the Coastguard lookout and, low down on the cliff face on the point Trwyn-y-Gwyddel, is Ffynnon Fair (St Mary's Well). Access is difficult, it is flooded by the sea at high tides but its water remains fresh and potable.

The crossing from Aberdaron to Bardsey is 5 miles, but with the strong currents and the possibility of wind against tide it is not always a feasible sailing trip even in reasonably good weather. There is a man in the village who takes parties across in a power boat twice a day, weather permitting. This is a time-saving and more certain way of visiting Bardsey and allows about two hours ashore. The landing point is on the east side of the island at Cafn Enlli, a narrow gully leading up from the north-east corner of Henllwyn Cove, a bite into the land which almost severs the larger northern part of the island from its tail on which stands the lighthouse.

Anchor in or just off the cove, bearing in mind that there are strong tidal streams all round the island. The Welsh name for the island, Ynys Enlli, means Island of Currents. Only the stump of a tower remains of the old abbey, but there are some impressive remains of semi-detached farmhouses with shared farmyards and big walls to break the gale winds. The yards have massive stone archway entrances and cobbled pigsties or cattle pens. The island population early in the last century was about a hundred, and it dwindled to thirteen in 1950. There is now only one family farming there, and the whole island is a Nature Reserve. The lighthouse first shone its light on Christmas Eve 1821. It is sad that while it is there to guide mariners and save their lives, it causes the deaths of many hundreds of birds every year who fly into its lantern at night. The old school house is now the base for the bird observatory.

After leaving Aberdaron, the coast runs roughly eastwards for about 12 miles to Trwyn Cilan, the most southerly point of the Lleyn Peninsula. Once past this high cliff promontory the twin islands of St Tudwal's West and St Tudwal's East come into view. They lie to the east of the high ground of Penrhyn Du. There is

a passage between the West island, the nearest to the shore, and Penrhyn Du
through St Tudwal's Sound which is clear of dangers with a depth of 7 fathoms.
Northwards of the Sound is St Tudwal's Inner Road off Abersoch Sands which is
a very popular anchorage during the season, despite the fact that there can be a
heavy swell in strong south-westerlies and surf in strong south-easterlies. Three
cables to the south-east of St Tudwal's East is a hazard, Careg-y-Trai, a patch of
rocks which dry to 9ft. These rocks are marked by a bell buoy to seaward.
Although a hazard, for which clearance lines should be drawn at night and in
poor visibility, they are – in calm settled weather – worth sailing close to for a
look at the seal colony.

Abersoch is the home of the South Caernarfonshire Yacht Club, the largest
sailing club in Wales, with a strong offshore-racing fraternity and very active
dinghy fleet. The harbour is up the estuary of the Afon Soch and forms a mud
basin behind the village. The channel is about 300yd long and it is possible to
wade up the centre of it at low-water springs. Visitors should anchor in the roads
and wave their flag for one of the club launches, which operate from 9am until
7pm during the season. Arrangements to be picked up later can be made by
telephone (075 881 2388). The club has a superb three-storey building perched on
the low cliff at Abersoch Point. Food, drink and showers are available, and
visitors from other clubs are welcome.

If a swell is running off Abersoch it is better to anchor in the outer road east of
St Tudwal's Shoal where the water is deeper and there is no danger of finding
yourself in surf conditions; but when there is a very heavy swell it is better to go
on across the bay to Llanbedrog Cove inside Llanbedrog Point. This is an
unlikely looking place seen from seaward, but worth a visit. The anchor should
be dropped just to seaward of the sewer-outfall marker beyond which it shelves
very rapidly into the bay. From there it is a fair row to the beach from which a
track goes up through trees to the village where there is a general store and a
good hotel. On the beach, which is a popular launching site for trailed boats,
there are donkey rides for children.

When it is blowing south-easterly – which may happen during March and
April and from the end of August to October – conditions will be bad at
Abersoch, but some shelter can be found just inside Porth Bach Point,
immediately west of the Sandspit buoy just behind the old lifeboat station on the
Point. With very strong winds from the south-east there is *no* shelter in
Tremadoc Bay except in the drying harbours. A short stone-and-concrete breakwater extends from the north side of Abersoch Point to the edge of the channel
into the harbour, inside which is a convenient place to dry out if you want to
attend to your bottom. The tide goes out nearly a further 3 cables at low-water
springs leaving a large expanse of sand.

Abersoch Boatyard (tel 075 881 2213) has one of the largest chandlery shops in
North Wales. There is a 5-ton crane for lifting boats arriving by road, a tractor
and low loader for taking boats in and out at all states of the tide, and facilities for

The drying inner harbour at Abersoch. It is virtually landlocked and is a favourite base for small, trailed runabouts and power boats

winter storage and repair work for boats up to 30ft. The other yard in Abersoch is Land & Sea (tel 075 881 2957) which specialises in powerboats and servicing outboard motors. They run five tractors which work during the height of the season from 8am until 10pm taking boats out over the beach and back again. At the back of their yard is the Abersoch Power Boat Club (tel 075 881 2027). They have a reputation for excellent meals based on a spit roast and a menu with thirty starters, but they are very heavily booked during the season. In the village are two pubs. The manager of The Vaynol used to live on Bardsey and would be worth talking to if you are going to take a look at the island. Tudwals is much favoured by the young with Plaid Cymru tendencies, but it sells Robinson's Old Tom – a Stockport beer brewed but twice a year and stored in rum casks. A potent brew which perhaps should not be drunk just before sailing!

In the nineteenth century Pwllheli, 5 miles along the coast, was a commercial port for sailing ships up to 300 tons, which were built on the farms along the coast and launched by horses down wooden slips. They sailed with slate to Newfoundland, and from there took salt fish to Naples. They had crews of five made up of the men of a family with perhaps a neighbour. Round trips took about six months, during which time the women and children, the lame and old, were left to run the farms. Ships in those days went up the Afon Erch 2 miles to

Abererch. In 1908 a harbour with half-tide lock was built at Pwllheli itself and was used by steam coasters up to 1939. During the war it was taken over by the Royal Navy. Today the lock is a ruin and this inner harbour has silted up and dries out completely. Only a few small local boats lie there.

The yacht harbour is the deep-water channel that leads to the inner harbour. Called the Pool, it is banana-shaped, 4 cables long, and has an average depth of 14ft at high water and about 8ft at low water. It is narrow, crowded and friendly with all the necessary marine facilities on shore. Pwllheli is recognisable on approach by Gimlet Rock, an isolated rocky mound just inland of Pwllheli Point. At the tip of the point a derelict jetty runs north-east to the edge of the shoals round the point. The outer buoy lies a cable north of the jetty, and newcomers should keep to seaward of it. The channel into the Pool is marked by closely spaced buoys.

There is a bar or sill and boats drawing 3ft will have to wait for the two hours either side of low-water springs before being able to get in. At low-water springs there is barely enough water for an inflatable to get over. However, this bar is never dangerous, it is just a barrier. In the Pool boats lie to chain moorings along the line of the fairway, and visitors have to pick up a vacant mooring (they are all marked with their tonnage) and contact the Harbour Master. If all are occupied there is quite good holding ground. The Harbour Master operates from a wooden hut near the lifeboat station, which is conspicuous. He can be reached by telephone (0758 2131), which is the council offices. He can accommodate six visiting boats between June and September and maybe a few more, depending on how many boats are away cruising.

There are two big boatyards – William Partington Marine (tel 0758 2808) and Firmhelm (tel 0758 2251). Both have large chandlery shops and undertake quite major work, glass and wood. Tony Evans Engine Services (tel 0758 3219) handle inboard and outboard engine repairs and also run the fuelling jetty (which is in front of the caravan site near the entrance) and the camp shop alongside the pumps. The local marine-electronics engineer is R. B. Rowlands at nearby Llanbedrog (tel 075 884 415), and Sailcare in the old ballroom on the front will do repairs and are Hood agents (tel 0758 3141).

The Pwllheli Sailing Club has a smart new building by Gimlet Rock opposite Partingtons. At the inner end of the Pool the Pwllheli Boat Club, which caters mainly for motorboat people, has a most convenient floating jetty out into the deep-water channel. Both clubs welcome visitors from the water.

A good walk north-east of Pwllheli is to the village of Llangybi, about four miles by country roads, for a visit to St Cybi's Well (429412). It can be found by following a path behind the medieval village church and across a causeway over a waterlogged field. The building round the well is of large stone blocks and is now roofless. It looks very much like a ruined farmhouse set at the foot of a wooded slope of ash and beech. The water was believed to have mystical qualities. It would tell girls if their lovers were faithful or otherwise; if a feather or bit of cloth was floated on the water and it drifted south all was well, if to the north it was bad news!

The politically minded and those with an interest in modern history might want to see the Lloyd George Museum at Llanystumdwy 8 miles east along the A497. Lloyd George was born in Manchester, but his father died when he was 2 years old and he was brought up by his uncle Richard, the local shoemaker, in a terraced cottage in the village. The nicest feature of the village is the little arched seventeenth-century bridge over the River Dwyfor – a picture-postcard bridge which causes something of a bottleneck for traffic in the holiday season. Lloyd George's grave is in a little wood near the bridge and is covered by a boulder on which he used to sit and watch the tumbling stream.

The old town of Barmouth clings to the hillside
above the Mawddach estuary and is appropriately
known locally as 'Gibraltar'

# 3 Three Harbours in Cardigan Bay

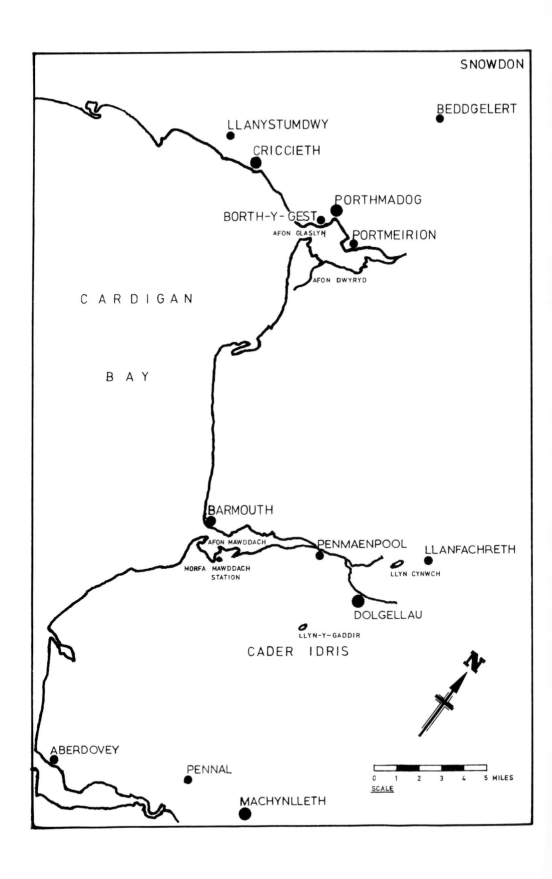

Sailing along the coast to Porthmadog it is worth going a little inshore for a look at Criccieth Castle perched on a rock on the edge of the water. The ruined building is thought to have been originally built by Llewellyn the Great and improved by Edward I in 1283. There is a small drying harbour below the castle which is used by local work boats, but it is no place for a cruising yacht. The town is largely Victorian in character and a fairly popular seaside resort. If you can anchor off it is only 1½ miles by road to Llanystumdwy.

The Harbour Master at Porthmadog has laid his own custom-made buoys down the channel, and he goes out once a month during the season to check the channel and adjust the positions of his buoys. When he was laying them one March, wading in thigh boots, he was bowled over by the force of the water rushing through the channel at 10 knots. Of course, it is unlikely to run that fast during the summer. At low water the whole of Tremadoc Bay, through which the channel runs, is a vast expanse of sand spreading seaward to roughly a line between Criccieth in the west and Harlech in the east. Through this sandscape flows the narrow channel of the Afon Glaslyn which has its source nearly 1,700ft up the Snowdon massif only 15 miles away and is fed by dozens of mountain streams on its way down to the sea. In the middle of the channel the Glaslyn is joined by the Afon Dwyryd flowing down from the tip of the Cambrian range in the east, which also contributes to the restlessness of the sandbanks.

As Porthmadog harbour is approached past the pretty bay of Borth-y-Gest, which dries completely, the number of bilge-keel yachts standing on the sand at low tide increases until the sandflats are left behind as the channel passes between Ballast Island and Tile Wharf. The island was artificially made by the local schooners offloading their ballast during the nineteenth century and into the early part of this century. If they got in and out without echo sounders, why not you? But do not try it for the first time at night. Visitors should pick up the most suitable vacant mooring and then contact the Harbour Master. He keeps about six moorings for visitors. Fin keelers have to take pot luck, but can usually be put alongside someone else or against the wall in the harbour. Ring him (tel 0766 2927) to say when you will be arriving and he will be there to meet you. No visitor will be left high and dry without a berth because all the owners of deep-water moorings are most co-operative and make their moorings available when they are out.

There are many good reasons for calling in at Porthmadog – the early nineteenth-century creation of William Alexander Madocks, MP, who constructed the mile-long cob across the river mouth to reclaim 7,000 acres of land and make the building of the harbour possible. In one corner of the harbour is the terminus of the Ffestiniog Narrow Gauge Railway which takes passengers on a truly breathtaking scenic journey high into the hills above the Vale of Ffestiniog. Tile Wharf offers a string of services to the visiting and resident yachtsman; there are two boatyards, a chandler and a marine engineer. At the seaward end is a slipway and the Porthmadog & Trawsfynydd Sailing Club, which was originally

Borth-y-Gest, on the way into Porthmadog. This pretty bay dries completely

The entrance to Porthmadog harbour, Tile Wharf on the left and the holiday-homes village right. 'There are many good reasons' for calling here, including a wide range of services and the Ffestiniog Narrow Gauge Railway

the Porthmadog Sailing Club before amalgamating with the Nuclear Power Station Sailing Club on its reservoir up in the hills. The club house is run on self-catering lines. All members have a key, and they take their own food into the kitchen and their own bottles into the bar. On the wharf they have a large dry-standing area for winter laying up and maintenance. Easter Saturday is the great day when a crane is hired and all the boats are lifted in.

The club has about a hundred cruising members, and runs a joint sailing programme with the Madoc Club of both racing and flotilla cruises to North and South Wales and a long weekend to Ireland. They really welcome temporary members who can use their showers and galley facilities, and some of their more experienced members are willing to accompany newcomers on day outings over the bar and around the local coast. On the town end of the harbour is the Madoc Club, a cosy and social yacht club in a nice old building. It is a great meeting place, and visitors from the sea are welcome to all the facilities which, on a small scale, are complete including showers, meals and ship-to-shore radio. The old dock on the west side of the harbour has a large public slipway. When spring tides conveniently occur in the mornings and evenings there is enough water for a boat of any size to get out and back in the same day.

Finally, the Harbour Master extends an invitation to any yachtsman who wants to bring his charts up to date to call in at his office in the harbour. Porthmadog is still classed as a commercial port and gets all the Admiralty Notices to Mariners, so if you want to bring your charts up to date, for anywhere in the world, you can take them there – but you have to do it yourself.

The town is a good place for shopping with plenty of eating places and pubs. The Blue Anchor Restaurant in the square has had a good reputation for some years. The Harbour Restaurant looks much like a chips-with-everything cafe, but its local fresh-fish dishes are recommended. There is an Italian bistro, and Joe Lewis is the fishmonger for local salmon. Near high water you can go up the Dwyryd estuary to anchor off the famous village of Portmeirion built by Clough Williams-Ellis in the Italianate style. Before leaving this area try to visit the Glaslyn Pass – a beautiful wooded valley with the River Glaslyn tumbling through it – which leads to the famous Snowdon village of Beddgelert, 7 miles away along the A498.

Sailing south to Barmouth and beyond care has to be taken getting past St Patrick's Causeway (Sarn Badrig, as it is shown on the charts). The east passage between the shore and the northernmost spur of the causeway is very narrow, the gap being no more than 2 cables. It is safe enough on a rising tide, but it should not be attempted at low water. For the visitor leaving Porthmadog near the top of the tide it would be safe to make for the east passage which is only one hour's sailing distance. Barmouth is a tricky estuary with a stream running out of the river at 4–5 knots and should be entered close to the top of the tide. Trying to get in against the spring ebb is almost impossible. It is not the best place for the sailor with a small outboard hung on the back. The Harbour Master is usually on Channel 16 at around high water and will direct yachts to suitable berths.

It is a town of two characters. The first and most evident is the crowded resort with a raucous fun fair on the front, souvenir shops and thousands of trippers stuffing chips and ice cream into their mouths and making the pavements almost impassable. Then there is Old Barmouth, built precariously up the face of the escarpment known as 'Gibraltar' or 'Penygraig'. It is both fascinating and good exercise to wander through the labyrinth of stone houses built on narrow terraced ledges hewn out of the rock face. They have tall chimneys of the Stuart period, and dormer doors to upper floors reached by stone bridges from paths and steps. Almost every small house or cottage has a tablecloth-size walled garden crammed with flowers and, although some are now let as holiday homes, there are still some old inhabitants. If you look genuinely interested and are not among a gaggle of tourists you may, as I was, be invited in to see one or another small home in the rocks. Next to the Harbour Master's office is a small, crowded but most interesting RNLI Maritime Museum with documents and exhibits going back to 1828 when Barmouth's first lifeboat went on station. Nearby is the Last Inn, once a shoemaker's shop, which is where the fishermen and boating people tend to congregate.

Inland is good walking country, and the most popular route is the Panorama Walk which starts from the east end of the town rising to 650ft above and alongside the Mawddach estuary with views across the water to the Cader Idris range. The south shore of the estuary is reached by a footbridge alongside the railway bridge to Morfa Mawddach station. From there the line of the old railway track to Dolgellau has been made into a riverside walk. It has the advantage, for the less active, of being on the flat and never more than a few feet from the wide waters of the estuary or, when the tide is out, the mud flats. After about six miles the track reaches the toll bridge at Penmaenpool where the estuary narrows to become the river. This point can be reached by tender working the tides with a stop at the George III Hotel, a restored seventeenth-century inn which has a riverside restaurant (Egon Ronay recommended). The old signal box has been converted into a bird observation post. There are plenty of waders and sedge warblers, reed buntings, grasshopper warblers and redpolls. On the other side of the toll bridge a bus can be taken back to Barmouth or a further 4 miles on to Dolgellau.

Dolgellau is an unusual little town of dark stone houses with black slate roofs lining narrow crooked streets which wander in all directions in maze-like complexity, the whole completely overshadowed by mountains. The square is dominated by a large market hall, but the motorist is dominated by the traffic wardens who reign supreme, for this town, once the junction of three Roman roads, is today a very busy triple throughway for legions of motorists touring the area. But there is a large and more than adequate car park on the edge of the town by the river. The ivy-clad Golden Lion Royal Hotel fronting its own small square is good for a drink or a meal, and in fine weather you can sit outside and watch the sightseers milling around. Some of the shops are a cut above average, and displays of souvenirs are fairly discreet. It was in Dolgellau that Owain Glyndwr summoned the last Welsh Parliament in 1404.

Two miles out of the town to the east is the Torrent Walk (OS 124, 752188) which is just what its name implies – but there is unlikely to be much torrent in the summer months. The steep path through the trees is charming, and the large rounded boulders in the ravine make a perfect scrambling playground for children. For more dramatic impact, but 3½ miles out of the town on the road to Llanfachreth, is the start of the Precipice Walk (746212). This is a contour path cut at 800ft above the Mawddach estuary around the precipitous escarpment of Foel Cynwch. It is a safe path, but needs a little concentration in places. The physically elderly, those unsteady on their feet and anyone who suffers from vertigo should give it a miss. The panoramic views of the estuary and Cader Idris are exceptional. The path goes round Llyn Cynwch, a very pretty lake. There are simple notices along the trail catering for those who cannot read a map or understand what they are seeing. The walk is a waste of effort on a hazy day.

For the serious hill walker Barmouth is, of course, the putting-in place for a walk along the top of Cader Idris. Crossing the estuary by the footbridge from Barmouth he could cover the length of the ridge and bus back from Dolgellau well within a day, or do it the other way round. The highest point is 2,928ft just below which is Llyn y Gaddir, one of four summit lakes. From there Fox's Path leads down to the Gwernan Lake Hotel on the Dolgellau road. That is the best point at which to come off the mountain and stop for rest and refreshment.

The last port of call before leaving North Wales is Aberdovey, which has a nasty bar. To find the outer buoy is easy enough, but sometimes the bar buoy lies almost flat in the turbulence and needs an eagle eye to pick it out. Great caution must be taken to identify the bar buoy, but once it has been found the rest is easy as the buoys come up in sequence. The bar buoy is altered every season, and should be passed close to either side. Aberdovey is a pleasant village with an Outward Bound School and hospitable sailing club, two hotels with friendly bars and restaurants. The only boatyard is up the estuary near the railway halt at Pen-Helyg among the sand dunes and can only be reached at high tide. It is advisable to pick up a mooring because the River Dovey rushes out at considerable speed, or go on up beyond the jetty and put down two anchors.

One very big caution – be very careful when going ashore in a dinghy, particularly at night. If the ebb is running strongly it is essential to wear a life-jacket. If anyone falls out, or the outboard stops, with a good 5-knot tide running you can be down to the mouth of the river and onto the bar in a flash. When the tide is out the estuary is a fantastic landscape of sand sculpted by the tide and a thousand rivulets. The wind funnels down the estuary between the hills, and sailing on an early ebb with the wind behind you go rocketing out over the bar and then perhaps within a couple of cables find yourself becalmed, or being headed from the opposite direction. The contrary situation can occur coming in. It is not advised to attempt to sail in as you will almost invariably be headed by wind coming down the estuary.

The hills behind the town, rising steeply to over 800ft, are veined with footpaths and bridleways making for easy walking and high views out over Cardigan Bay. The Dovey has a narrow channel winding between acres of sand at low water, and I once spent a day exploring the river by rubber dinghy as far as Machynlleth. Much of the way was on foot pulling the inflatable behind me. The locals thought I was mad, but the only danger, if you go up and down with the tide, is getting out of the boat when it grounds and stepping into a hole and up to your waist in water. For miles the only signs of life are the sheep on the hill slopes either side of the broad flat valley.

There is little difficulty getting up the first 6 miles of river to Pennal, a nice little village near the river. It is set among hills for climbing and streams for fishing. Nearby is Cefn Caer, the site of a Roman fort. Access to the village is through the park-like grounds of the Riverside Hotel. As I approached the main entrance the manager came out, looked at my clothes which were perhaps ill-suited to a country hotel, and asked me what I was doing in his grounds. I had to show him the boat to convince him because nobody had ever arrived by boat before and he believed the river to be unnavigable. It is my opinion that yachtsmen do not use their tenders often enough to make little voyages of exploration inland. There are many quiet waters waiting to be 'discovered' all round Britain's coasts and for them you do not need a yacht, nor even a trailed boat. A little inflatable or small car-top craft will suffice.

The harbour at Cemaes where everything is on a
small scale. The clifftop walk provides breathtaking scenery and three historical sites

# 4 Menai Strait, East and North Anglesey

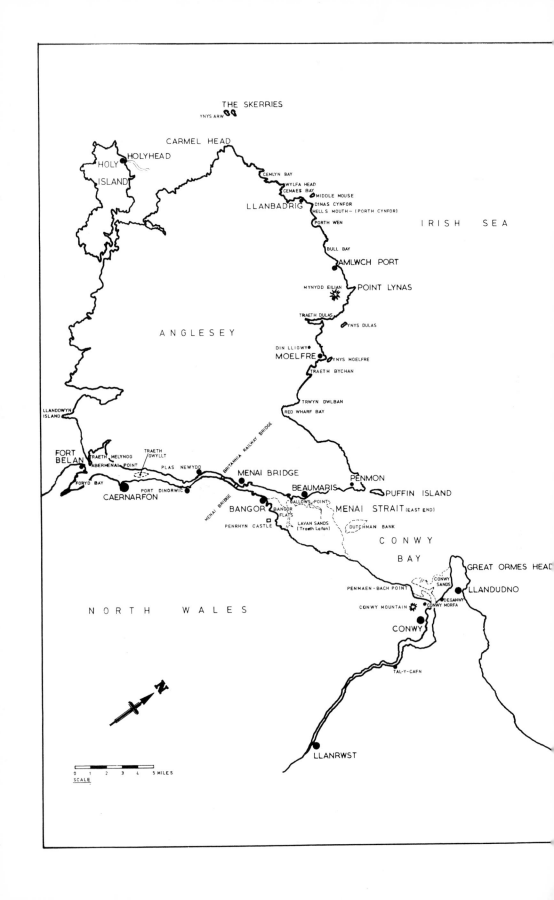

In the Menai Strait there are many confusions and some hazards, but it is a delightful and picturesque stretch of sailing water even if a little deceptive to the newcomer. The confusions are the extensive sand flats and bars which dry for square miles at each end of the Strait and make large areas of tempting water into 'no go' areas; there is the phenomenon of tides flooding and ebbing at both ends of the Strait but not synchronising, so that it is possible to punch an ebb tide going out and vice versa, and the time and location of slack water in one half of the Strait is constantly variable. Fluky winds and miniature squalls puffing out of the mountains and round belts of trees add to the complications. The hazards are the very strong tidal streams which make a good anchor, plenty of chain and a reliable and powerful-enough engine essential for the cruising man who is going to stay around in the Strait; another, if entered at the wrong time, is the Swellies, a mile-long race between just-submerged rocks and through sucking whirlpools. Arriving on the 'dry' Sabbath is, to some, another kind of hazard, but there are plenty of hospitable sailing clubs which welcome bona-fide cruising crews to their Sunday bars. The channel is plenty wide enough for easy tacking except through the Swellies, when it is most advisable to use the motor.

Caernarfon, just inside the Menai Strait, is a most obvious stop. Edward I's great castle is a truly magnificent sight from the water, and set in the town walls are two of the friendliest sailing clubs I have ever been invited into. The local pilots are Jones & Son and, in my opinion, no cruise in these parts is complete without making the acquaintance of one of that entertaining and helpful family. The Harbour Master, Capt Raymond Phillips, whom you will have to see anyway, is a very knowledgeable and helpful man too.

But first you have to get into Caernarfon over the bar which is not always possible and, once inside, there is the risk of being unable to sail out again for a day or two if conditions over the bar turn against you. A short term of imprisonment in the Strait, however, is no tragedy, unless you are in a hurry, because it offers 17 miles of very interesting sailing in sheltered waters in exceptionally picturesque surroundings with four boatyards, ten clubs, four towns and three castles to visit. A good time to be there is during the Menai Strait's Fortnight (which starts at the end of July or the first week of August) when upwards of 300 boats, from ocean racers to old gaffers, and hundreds of dinghies race in different parts of the Strait every day and fill the narrow water with life and colour.

There is an inshore passage from Llanddwyn Island to the entrance to the Strait at Aber Menai which can be used by boats of shallow draught in good weather conditions during the period above half tide. But since there are places where there may not be more than 1 fathom of water it should not be attempted when there is a heavy swell running or in breaking seas. Except when using the inland route from Llanddwyn Island, the approach to Menai Strait and Caernarfon is from the south-west through the channel over the Caernarfon bar. It is important to locate the fairway buoy and then follow the buoys all the way in.

Caernarfon inner harbour. At one time boats lay only against the slate quay or in the deep-water channel just off it, but now drying-out moorings extend up the River Seiont

Both north and south of the fairway channel there are sand banks which dry to up to 6ft with several isolated drying patches in between them, and at times the depth over the bar at low-water springs can be down to ½ fathom. The channel is continually changing, and the buoys may not be where they are marked as being on your chart.

You have only to mention the Caernarfon bar to some people and they blanch, and there are some in the Strait with very good boats who have never ventured over it. But the bar is only bad in bad conditions, and perfectly safe when conditions are right which, during the summer, they are about 80 per cent of the time provided you follow the buoys and work the tides. If there have been a number of days of strong sou'westerlies then the Atlantic rollers come up into St George's Channel and land on the doorstep of Caernarfon. That is the time when you can be badly bounced on the bottom as you drop into the troughs over the bar. The prevailing winds are westerly or sou'westerly, which makes the entrance in reasonable weather a nice broad reach. One oddity though – periods of high pressure in summer can change the prevailing wind to north-easterly. If taken at half flood there will be a margin of ¼ mile to tack all the way in. If the wind is from the north-east it is sometimes lumpy and it would be easier to motor-sail in sticking to the channel rather than have the strain of worrying where the banks are while tacking. There is a minimum depth on the bar of about 11ft at half tide.

It is, of course, possible to motor in against the tide in good weather and even to sail against the tide over the bar itself where the ebb has started to fan out. But in the gap between Aber Menai and Fort Belan the tide can run at over 4 knots at springs and over 2 knots at neaps. It is unwise to get too near to the South Sands on a falling tide as they shelve steeply and are most unlikely to be where they are shown on your chart. Once through the gap it is simple pilotage up the Strait. The channel runs close in to the Caernarfon shore after passing the mouth of Foryd Bay (all of which dries) just beyond Fort Belan. There is a small dock behind Fort Belan, but you will not be welcome there; it is the private property of Lord Newborough and he likes to keep it that way, only welcoming paying visitors by road.

The last buoy is No 9 starboard hand, after which port- and starboard-hand buoys change sides as Caernarfon is considered the head of navigation. Immediately due south of No 9 buoy is a nice flat sand spit on which twin-keel boats often take the ground, out of the tidal stream, instead of going into the harbour. The harbour, which is in fact the old slate quay below the castle walls and the drying mouth of the little Seiont river, has a very narrow entrance with no more than a trickle of water at low-water springs. After passing No 9 buoy there is a green conical Cardinal East buoy immediately to starboard, followed by a series of stick buoys marking the outer edge of the channel into the harbour. It is only about 30ft wide between the sticks and the sea wall, and it is best to keep close up to the sticks as there are some rocks and two slipways off the wall. The channel bends round the end of the castle and into the river. But there is a snag in the form of a swing bridge which will open during the four hours before and the four hours after high water, and remains open between 2300 hours and 0700 hours. If it is closed it will be opened by the operator if given a signal of one long and three short blasts. Shallow-draught boats without masts can get under it during much of the other four hours at neaps, but not sailing boats unless they can lower the mast.

Inside the river is packed with boats, many of them lying against the quay. The only thing a visitor can do is to lie against some stranger and make his peace with him; from my own experience making that peace is no problem. The boats are crowded in Caernarfon but it is, by comparison with other places, a small crowd and friendly too. They do not get too many strangers, so they do have a curiosity value! The Harbour Trust Office is at one end of the quay – which is also a big car park for visitors to the castle. If you are going to be there for a night or two the Harbour Master will be very helpful. There are two clubs – the Royal Welsh Yacht Club and the Caernarfon Sailing Club. Both welcome visiting yachtsmen and offer their facilities on the usual free basis. The Royal Welsh, which is housed in the two towers of the city gate overlooking the entrance to the Strait, is closed on Thursdays. The Sailing Club, which occupies the former battery at the end of the city wall overlooking the Strait, is open every evening and Sundays, being very much the local businessmen's club. The two clubs are the only source of wet stores on a Sunday.

In the harbour you are virtually in the centre of the town with plenty of shops and a public lavatory on the quay. Scrubbing down and other work on the bottom can be done on the foreshore of the river alongside Caernarfon Marine, who can do some repairs and also supply fuel. The castle, built between 1283 and 1322, is one of the best-preserved monuments of the Middle Ages, and that part of the town which is within the walls (parts of which are still intact) contains several buildings of historical and architectural interest. It is the best starting-off point for a tour of Snowdonia and for the Lleyn Peninsula. It would be a pity to sail round the periphery of Snowdonia and not make at least one expedition into the mountains, but even the foothills are a very long walk from the water – although some people actually run from Caernarfon to the top of Snowdon once a year on the Three Peaks Race. However, there is an easy way to reach the mountains from a boat; use the Snowdon Sherpa bus service. This is a fleet of minibuses which run Monday to Saturday from the end of May to the end of September linking Caernarfon and Porthmadog to the footpaths up to Snowdon. Timetables can be had in advance from Snowdonia National Park Information Services, Penrhyndeudraeth, Gwynedd LL48 6LS. Also a good bus service from Caernarfon square connects with the Inter-City train service at Bangor station. Caernarfon is a teeming tourist centre during the season, but while there are good cafes for bacon-and-egg breakfasts it is not the place for those seeking an interesting dinner when they come ashore; after 9 o'clock in the evening the choice is Chinese or fish n' chips.

There is a commercial harbour at Caernarfon, Victoria Dock – or at least what looks like one. It was built as a timber dock for floating logs, not boats. The Harbour Master prefers all fin- and single-keel boats to use the Victoria Dock as he is concerned about them falling over or being left unattended in the river. Yachts should turn to port after entering the Dock and dry alongside the wall. The entrance, just beyond No 9 buoy, can be entered about half tide by most boats, but care is needed because the tide sweeps very fast across the entrance on both ebb and flood. Behind the Sailing Club is an old steam dredger, which is part of a small maritime museum on the harbour wall.

The alternative to putting in to Caernarfon is to use the anchorage behind Aber Menai Point. This is a favourite place with some of the locals who go down to their boats on a Friday evening and, if the tide is right, push off to Aber Menai for a night of solitude. On Saturdays and Sundays during the summer it can be crowded with family boats stopping there for picnics and for digging up the excellent cockles on the foreshore. Going from Caernarfon to Aber Menai is very easy. You go out with the ebb and just before being swept through the gap turn

90° to the north. At that moment you may need to put your engine on because from going with the ebb you will suddenly meet a head-on tide coming over the banks of Traeth Melynog Sands into Aber Menai Creek. It is the water from the north side of the Strait turning south to meet the main stream going through the gap plus the water draining out of the River Braint.

Inside the point there is good firm sand with a gentle incline so you can nose onto it and then drop your anchor. Make sure it is holding firm otherwise you can be in trouble with other moored boats as the south-going current tries to take you back south again. The tide will recede slowly and leave you on a good clean stretch of sand sheltered by 6–9ft-high dunes to the west and the 2ft sandbank north of No 8 buoy to the east. Tucked well in behind the point you will be out of the main tidal stream when you float again, but it is an uncomfortable anchorage in north-easterlies until the water goes away. In those circumstances it is more comfortable to anchor on the seaward side of the point. If making for the Aber Menai anchorage from the sea, coming in with the flood, it is almost essential to use the engine. Otherwise the water rushing in through the gap suddenly fans out and, running obliquely into Aber Menai Creek, it can carry you onto the bank. Then if your anchor does not hold you will be bounced further and further onto the bank and, as has happened, you could break up. Aber Menai is a nature reserve and, more often than not, free of humans. It is wonderful to wake up in the morning to the sound of birds, surrounded by miles of sand and, if you are lucky, not another soul or boat in sight with time for breakfast and a bit of a bottom scrub before the water reaches you.

On leaving Caernarfon it is essential to keep well into the mainland side as there is an enormous sandbank, Traeth Gwyllt, stretching from the Anglesey shore well over the middle of the Strait. On the Anglesey shore behind the sandbank is the Mermaid Inn which can be reached from a broken-down old pier which dries. The inn was burned down, but has been rebuilt. Unfortunately its local character has gone and it now caters more for the disco addict than yachtsmen. Plas y Deri, one of the best National Outdoor Pursuits Centres in Britain, is situated on the foreshore between Caernarfon and Port Dinorwic and just beyond the low-lying Ferodo factory. It has an active and well-equipped sailing complex with a big slip, changing rooms, showers, cafeteria, bar, workshops and sail loft. They run dinghy and cruising courses, and passing yachtsmen are welcome to call in and make use of any of those facilities for a small charge. If the philosophy of John Jackson, the founding director, is maintained Plas y Deri will become very much integrated in all local activities as well as its own and yachtsmen can regard it as they would a sailing club.

On the mainland side just before Port Dinorwic are two shallow bays which would seem to have nothing to recommend them but are, in fact, useful anchorages when the wind is blowing hard from the south-west. The shelter is provided by the configuration of the land, not the depth of the bays, which is hardly perceptible. Beyond them is Dinas, a blunt point cutting off the full view of Port Dinorwic. It was there that both Suetonius Paulinus in AD 61 and Julius Agricola in AD 76 are believed to have encamped before invading Anglesey. The Welsh placenames on the other side include such significant ones as Field of the Long Battle, Field of Bitter Lamentation and Hill of Graves. The parish behind Dinas, Llanfairisgaer, means the Church of St Mary below the Camp. The Romans invaded Anglesey for her copper, and also to control what was then the 'Granary of Wales'. So here you are literally sailing through ancient history.

Port Dinorwic, which is midway along the mainland side between Caernarfon and Bangor, was formerly a slate harbour, but is now taken over by yachts. It lies in a bay offering shelter from the run of the tide. The small town is reached up steep streets and boasts one of the best fish n' chip shops in North Wales. All within a few yards of the water are the Seahorse restaurant – a little expensive but with very good cuisine, the very active Dinorwic Sailing Club, and also the Gardd Fôn public house which is very much a boating-man's pub. There is plenty of room to anchor in 2 fathoms at low-water springs about a cable off the shore, but the bottom is very encumbered so always buoy your anchor.

Then there is the so-called Menai Marine development occupying the whole of the north-western half of Port Dinorwic. In the early 1970s a caravan-site developer managed to persuade all the local authorities to allow a development which could have turned Port Dinorwic into a superb yacht marina for those who like superb yacht marinas. The tidal basin was to be dredged with a channel to make it available at all states of the tide and pontoons were to be installed. The old slate-quarry port with its locked basin and dry dock was to be improved with plug-in services and shoreside facilities. An hotel, restaurant and shops were to be built, and the potholed dock roads and waste ground landscaped and made all pleasant for promenading visitors. The wooded hill on the north-west tip of the bay with its public walk along the shore was to become an architect-conceived holiday-and-retirement village with beautiful views across the Strait.

The houses were built and sold, the marina never happened, the existing facilities left over from the slate-quarry days are no better than they were, parts of the wall of the tidal basin collapsed, and so did the company running the whole unhappy venture. However, it was still operating in a fashion in 1981. The tidal basin can be used by twin keelers and those who wish to lie against the rough stone wall and floating berths are available in the locked basin, but there are no shoreside facilities.

From Port Dinorwic to the Britannia railway bridge is a gently curving 3 miles, with steep wooded hills on the mainland shore and the sloping parkland of Plas Newydd on the Anglesey side. Plas Newydd is *the* big attraction in North Wales for those who enjoy stately homes and gardens. The late eighteenth-century house, its contents and 169 acres of garden, park and woodland were given to the National Trust by the Marquess of Anglesey in 1976. He still lives in part of the house. The stables, the north wing and several outbuildings were at one time occupied by HMS Conway training school, but are now leased to the

Lady Anglesey's pink-and-white bedroom at Plas Newydd. The window beside the bed looks down the Menai Strait to Caernarfon

Cheshire County Council as an outdoor-activities centre. Their sailing activities are based in the toytown-size harbour on the foreshore below the house and during the summer their day boats are moored in a line in front of the house. At the foot of the sweeping lawn there is a landing stage for the tripper boat *Snowdon Queen* out of Caernarfon. It is not available to yachts, but a landing could be made by tender. If visiting by sea it would be politic to first contact the administrator (tel 0248 714795) as there is the question of buying a ticket to go into National Trust property.

To walk through the house and absorb what there is to see needs at least an hour. Each person will find his own points of special interest – the Gothick Hall, the rooms in Neo-Classical style, the Rex Whistler Room, the Cavalry Museum. There is also Lady Anglesey's Bedroom, a pale-pink-and-white confection with a four-poster bed muslin-hung and painted with trailing ivy in the Sheraton style, and a view of Snowdon through the windows. The Cavalry Museum is where I browsed the longest. It is devoted to the campaign relics of the 1st Marquess who was second-in-command to Wellington at Waterloo. Most bizarre of the exhibits is his articulated artificial leg, the prototype for many of the same design sold for years as 'the Anglesey leg'. The garden is at its best in May and June, but the trees and sweeping lawns, the woodland walks and the bird life are a tranquil pleasure at any time. In the middle of the lawn fronting the turreted and castellated stables is one of the best-preserved cromlechs to be found. It marks the

The Swellies and the suspension bridge with Snowdonia in the distance. Telford's famous bridge of 1826 completed the great London–Holyhead road scheme, now part of the A5

burial chamber of one of the seaborne invaders of Anglesey long before the Romans came there. The tiled milking parlour has been pleasantly converted into tearooms with home-made food and a National Trust gift shop.

Going on towards Bangor and Beaumaris the approach to the Swellies should be made keeping more to the mainland side to pass under the Britannia Bridge leaving the Britannia Rock (on which the bridge's centre column stands) a little to port, and then making towards the stone triangular beacon on the shore ahead. Pass the beacon about 20ft offshore. At the moment of passing look astern and alter course slightly to port to bring the two green lights fixed on a gantry under the bridge in transit one above the other. That gives the clearance line for Cribbin Rock on the port hand. When Price Point metal beacon with a light on top is abeam on the starboard side adjust course to pass midway between that beacon and the buoy on the Swelly Rock just ahead to port. Once past the buoy pick up a line between the flag pole (astern) on Gored Goch (an island with a house on it), roughly the centre of the suspension bridge and a beacon (lit red) on the shore just beyond the bridge. This line will clear the Platters – a nasty shoal off the shore about 2 cables before the bridge. Once under the bridge move over to the centre of the Strait and continue keeping well clear of the rock with a beacon on it 2 cables beyond the bridge on the Menai shore. The rock submerges at high water, but the beacon is always visible. It sounds simple and it is, but only if the passage is made at high-water slack. In the Swellies slack water occurs approximately two hours before high-water Liverpool and one hour before high-water Holyhead. At high-water slack the tide is turning from running from Caernarfon to Bangor to running from Bangor to Caernarfon. So if you are going on past Menai Bridge you need to arrive at the Swellies just before slack water, and if going the other way arrive just after for a good rate of tide down to Caernarfon.

From the suspension bridge going on north-west the Strait starts to broaden out little by little, but for some time has the appearance of a wide gorge with wooded slopes as far as Bangor Pier. Visually it is a wonderful stretch of water, as picturesque as any that people will sail days and weeks to find in foreign parts. On the mainland shore there is no suitable anchorage or landing place before Bangor. On the island side there is the small town of Menai Bridge in the shadow of the bridge itself.

About 4 cables on past the bridge on the Anglesey side is St George's Pier, formerly built for the excursion steamers which used to ply the Strait. In the late 1970s it fell into great disrepair and was closed, but has since been rebuilt with a large floating stage at the end which is the ideal place to go alongside. The charge is reasonable during the day, but very expensive for an overnight stop to discourage boats rafting up against it as they did in the old days, to the botheration of the local angling and fishing boats. The pier gives immediate access to the middle of the town, and water can be taken on from the stage.

It is also possible to moor alongside a string of old concrete barges permanently anchored about a mile above the bridge. There are notices saying 'No Mooring' but people seem to ignore them. The barges are rough old things so you need plenty of fenders, and it is also a long and possibly dangerous run ashore in a tender. The tidal currents are not only very strong but they move about in mysterious ways and, if the outboard should fail, tender and crew could end up spinning through the Swellies. I know of one drowning in recent years which happened in exactly that way. Never attempt to put an anchor down in the vicinity of the barges because there are some very deep holes below. Inshore of the barges there are some tempting creeks and backwaters round islands but, although local boats may be seen afloat in them, when the tide goes out they dry overall and the bottom is a mixture of mud, rock and ground tackle galore.

The Welsh name for the town of Menai Bridge is Porthaethwy; its English name, taken from the suspension bridge, dates from 1826. If you have time to do more than essential shopping ashore there is an interesting town trail which will take about an hour at a leisurely pace. Coming off the pier turn left along St George's Road and Beach Road towards the bridge. About 300 yards before reaching the bridge a flight of stone steps leads up to a cottage, Old Cambria House, which is private property. It was built in 1686 by Coningsby Williams, who was the king's tenant of the Porthaethwy Ferry, as a habitation for the ferryman. Later it became the Three Tuns Inn and was used by the cattle drovers who made their beasts swim across to the mainland at this point. Later still it was converted and became the Cambria Inn. Nearby are Stablau Newydd, which were the stables for the Cambria Inn and were used by Telford as a foundry when building his suspension bridge.

Go down to the waterside again. Just before the bridge there is a small quay which was the landing stage and crane site during the building of the bridge. Passing under the bridge there is an iron door set into the rocks, which covers the entrance to a service tunnel leading to the anchor points of the bridge. The path now becomes a metalled road called Belgian Promenade because it was built by Belgian refugees during World War I. All along this waterside walk you get a variety of perspectives of the suspension bridge which is 1,000ft long and 100ft above the water. It was only the second chain suspension bridge ever to be built; the first was across the Tweed in 1817. The limestone for the pillars came from a quarry at Penmon on the north-east corner of Anglesey, and the wrought-iron rods were forged in Shropshire and brought to the site by horse transport. At the end of the Promenade a causeway crosses the water to Church Island on the edge of the Swellies. The little church of St Tysilio was built about AD 630 and was the beginning of the community which was to become Menai Bridge. The graveyard covers most of the island. In the centre is a small hill with a Celtic cross war memorial on its summit, from which you get a wide view of the Swellies down to Britannia railway bridge. Originally the bridge was a tubular structure, but that was seriously damaged by fire in 1970 and it has been rebuilt as an arched bridge with a road running above the railway line. It is named after the rock on which its centre tower stands.

The Gazelle Hotel, opposite Bangor, is a popular yachtsman's pub. Anchoring is possible above and below it on the edge of the fairway

Coming off the island, walk up the steep path through the trees to the A5 on the outskirts of the town. Then if you have the time, and only if the air is clear, walk a mile along the road to the Marquess of Anglesey's Column and climb its 115 steps for unrivalled views over the whole area and the mountains on the mainland. The column was built in 1816 to commemorate the heroism of the 1st Marquess who lost a leg but won his title at the Battle of Waterloo. Back in the town there is the Museum of Childhood in Water Street. This is a small private museum crammed with old-fashioned toys, dolls, gramophones, musical boxes and a variety of childhood bric-a-brac. The Tegfryn Gallery near the end of the town going towards Beaumaris houses the work of North Wales artists. Should you be sailing in the Strait as late as October that is when Menai Bridge holds its annual Ffair y Borth, the largest of its kind in Wales and held regularly since the sixteenth century.

Further on towards Beaumaris there are dozens of laid moorings off the island opposite Bangor Pier with the Gazelle, a popular yachtsman's pub, right on the waterfront below cliff-hanging houses and a large white block of flats. It is quite feasible to anchor above and below the pub on the edge of the fairway, and there is a slip beside the pub. The road which hairpins down to it is much used by people trailing dinghies, and on club sailing days the hard is a scene of tight manoeuvring of cars and trailers. The dining room of the Gazelle faces onto the water and the Snowdon hills in the distance. Bangor Pier, a delightful example of Victorian seaside architecture, is 1,550ft long and runs out two-thirds of the way across the Strait; the end of it conveniently marks the edge of Bangor Flats and the channel. At the time of writing it had been closed for some years and was deteriorating rapidly into a dangerous rusty structure, but plans were afoot for its restoration and there is hope that it will open one day and once again be available as a grandstand on regatta days. Meanwhile it is no place to go alongside.

A sharp turn right past the pier leads to the stone breakwater of the best-known boatyard in this area, Dickie of Bangor. They offer every service from small repairs and getting engines going again to building fine boats. They have no moorings, but cruising yachtsmen are welcome to lie alongside their breakwater, which dries, for one or two nights; they are not interested in long-stayers. The end of the breakwater is accessible approximately three hours either side of high water. From there it is a mere 100 yards to a post office, shops and three pubs. The Garth Hotel is a typical fishermen's and longshoremen's pub with a sprinkling of yachtsmen, and the Union is similar. Bangor is a gastronomic wilderness, but it is on the Inter-City London–Holyhead line, it has a cathedral, its university college and, 1 mile to the east, is Penrhyn Castle which is open to the public.

Port Penrhyn – ½ mile away from Dickie's boatyard and isolated in the middle of Bangor Flats at low water – is a commercial port, but yachtsmen may use it if they do not mind lying against rough walls and having a long uphill walk into the town. From Bangor Pier onwards the Strait opens out and the channel is along the island shore, with the mainland side drying about 5 cables at Bangor Flats north-west of the pier to nearly three miles opposite Beaumaris. Gallows Point is a flat spit about 300 yards long which forms the south-western end of the shallow bay of Beaumaris. The Anglesey Boat Company has a large chandlery shop, petrol pumps and extensive workshops there, and all around the shoreline there is dry standing. Bilge keelers can get close in to the shore at high water and sit on the mud anchored to the shore. It is a great do-it-yourself place.

Also on the spit is the club house of the North West Venturers Yacht Club, membership of which is restricted to those with genuine cruising boats. It is a self-help club with each member holding his own key. The club house has a large sitting room with glass walls overlooking the bay and Puffin Island and, in the distance, Great Orme. Cruising crews are welcome, and the club keeps a library of members' logs of cruises round Anglesey, the North Wales coast, to Scotland, Ireland and as far away as the Mediterranean. They could prove useful reading, and there is no objection to visitors looking at them. Visitors to Beaumaris can either contact the Royal Anglesey Yacht Club which has a few visitors' moorings, or Peter Brimecombe who has a shed on Gallows Point (tel 0248 310). In his shed he builds small boats and does repairs in wood in the traditional manner. He is one of the dying race of adze fanciers, and his work is superb. He is also the Mooring Supervisor for the Anglesey Borough Council. There is no Harbour Master at Beaumaris nor, for that matter, for any part of the Strait

Beaumaris Castle, begun in 1295 by Edward I as his eighth and last castle in Wales, was never finished. This viewpoint from above the northern gatehouse looks down into the Inner Ward and across the Menai Strait to the mainland

The ancient dock of Beaumaris Castle, once fed by the sea, which is beside the gateway into the castle

above the road bridge. At the Caernarfon end of the Strait everything is well organised by Capt Raymond Phillips.

Beaumaris is an excellent place to go ashore. The castle, begun in 1295 by Edward I as his eighth and last castle in Wales, was sufficiently ready to be occupied after only three years, but was never put to use and was never finished. However, there is enough there for it to be a huge and spectacular monument. With almost perfect symmetry of design, it is a good example of concentric defence. The inner ward is rectangular with two gatehouses and six great towers; the outer ward is octagonal with two gates and twelve towers. The high walk around the top of the walls of the outer ward still makes an almost complete circuit providing plan views of every part of the inner ward, its walls, towers, the great hall, chapel and the other departments of the castle which are all roofless. Beyond the outer walls the view is of rolling pastures inland to the west and the broad stretch of the Strait to the east. The entrance by the gate next to the sea – now well inland behind the broad expanse of The Green – is reached over a wooden bridge which spans what was a small dock into which boats sailed and moored right by the gate. It is now merely a part of the moat but one mooring ring is left. At the height of the building work 400 masons and 2,000 other craftsmen and workmen were employed. One wonders where they were found in those days; the population of Beaumaris today is but 2,000.

The Green, which runs from the short pier to beyond the town along the waterfront, gives Beaumaris its unique character. In summer there is much picnicking on the grass, camels may be grazing there when the circus comes to town, and the low sea wall makes a perfect viewing stand for the club and regatta racing. The pier served as the ferry point to and from the mainland for many centuries until the Menai bridge was opened in 1826. At low tide passengers had to walk to the edge of the treacherous Lavan Sands, which cover several square miles off the mainland shore, to be picked up by the ferry boat. There were many cases of people being caught by the incoming tide and drowning in the fast-running current. Fronting the Green is Victoria Terrace, a row of tall classical houses built 1830–35 by Joseph Hansom, the designer of the Hansom cab. Next to them is Green Edge, a more modest terrace with trellised verandahs built by John Hall of Bangor a few years earlier. Behind is the Court House opposite the entrance to the castle. This dates from 1614 and still has its original hammer-beam roof. It is the only known court in which the jury sat on a higher level than the judge. It is now used as a magistrates' court, but is open to the public.

The walk from the Court House to the Gaol takes in the whole length of Castle Street, in which several medieval buildings survive in excellent condition. The Tudor Rose, built c1400, is one of the oldest houses in Britain and retains its original woodwork. Ye Olde Bull's Head, built in 1472, houses a collection of antiquities including a ducking stool and water clock; it is a good pub and hotel. The door leading to the courtyard and stables is the largest simple-hinged door in Britain and big enough to have allowed mail coaches through. The 1829 Gaol is a well-preserved example of the harsh justice of the early Victorian age. Visitors can walk in and out of the tiny cells, along the condemned man's walk to the scaffold and to the last remaining treadmill in Britain which is still in good order. It was not only a tiring punishment, it was functional as well, providing the manpower to pump up the prison's water supply. A display of prison documents and illustrations of prison life are as educational as a tour of the grim building itself. The Parish Church of St Mary and St Nicholas, across the road from the Gaol in Steeple Lane, is in parts almost as old as the castle. For meeting people go to the Liverpool Arms where most crews off boats go to drink. The landlord served on the Royal Yacht *Britannia* and has made his bar into a gallery of naval and maritime photographs, drawings and paintings.

Four miles on by sea up the Anglesey coast is Penmon, one of the prettier spots on the island with its priory and church of St Seiriol, holy well and dovecote. It is then just a short walk to Penmon Point and Menai lighthouse (also known as Penmon lighthouse) overlooking the north-west entrance to Menai Strait between the Point and Puffin Island. If going there by boat turn inshore by the black conical buoy B1 and drop your hook about 2 cables off the shore opposite the quarry marked by a chimney. Bilge keelers can go close inshore and dry out, but it is sand and boulder so it may be necessary to be on board as the last foot or two of water goes out. An alternative anchorage is in Lighthouse Cove, round the far side of the lighthouse; it is a rock-bound pool. A bus from Beaumaris is a less troublesome way of getting there.

The priory was founded in the sixth century by St Cynlas and given as a gift to his brother St Seiriol. It was largely destroyed by marauders, and rebuilt in Norman style between 1120 and 1170. The church walls are massive for a small building and the interior, lit by tiny windows, is dark and mysterious. A roofless ruined thirteenth-century refectory with a first-floor dormitory occupies one side of the cloister with later buildings attached. The prior's house is still lived in, which helps to bring this religious site to life. Nearby at the base of a rock outcrop and well hidden by trees and bushes is St Seiriol's Well in a cell with stone benches. Another oval-shaped cell in the rock close by is believed to have been the saint's actual dwelling, and the cell with the well in it was probably his tiny church. Another and unique building well worth looking at is the large domed dovecote built c1600, probably by Sir Richard Bulkeley. It is entered by a low doorway and in the centre a stone pillar rises almost to the roof with corbelled steps which were used to lodge ladders to reach the 1,000 nests lining the walls. The point is a popular place for picnics to the accompaniment of the sea swishing in and out of the rocks and the melancholy note of the fog bell which tolls, fair weather and foul, in the lighthouse. The light is automatic, coming on when daylight falls below a certain intensity.

From Beaumaris the way out of the Menai Strait is by the well-buoyed channel which runs close to the Anglesey shore and then through Puffin Sound, a bottleneck of barely more than a cable's width at low-water springs. There is another exit – straight on north-east past Puffin Island, but it is not recommended. To the east of the channel towards the mainland are Lavan Sands drying in places up to 14ft and, further up, Dutchman Bank drying up to 10ft blocks the way out to the north-east. Along the whole channel from Beaumaris to Puffin Sound there are four shallow bays which dry, and their sand and shingle are liberally sprinkled with boulders. The mainland can offer a spectacular skyline of the northern end of the Snowdon range. Before breakfast on a bright summer morning the mountains stand black silhouettes entwined in strands of mist, their tops rim-lit by the early sun. In the evening the low mellow sun throws them into relief and brings out every detail of their shape and colour.

The decision when to start for Puffin Sound should be based on a careful study of the tidal system. If the wind is the prevailing one from the south-west then there should be no problems in making a passage round the north coast of Anglesey to Carmel Head and Holyhead, away to the Isle of Man or wherever. But if the wind is anywhere in the north it would be better not to go as it would mean sailing along a lee shore with very strong tidal streams, plenty of hazards and no safe refuge at all. That condition is only common at the beginning and end of the season, but there is always the exception to the rule – sometimes in mid-August. If the wind is from the north to north-east it will be quite apparent in the Strait, but if it is blowing from the north-west it will not be noticed at

(*Above*) Looking across Red Wharf Bay from the Ship Inn. At low water the sands are shared by riders and yachtsmen; (*opposite*) Porth Llongdy, a possible first port of call after the Strait. A natural harbour which dries, it can be entered in reasonable weather by boats with up to 5ft draught one hour before HW neaps

Beaumaris, which is in the lee of the island, and the first squalls will not be encountered until near Trwyn Du just before reaching Puffin Sound.

Puffin Island Beacon (or Perch Rock Beacon) marks the eastern side of the entrance to the Sound, and the black-and-white-banded lighthouse off the end of Trwyn Du marks the western side. Coming out through the Sound with the wind in the north or west and a strong ebb under you can be a little alarming as you hit a nasty lolloping sea after leaving the lee of Anglesey. Although the Admiralty Chart shows a maximum tidal stream off the north coast of Anglesey of 3.4 knots, there are parts when it runs 4 and 5 knots, and between Point Lynas and Carmel Head the sea inshore can become increasingly rough owing to a number of overfalls which get severe off the Skerries. Wind direction and tides are more crucial than usual along this stretch of coast, and cruising close inshore to visit anchorages and harbours should only be considered in settled weather with offshore winds.

But, given the right conditions, there are a number of fascinating places to visit. The first stop after the Strait could be Porth Llongdy in the western corner of Red Wharf Bay. The whole bay, 2½ miles wide and 1½ miles deep, dries out and its inner circumference is a giant beach for family fun. The channel into Porth Llongdy runs south close inshore past Trwyn Dwlban and is the mouth of the

Afon Ceint, but at low-water springs is no more than a rivulet in the sand. It runs about eighty yards off the shore to a pool opposite the Min Y Don Hotel. Above the pool the river splits; one arm going east across the sands, the other curving round a high shingle spit into Porth Llongdy, a natural harbour which dries. The channel can be used in reasonable weather by boats up to 5ft draught 2 hours before high-water springs and 1 hour before high-water neaps.

A ¾-mile diversion is worth making for a visit to the Ship Inn opposite the Shingle Point which was, many years ago, a grain warehouse with two adjoining stone cottages. Inside, the inn is old and unspoilt with a super log fire on chilly days and good bar meals. The cottages are a restaurant formed of several low-ceilinged stone-walled rooms leading one into the other providing intimate and cosy nooks. The telephone number (which you will need to book a table) is 024 874 2568. It might be possible to get in, have a quick meal and get out again on a spring tide, but normally it would mean taking the ground in between. The Red Wharf Bay Sailing Club, an active dinghy club, have their clubhouse, slip and boat park in Traeth Bychan 2 miles further along the coast. It is a little bay which dries out about 300 yards, but there is anchorage of about 4ft at low-water springs just inside the entrance points.

A mile to the north is Moelfre, which gives protection against winds from the south-west. There is good holding ground, but strong south-westerlies blast like mad through a gap in the land and the boat will shake; it is then wise to put plenty of chain out. Moelfre is quite untenable in a north-easterly, but in a north-westerly gale it offers uncomfortable safety in the anchorage tucked in under the old lifeboat house. On the point which is opposite the island, Ynys Moelfre, there is a Coastguard lookout and the lifeboat station, so there is plenty of authoritative local knowledge available. *The Royal Charter*, coming back from Australia with returning gold diggers and their gold, foundered on this point on 26 October 1859. She was an iron fully rigged sailing ship of 2,719 tons with a 200hp auxiliary steam engine and one of the finest ships of the Liverpool and Australian Navigation Company's fleet. As she rounded the Skerries on her way to Liverpool the wind veered to the north-east and blew a hurricane. Her position on a lee shore became precarious; the engine was not powerful enough to hold the vessel on her course, and she was driven ever closer to that treacherous lee shore. With two anchors out, her masts cut away and the engine going full steam, she was still driven onto a ledge below the cliffs of Moelfre. 459 people perished. During the days that followed many a small fortune was picked up in the pools and on the beaches nearby. Even so, £300,000-worth of gold was salvaged from the wreck.

Moelfre village has a small shingle beach where a landing can be made, steep streets and a few old cottages. One thing that a crew with time should go and see is Din Lligwy, 1½ miles away by road. It is a fourth-century British defensive settlement built during the Roman occupation of Anglesey. This is not one of those remains which looks like nothing but a heap of stones to all but the expert.

A round house in the fortified village of Din Lligwy. The doorstep and walls date from AD 380–385

The defensive wall is almost intact to several feet in height, and so too are the square and circular walls of the huts. There are even front doorsteps and parts of doorways. It is all so obvious and clear that one can easily rebuild the walls and people the settlement in one's imagination. Of course, it is on a hill and there is a clear view across the next bay, Traeth Lligwy, and the island of Ynys Dulas beyond.

If in search of solitude and bird life put into Traeth Dulas, an almost entirely land-locked lagoon with an anchorage with 2 fathoms at low-water springs 200 yards off the easternmost point of the sand spit, Morfa Dulas, which almost closes the entrance. From there it would be better to explore the serpentine channel by dinghy. Somebody does keep his boat well up the channel – which is the Afon Goch – moored to a large tree stump which has been imported onto the saltings. Off this bay is Ynys Dulas, a long low-lying rocky island with a pepperpot tower in its centre; well worth a visit on a calm day either in the dinghy or at high water in a shallow-draught boat. It has a large seal population, and sea birds which are so unused to humans that they just sit on their nests and stare at you as you clamber about near them.

Next comes the north-east point of Anglesey, Point Lynas, a ½-mile-long headland facing north from the foot of Mynydd Eilian, whose peak is a mile inshore. The headland is recognisable by its white lighthouse which looks like a fort. The squat lamp house is surrounded by castellated walls, behind which are the cottages of the lighthouse keepers. On the east side of the headland is a high pier with a stairway down to a jetty used by the Liverpool pilots. The ships going

A rare sight: the beacon on Middle Mouse being painted by Trinity House

to and from Liverpool pause a mile or two off Point Lynas. On the flood a race runs out north-east – and on the ebb north – from Point Lynas and, although rarely dangerous, it is most uncomfortable and very nasty with wind against tide. Even in good weather it can be a rough patch. It is more comfortable to pass close in about 1½ cables off the point, but if the wind does not make that possible or advisable there is little choice but to plough through the turbulence of the race.

Out to sea approximately two miles north of Amlwch Port is the Marine Terminal Buoy, a very large orange monster to which tankers attach themselves to pump oil ashore. The area should be avoided, not only because of the tankers but because there will often be diving personnel at work in the vicinity. The shoreline now becomes more precipitous and the tidal stream gets stronger, up to 5 knots at springs. Round the next headland, Dinas Cynfor, with Middle Mouse lying ¾ mile offshore, is Cemaes Bay which actually embraces four bays or coves. In the deepest of them, Porth Mawr in the south-east corner, is the harbour. In fair weather Cemaes Bay is a good stopping place, and for a change from a cramped cockpit there is a National Trust clifftop walk from the village all the way to Bull Bay, about five miles. You can get a bus back.

I must emphasise that Cemaes Bay is no sanctuary in northerlies, nor when the tide is out. If it blows strong from the north the rollers crash into the bay and right over the breakwater. In extremis it might be possible to go into Porth-yr-Ogof in the far western corner of the bay to shelter from a north-west gale; uncomfortable, but you would survive. With a north-north-easterly to easterly wind Llanbadrig Cove in the eastern extremity of the bay is partially landlocked and safe. But in either case one might have to get through a wicked sea to get in.

Cemaes Bay has two aspects: the old village of stone cottages clustered round the harbour and short steep winding streets giving it a picturesque character, and the ugly housing estates on the hill above the bay. Of the forty or so old buildings, only three are still lived in by local people; the rest are holiday homes. So, like many an old fishing village, it is, out of season, a well preserved but dead place. During the summer months it has a bustling character provided by visitors who fill the small village pubs and shops and crowd the small beach when the sun shines. Everything is on a small scale, even the angling business – just two motor boats. The clifftop walk towards Bull Bay provides breathtaking scenery and three sites of historical interest. The cliffs above the two western coves overlook the whole of Cemaes Bay across to Wylfa Head with its atomic power station (capacity 1 million kilowatts), a giant cubic monolith spoiling the natural scenery but impressive nonetheless.

At Llanbadrig there is a small restored church (OS 114, 376948) dedicated to St Patrick and reputed to have been founded by him in AD 432. It stands at the end of a short lane looking over the sea to Ireland. A mile further on is Dinas Gynfor, the most northerly point of Anglesey and the site of an early British cliff fortress. Ramparts, entrances and a redoubt can be traced and defensive works overlook the dramatic Porth Cynfor (Hell's Mouth). There are also the remains of

The abandoned brickworks and quay, Porth Wen, a 'remote, cliffbound, almost circular "bite"', is the most surprising find on a walk from Cemaes'

This view of Porth Wen shows the characteristic topography of the north coast of Anglesey

buildings in the vicinity left over from the time when china clay was quarried there. Porth Wen, a remote cliff-bound almost circular bite, is the most surprising 'find' on this walk. Seen from above on a calm day it is a blue lagoon with a beach. It looks a perfect anchorage, but it is a trap in onshore winds and even in calm weather it can become disturbed by a nasty swell, possibly caused by big ships passing close by on their way to and from Liverpool. Seven boats cruising in company went in there a few years ago, the wind picked up, and they were all written off.

The surprise comes on looking over the clifftop into Porth Wen to see spread out on a ledge below a large brick works with a chimney rising almost to eye level. Although closed in the late 1930s, the ruins look like something still under construction. Far from any pollution and washed by damp sea breezes, the brick work of this hidden example of recent industrial archaeology looks as good as new. The way down is along a path which was once a railway track up and down which bogies were winched. But most of the bricks were shipped out by sea from the quay alongside, and coal came in the same way to fire the beehive kilns. The

setting is quite beautiful, although the brickworkers probably did not appreciate it as much as the visitor can today. After the war a doctor from Liverpool converted one of the kilns into a house in which he spent his summer holidays. Alas, when the permissive age reached Cemaes it was frequently broken into and used by so-called courting couples who added injury to insult by emptying his drink cupboard. The doctor eventually left it to the vandals. In the pubs in Cemaes I have been told by good chapel-going married men that the doctor's kiln was beautiful inside!

West of the Wylfa atomic power station is Cemlyn Bay, a possible anchorage in fair weather with winds in the west and south but hopeless in northerlies. A reason for stopping here is the sand spit which separates the bay from an inner lagoon, which is a bird sanctuary, more interesting in winter when it is crowded with wildfowl than in the summer months. The walled garden of the house there is a stopping place for many migrants; it was formerly owned by the millionaire pioneer aviator and racing driver Capt Vivian Hewitt.

From there on round Carmel Head to Holyhead there is no really suitable shelter. It is possible to land on the Skerries and visit the lighthouse in calm conditions, and very interesting it is too. The anchorage is in a lagoon between

the south-west island, Ynys Arw, and the main island and is entered from the north or west on either side of Trench Rock. White leading marks are painted on the rocks, and there is a stone jetty for landing. The lighthouse keepers invariably come down to take your lines and make you welcome. The Skerries have big colonies of seals and black rabbits, and the keepers keep a 'visitors book' of all the interesting birds which land there. The first Skerries light was lit in 1716. It consisted of a brazier which burnt about 100 tons of coal a year. It was the last lighthouse in the country to be privately owned, and a succession of owners lost money trying to collect dues from ships which benefitted from the light until, by 1840, the trade into Liverpool had so increased that the light dues became very profitable, amounting to over £20,000 a year. In 1841 Trinity House bought the lighthouse for nearly £½ million. The present lamp is 4 million candle power, the electricity being supplied by diesel generators which also drive the pumps for the large compressed-air tanks for the foghorn.

One can only go one way at a time, so I have had to leave Conwy on the north-east entrance to Menai Strait to the end. But, like marzipan on a Christmas cake, it is worth leaving to the end. The approach to the Conwy fairway buoy coming from Beaumaris is 122°mag from the north-east tip of Puffin Island. There is a channel between the south-east side of Puffin Island and Irishman Spit which lies approximately 2 cables off the island shore with a depth of 1 fathom at low-water springs. Careful note should be taken of the tidal system before making the passage. The Conwy channel is well defined with buoys, but it does change slightly and the buoys are not always in exactly the right place. If coming in near low water you must be prepared to go aground and sit it out for an hour or two, but the newcomer should time his arrival in the river itself at dead slack water springs or within an hour either side at neaps. Both at springs and neaps there is a rip off the narrows of up to 6½ knots at times. If an engine fails while looking for a mooring a boat can be swept under the bridges and lose mast and rigging at the very least, or be swept back onto a sandbank and possibly neaped.

On the subject of that rip, more than a few people have been drowned trying to board a dinghy, and in no way can a dinghy be rowed ashore when the rip is running. To avoid any mishap, damage to other boats and panic on board, the cruising man visiting Conwy should do a little pre-arrival arranging. He should telephone either the Harbour Master (049 263 6253) or Deganwy Yacht Services (0492 83869) to agree a definite plan on arrival so that he knows where he is going to go and what he is going to do. The Harbour Master does keep a few spare moorings among the 700-plus in the estuary, or he may be able to allocate someone else's for a short stay. Deganwy Yacht Services on the opposite (north) shore can offer a mud berth inside the old railway dock or, in an emergency only, an overnight deep-water mooring outside. They can do almost any type of repair

The Skerries Lighthouse from the anchorage in the lagoon. It is possible to visit it in calm weather and the keepers make you welcome

work. At Conwy there is a quay in front of the town wall, but it is likely to be occupied by the local fleet of trawlers. On the quayside there is a large chandlery and marine engineers. The North Wales Cruising Club (tel 049 263 3481) also have a few moorings. The Conwy Yacht Club in Deganwy has the fleet of Conwy One Designs, and for those who moor on that side they have changing rooms, showers and a bar. The Liverpool Arms on the quayside at Conwy has great charm and good home-made pies and bar snacks. The landlord is very sympathetic towards yachtsmen.

The castle is the main attraction at Conwy. It is best viewed from the water about halfway between Conwy and Deganwy when its eight great towers and the whole of its north and east walls can be seen against a backdrop of rounded hills. You will be looking due south, so early morning or early evening give the best lighting. Below the castle are the three bridges which cross the Conwy river. In the foreground is the elegant arched road bridge completed in 1958 which, unfortunately, obliterates the view of Telford's delicate suspension bridge of 1826 with its castellated cable towers to complement the castle. Beyond, also hidden from this viewpoint, is Robert Stephenson's tubular railway bridge, a small-scale forerunner to the one he built across Menai Strait. Telford's bridge is now National Trust property and used only as a footbridge. Its design can best be appreciated from on top of the East Barbican wall of the castle. Although sailing boats cannot get under these bridges, the river can be navigated by the adventurous in a small boat for 12 miles as far as Llanrwst – a market town with a bridge dated 1636 which was designed by Inigo Jones. At high tide it is a wide expanse of water with thickly wooded hills on both sides. When the tide goes out it becomes a network of meandering channels between acres of shining mud, and most of the channels are false ones. River trips are run from Conwy to Tal-y-cafn, 4 miles up river, for visits to Bodnant Hall with its 50 acres of garden owned by the National Trust and open to the public.

Conwy Castle was built by Edward I between 1283 and 1287 as his head-quarters in his war against the Welsh. It was nearly his undoing in 1294 when he and a few followers were trapped there by the river in flood, and narrowly escaped capture when a strong Welsh force came down off the mountains to attack. The floods subsided just in time for his army to come to his relief. The town walls, contemporary with the castle, with 21 towers and 5 gates are virtually intact, and there is a ½-mile walk along the top completely encircling the old town. Here the streets are narrow and can become very congested in summer. Plas Mawr, an Elizabethan mansion built 1576–1580, is the most interesting building and is now the home of the Royal Cambrian Academy of Art. Near the gate leading to the quay is Aberconwy, a medieval house of about 1500 with its richly decorated upper part hanging out over the pavement above an antique shop. On the quay is the smallest house in Britain furnished as a mid-Victorian Welsh cottage. It has two rooms, one above the other, and in each there is space for only two or three people to stand. Whether it is genuine or not, the tourists queue to go in one by one. The quay is at its lively best when the fishing boats are in with a catch, particularly if it is of Conwy dabs.

For a much higher view over Conwy and the whole of the Bay take a walk up to the top of Conwy Mountain (809ft); a path leads to the summit from Mill Gate. The northern side of the mountain is a sheer escarpment down to the shore ledge, along which run the A55 to Bangor and the Holyhead railway line. If you look out to sea from above Penmaen-bach Point at low water of a big spring tide you may discern the remains of foundations of buildings, causeways and tree stumps along the low-water mark. Legend has it that there was a fertile valley with farms and a palace, Llys Helig, between Bangor and Great Ormes Head but that around the sixth century there was a sudden land subsidence which submerged it, and thus Conwy Bay was formed. Round Great Ormes Head is Llandudno, the most famous resort in North Wales, which is only 2 miles by road from Conwy. There a cabin lift from Happy Valley will take you to the 679ft summit of Great Ormes Head where there is a nature trail, an hotel where Lewis Carroll wrote *Alice in Wonderland* and, at its western extremity, a lighthouse. When the tide is out you will see the square miles of Conwy and Lavan Sands – the same sand, no doubt, that the Walrus and the Carpenter 'wept like anything to see such quantities of . . .'. In 1985 work is due to start on the A55 tunnel from Deganwy to Morfa Conwy, so Conwy harbour will be disrupted for the next 4 or 5 years. The Harbour Master should be contacted for advice when the time comes.

After several years of visiting North Wales and different parts of its coastline and seaboard by road and by boat, but without ever having had the time to make a complete circumnavigation, I finally had the opportunity of joining a boat out of Porthmadog for a cruise round Anglesey and back through Menai Strait; at least that was the intention of the skipper and myself. But after clearing Bardsey Sound a sense of adventure took hold of the crew. They wanted to go across the sea to Ireland, not coast-hopping round Wales. I was out-voted five to one and hijacked to Wicklow. Frustrated at the time, I have long since forgiven them for it became the start of a love affair with the Irish and their coast.

After this chapter went to press another referendum was held in Wales on Sunday licensing, the outcome of which restored Sunday opening over nearly the whole of north Wales. The only part which still has a dry Sabbath is the Lleyn Peninsula. All round the coast, including Anglesey, the pubs are now open on Sundays except between Nevin (Porth Dinllaen) and Porthmadog.

Another new development which will be good news to yachtsmen is that work has started on the dredging of the inner harbour at Pwllheli and the construction of a marina.

'We picked up a mooring [at Dun Laoghaire]
right opposite the Royal Irish Yacht Club and
very soon one of their launches took us ashore to
use their showers'

# 5 Dublin to Wexford

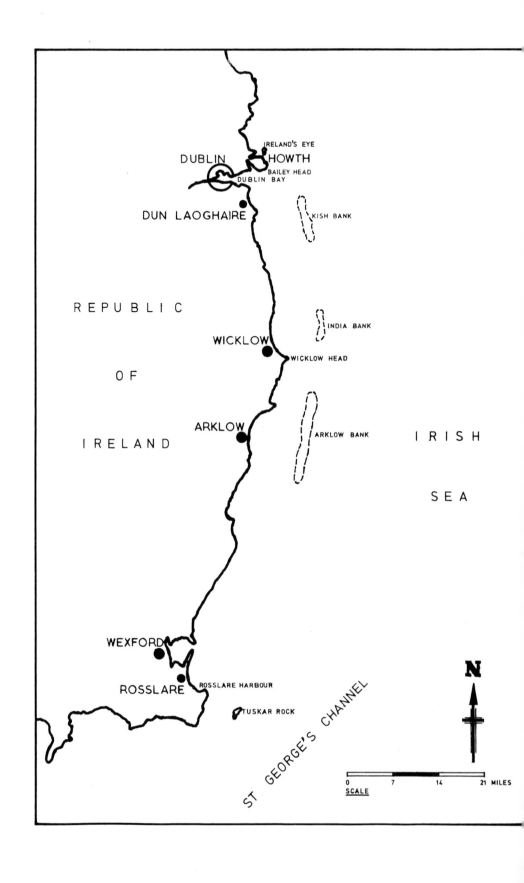

DUBLIN
IRELAND'S EYE
HOWTH
BAILEY HEAD
DUBLIN BAY

DUN LAOGHAIRE

KISH BANK

REPUBLIC

OF

INDIA BANK

WICKLOW
WICKLOW HEAD

IRELAND

ARKLOW

ARKLOW BANK

IRISH

SEA

WEXFORD

ROSSLARE
ROSSLARE HARBOUR

TUSKAR ROCK

ST GEORGE'S CHANNEL

N

0    7    14    21 MILES
SCALE

The east coast of Ireland can be difficult to approach because it is guarded along most of its length by a string of banks lying in the same north-south direction as the tide, which can so easily set you above or below the 'gate' you must enter. Also they are some 5 to 6 miles offshore, and conditions may be such that you will be on one of them before you can see the land. Therefore navigation must be more accurate than dead reckoning with visual bearings at the end. In fact for a worry-free passage it is essential to be able to get good DF fixes. In rough weather or bad visibility you cannot afford to get your position wrong. If you went onto one of the banks, particularly the Arklow Bank which dries, there would be a very real danger of losing the boat. On the east coast there are virtually no safe anchorages, and the harbours are all about one tide's distance from each other. The banks do, however, have some moderating effect on the sea inside them.

The return home in bad weather also has its problems. Holyhead is the only sure haven on the North Wales coast in any weather and at any state of the tide. Even so, despite its 1¼-mile breakwater, in north-easterly or easterly gales it can be most uncomfortable. Altogether sailing the Irish Sea and along either coast requires more seamanship and careful calculations than sailing about the south coast of England or even the west of Scotland where, although the winds are usually stronger, the tides are less potent and there is always a safe anchorage within easy reach. Every skipper will plan his own cruise route and strategy and do his own arithmetic. But the following information and suggestions on cruising from North Wales to the east coast of Ireland may be useful to first-timers.

From Bardsey Island it is roughly a 60-mile passage to Howth or Dun Laoghaire which, at a speed of 5 knots – if you are that lucky – gives you exactly a flood and an ebb or an ebb and a flood cancelling each other out during the length of the passage. Bardsey Sound should be negotiated at slack water, either high or low as near as possible, or with a fair tide and wind. Going westward, slack-water low is obviously better in case you leave it a little late when at least the first of the flood will see you through – although it might be uncomfortable with wind over tide. Also if the Sound is left at the start of the flood for a passage to Dublin Bay it is a reasonable bet that you will arrive off the Kish Bank at low-water slack or early in the new flood and have the flood to keep you clear of the bank and take you nicely into Dublin Bay or round the Bailey into Howth. Not that the Kish Bank is a lurking hazard; the light tower is large enough to be seen for miles in anything but very bad visibility, but there is always the possibility of arriving in the area with little or no wind and an engine which will not start. Then an adverse tide could pick you up and whip you across the bank.

It would also be wise to arrange the same timing when making for Wicklow in case you should end up south of Wicklow Head, when you would need the flood to take you round to Wicklow itself. There is a 5–6-knot tide round Wicklow Head, and if you arrive off the head or just south of it on the ebb you will be carried down inside the banks towards Arklow. The 'gate' into Wicklow is between the India Bank (the continuation of South Ridge) about five miles NE of Wicklow Head and the northern end of the Arklow Bank, about four-and-a-half miles offshore just south of Wicklow Head. Arklow Bank is awash in places and liable to change, which is another good reason for arriving off Wicklow on the flood. The gap between the two sets of banks is about ten miles. Codling Lanby buoy is a good mark when approaching from the east. Setting out from Holyhead for Howth or Dun Laoghaire it is best to leave at high water so that the first of the ebb will help to take you clear south of the Skerries and then, with luck, you will make the 40 miles to the Kish light with the last of the succeeding flood still with you. All these calculations only apply, of course, if you have a fair wind or, if too little or no wind, you use your engine to achieve the necessary average speed. Otherwise, as I mentioned earlier, you can go up and down with three or four tides and spend twenty hours or more on passage.

When doing a round trip in the season when the prevailing winds are south-westerly it usually pays to sail anti-clockwise – go over to the north and work your way south down the Irish coast. Then the chances are that you will have a fairer wind to get back. The Kish light has a radio beacon which is supposed to have a range of 50 miles, but you may have to get within 10 miles for an accurate fix. Behind you is the Skerries beacon, and to the north is Craigneish beacon, Isle of Man, which is one of the most powerful and audible all over the Irish Sea. Wicklow Head beacon is ahead of you, and Tuskar Rock beacon is useful once south of Wicklow. A beacon is scheduled to start operating on Bardsey Island, but at the time of writing was still not operational.

I sailed over to Ireland on a six-day cruise out of Pwllheli with John Mills, who charters a 30ft Halmatic, across to Howth, down the east coast to Wexford and back. Despite losing a day's sailing because of bad weather, we managed to include a few hours in Dublin, an afternoon and a night in Wicklow and a whole day in Wexford. We were through Bardsey Sound at 0630 and on a course of 315° for the Kish light. Winds were SE 2–3 all the way, and the engine was used part of the time to keep our average speed right. Passing the Kish the wind increased to SE 6 and we romped the last leg into Howth. The approach into Howth is easy. From the Kish light you can see the gap between Bailey Head and the island called Ireland's Eye which has a small stack off its east end. There are a few isolated rocks off the south side of the island protected by buoys, so the prudent course is to keep in more towards Bailey Head. We picked up a buoy in Howth at 1845, 12¼ hours and 63 miles on the log from Bardsey.

Being a Sunday evening the harbour was already crowded with yachts, and there were still more to come. Every few minutes an Irish boat would come reaching in between the harbour walls and tack through the crowd to its own mooring. Big or small, none used its engine but sailed with great panache. The Howth Yacht Club was spacious with a big bar to match and every facility. We were all strangers to the club, a situation which lasted a full 5 minutes. We finally left awash with Guinness, and our heads full of goodwill towards the natives and more local knowledge than we could digest. When I was last there in 1981 a vast civil-engineering project had started to provide the club. with a 200-boat marina and new clubhouse, so by now the whole character of the place will have changed.

Howth is 9 miles by road from the centre of Dublin to which there are bus and train services. The Hill of Howth forms the northern horn of the crescent of Dublin Bay. The summit of this rocky promontory is encircled by a pathway from which one can look over the bay to Dun Laoghaire to the south, and to the north across Howth Sound to Ireland's Eye, a favourite picnic place with the local dinghy owners. In the town are the ruins of Howth Abbey, the sixteenth-century Howth College, and Howth Castle dating from 1654, the public gardens of which are best when the rhododendrons and azaleas are in bloom. King Sitric is a restaurant for superb fish food and good wine, but in the expensive bracket.

From Howth it was decided to make for Wicklow 25 miles south, an easy day sail inside the banks on the ebb tide except when there is strong wind against tide, as there was that day. A force 6 southerly made it most uncomfortable and wet. After about two hours of the type of conditions which most people hate, but enjoy talking about afterwards, it was agreed that we turn and run for Dun Laoghaire. There we picked up a mooring right opposite the Royal Irish Yacht Club and very soon one of their launches took us ashore to use their showers. The Royal Irish is an imposing Georgian building overlooking the harbour and the atmosphere seems rather grand and a touch formal, but everyone was every bit as friendly as they are in the smallest boat club or waterside pub anywhere else in Ireland − except on the question of dress! It would have been most pleasant to have dined there for the club has preserved an air of elegance which is not easily found these days unless you have the money and the connections. As visiting yachtsmen we were accepted as honorary members. But, alas, none of us had brought the mandatory tie and jacket.

So instead we took a 20-minute train journey into Dublin and engaged a taxi driver to take us to a good restaurant which I knew of. Being Monday night it was closed − so much for my local knowledge; and after an hour the driver dropped us off 100 yards from where we had hailed him and the charge was £3. But in the intervening hour he had taken us on a tour of Dublin giving us the while a most humorous historical commentary immaculately edited for English ears. The rest of the evening was spent exploring the pubs of which we had all heard so much. But, being strangers to the city, we never did find any of the more famous ones. With beginners' luck we jumped on a moving bus at 11.30 which off-loaded us at Dun Laoghaire harbour. We did not know it then, but last buses leave the city centre for suburban destinations at 11.30pm sharp.

If making a week's visit to the east coast of Ireland (on a charter boat it will probably only be six full days) and a day is spent in Dublin, there will only be time left to visit two out of the four remaining ports, leaving a margin for getting back across the Irish Sea in time. Rosslare is nothing more than an artificial harbour and car-ferry terminal, of little interest, the furthest away and so reduces the choices to Wicklow, Arklow and Wexford.

The morning after our visit to Dublin, with the wind NW force 3, we had an uneventful reach to Wicklow, leaving at 1130 and arriving at 1515 with 15 miles on the log. Going down inside the banks from Dun Laoghaire is a matter of buoy hopping, or rather buoy passing. They come up within sight of each other through the binoculars. The main thing to watch is that you do not go too far offshore and therefore too near the banks, as the tide tends to set you onto them anyway. In strong winds from the east the banks break some of the force of the sea. Always try to make Wicklow from Howth or Dun Laoghaire (and thence Wicklow to Arklow, and so on) on one ebb unless you have a very strong fair wind to stem a foul tide. If you are beating and the tide turns on you, then you will be wasting your time. The entrance to Wicklow harbour, which lies to the east of the town, is straight in between the two quays. If the wind is from the north or east it would be best to go right in, round a right-hand bend, and into the river where there are always several yachts moored. Otherwise it is quite comfortable to lie inside the east quay a little way off the lifeboat slipway.

The delights of Wicklow are not to be found in the harbour but in the Grand Hotel (where you can eat extremely well) and the Wicklow Sailing Club (which opens when you need a shower and stays open as long as there is good company still awake). There is a small but very active cruising fraternity who have developed a special relationship with their opposite numbers in North Wales. The yacht traffic between Wicklow, Holyhead and Pwllheli is constant throughout the season. There is not a great deal to do or to see in Wicklow itself; it is the welcome and hospitality of the people that give it its character. There is an interesting and instructive 2-mile walk along the clifftops to Wicklow Head which gives extensive views of the banks and, on a clear day, the Codling light. On the way there is Peadar's Rock on which, according to the eighth-century Book of Armagh, St Patrick once landed; the Black Castle built in the twelfth century with an underground passage linking it to the town; and some old cannon from the Napoleonic Wars. On the head there are three lighthouses.

Two were originally built on Wicklow Head by the Revenue Commissioners, and were lit for the first time on 1 September 1781, each lantern containing twenty tallow candles and a large reflector. One tower is still in situ minus its 8-sided lantern which was replaced by a brick dome in 1866 to protect the tower from the weather. Two lights were considered necessary to warn mariners of the dangerous sand banks off the Wicklow coast, and also to lead vessels through the Wicklow Swash – the safe passage between the banks – when the lights were in line bearing WNW and one above the other. Two new lighthouses were erected to take over from them in 1818 but on the same bearing; their lanterns housed fifteen oil lamps and a reflector each. Then in 1865 the upper or inshore of the two lights was discontinued to give way to a lightvessel, the Wicklow Swash,

Wicklow Head lighthouse. Originally there were two to lead vessels through the Wicklow Swash; later the inshore light was replaced by light vessels and today by Lanby buoys

which in turn was replaced by the Codling and North Arklow lightvessels in 1867. Meanwhile the remaining 1818 light was converted to gas which continued to be used until 1906 when it was given a paraffin-vapour burner, and also a 500mm revolving optic. In 1976 paraffin gave way to electric, and only two months later Lanby buoys took over from both lightvessels. In 1978 a radio beacon was added to the station which is linked to five others around the Irish, Welsh and Isle of Man coasts.

After leaving Wicklow we wanted to go into Wexford, but the bar shifts frequently, there is a large shallow lagoon to negotiate which at that time was unbuoyed, and the *Sailing Directions* said: 'It would be foolhardy to attempt to get into Wexford without someone on board who has local knowledge'. Anywhere else we might have had to drop the idea, but Harry Jordan, the then Commodore of Wicklow Sailing Club, after a quick telephone call, arranged that we would be met by a pilot if we were off the Wexford Bar at 1930. Our pilot turned out to be the local chemist, John Sherwood, who had brought some of his family with him for the 5-mile trip out to the bar to meet us. He led us through the gap with breaking water within 50 yards on either side of us, past patches of water on which sea birds were standing, past a perch behind which were what looked like small rocks but are, in fact, the ruins of an inundated fort and village awash at high water. We entered a featureless lagoon some 3 × 5 miles in extent and, after making several incomprehensible changes of course with our echo

Wexford: 'after making several incomprehensible changes of course . . . we arrived alongside the town quay'

sounder showing a foot or two to spare, we arrived alongside the town quay having taken 1¾ hours to negotiate the channel under engine.

When we were tied up John Sherwood and family joined us on board for a drink, and I asked him if many 'foreign' boats came into Wexford. 'Two years ago, in 1976, we did have 14, maybe 15.' But he was hoping that things might improve in the future and life become more exciting for the locals because the Wexford Harbour Boat Club, with the co-operation of the local fishermen, were about to buoy the channel for that season and repeat the exercise annually with necessary alterations; this they have done. We were picked up by cars at 11.30 that night and taken to a hastily arranged party in our honour at the Boat Club a mile up the river. Needless to say, we did not make the morning tide as planned and so spent the day in Wexford – some of it sitting in the bar of the local undertakers listening to stories about the days when the harbour was full of schooners and barquentines. The facia clearly states 'Con Macken, Bar Undertaker'. There is a window either side of the doorway, one displaying bottles and the other wreaths and crosses. It is a practical arrangement; the undertaker gets to know his future customers well ahead of time and, when their time comes, their relatives can have a few drinks while making the funeral arrangements and ordering drink for the wake.

On a later visit to Wexford I found the Crown Bar in Monck Street. Small and insignificant from the outside, it was once Kelly's Crown Hotel, a stage-coaching inn and thought to be the oldest licensed premises in the British Isles. It has been in the Kelly family since 1841, but what makes it more extraordinary than any other pub is that crammed into every inch of wall and ceiling space is the largest collection of antique weapons and militaria outside a museum. They are the lifetime's collection of the last Kelly landlord who died a few years ago. His elderly widow now runs the pub, opening only in the evening and on Saturday mornings. Whether the Crown stays in the Kelly family and keeps its collection intact will depend on Mrs Kelly's daughter, who is a nurse, and when I was there had still not made up her mind whether to change her vocation. The old granary near the edge of the town has been very well restored, and is now a restaurant of the same name where I had a first-class dinner. Like so many restaurants throughout Ireland, their portions are so generous that I was not able to face anything from the staggering sweet trolley. Worth mentioning here – Irish men seem to have insatiable appetites, and will often order three different puddings to round off their meal.

Wexford is fronted by a long quay once lined with coastal shipping, now deserted but for a few fishing boats and the occasional yacht. Berthed alongside is an old lightvessel which is now a maritime museum. On the quay is a statue to John Barry, founder of the US Navy, who was a local boy. The streets are narrow – in places you can almost shake hands across the road, and a small gem in this small town is the Theatre Royal, a restored Regency theatre where top international singers perform during the annual October Opera Festival, one of

What better way to get to know your undertaker? This very Irish combination of trades is in Wexford

A corner of the little maritime museum in Arklow, typical of similar museums to be found in Irish coastal towns

the events in the Irish social calendar. There are also many fringe events at the time including, so late in the season, yacht racing. Two miles out of the town on the north arm of the lagoon known as the North Slob there is a wildlife sanctuary where a large proportion of the world's population of Greenland whitefront geese winter, and it is a refuge for many species of wildfowl which migrate there. The Tuskar Rock and lighthouse, only 6 miles off the coast, is a rich area for sea angling.

We sailed at 1940 to find our way out through the shallow lagoon to the bar. At a time when we really needed the echo sounder it decided to go on the blink, but fortunately our skipper had not neglected the old skills and he guided us out with a list of bearings, taken the previous night, in one hand while expertly swinging the lead with the other.

Arklow, which we missed out on that trip, is an active fishing port with some commercial shipping. Once inside the basin it is as safe as houses, but the narrow entrance between two north-west-pointing walls can be dangerous in a strong onshore wind particularly around low water. It is definitely unsafe in strong south and south-easterlies. Because there is always water running out and the walls blanket the wind, it is advisable to motor in. Every facility except sail making is available from the yard of the great man himself, Jack Tyrrell, who never built a bad vessel and who still builds them in wood using locally felled oaks. He it was who built *Gipsy Moth III* that took Sir Francis Chichester round the world, despite his grumbles about her. More recently he designed and built the Irish Sail Training brigantine *Asgard*.

The town's famous pottery products are exported worldwide, and the company has a large bargain shop on the side of the dock. Prices are low, design is mundane and the staff, surprisingly, is Japanese, as is the management. You can join a conducted tour of the pottery, but rather more interesting to sailors is the little maritime museum up in the town. It has some pretty macabre souvenirs of the *Lusitania* – Arklow fishermen went to the rescue of the torpedoed passengers – including a medal struck in Germany to celebrate the submarine's 'heroic victory' over an unarmed liner. If stopping a while there are good beaches either side of Arklow harbour, and 4 miles from the town are the botanical gardens at Mount Usher, Ashford, open to the public on Sunday afternoons.

Tintern Abbey by Bannow Bay, Co Wexford, was founded by William, Earl Marshal of England, about 1200 and first occupied by monks from its namesake in Wales

# 6 The South Coast of Ireland

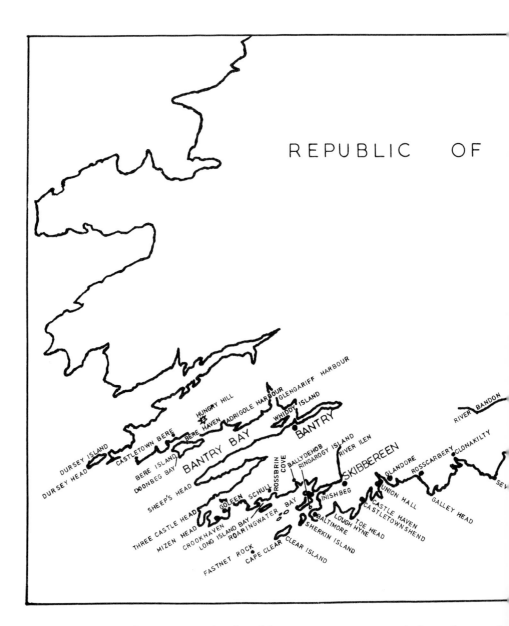

REPUBLIC OF

RIVER BANDON

GLENGARIFF HARBOUR

HARBOUR

HUNGRY HILL

ADRIGOLE HARBOUR

BERE HAVEN

WHIDDY ISLAND

BANTRY

BANTRY BAY

DURSEY ISLAND

CASTLETOWN BERE

DURSEY HEAD

BERE ISLAND

DOONBEG BAY

SHEEP'S HEAD

BALLYDEHOB

RINGAROGY ISLAND

RIVER ILEN

ROSSBRIN COVE

SKIBBEREEN

GLANDORE

ROSSCARBERY

CLONAKILTY

THREE CASTLE HEAD

GOLEEN

SCHULL

UNION HALL

GALLEY HEAD

MIZEN HEAD

CROOKHAVEN

LONG ISLAND BAY

ROARINGWATER BAY

INISHBEG

BALTIMORE

LOUGH HYNE

CASTLE HAVEN

CASTLETOWNSHEND

TOE HEAD

SHERKIN ISLAND

FASTNET ROCK

CAPE CLEAR

CLEAR ISLAND

SEV

The east coast of Ireland, south of Dublin, is interesting enough for a short and introductory Irish cruise, but a fortnight along the south coast from Dunmore East to Bantry Bay would be tenfold more rewarding. To go further on into the Kenmare River, past Valentia, round Dingle and up to Galway Bay is a cruise of which dreams are made, and I have never had the time to make it. However, Bantry Bay is comfortably reached from North or South Wales within a fortnight stopping at a different place each night, if an Irish Sea night passage is made at the beginning and at the end. The places which I will describe were not, I must admit, all visited within a fortnight's cruise, but during the course of three trips to that coast. The ground that you can cover and the number of places where you

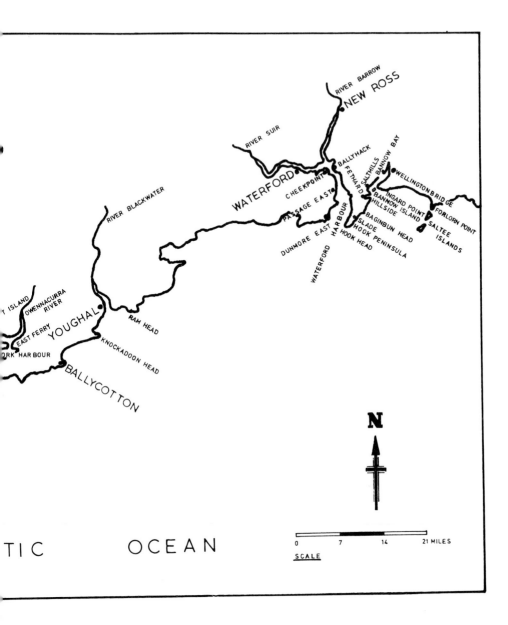

RIVER BARROW

NEW ROSS

RIVER SUIR

BALLYHACK

BANNOW BAY

WATERFORD

CHEEKPOINT

PASSAGE EAST

FEETHARD

SALTMILLS

WELLINGTON BRIDGE

INGARD POINT

FORLORN POINT

RIVER BLACKWATER

BANNOW ISLAND

HILLSIDE

BAGINBUN HEAD

SALTEE ISLANDS

DUNMORE EAST

WATERFORD HARBOUR

SLADE

HOOK HEAD

HOOK PENINSULA

T ISLAND

OWENNACURRA RIVER

EAST FERRY

YOUGHAL

RAM HEAD

RK HARBOUR

KNOCKADOON HEAD

BALLYCOTTON

N

TIC        OCEAN

0        7        14        21 MILES

SCALE

can call in in a given time are governed not only by the weather, but also by how willing you are to use your engine because the south coast of Ireland is a succession of headlands so tacking to get round them can use up valuable hours heading out to sea and back again.

Dunmore East is the obvious first port of call after crossing the Irish Sea and passing outside Tuskar Rock and Coningbeg Lightship to avoid the Saltee Islands. The *Sailing Directions* call it a 'small artificial' harbour on the west side of the entrance to Waterford Harbour. But after a long crossing, and possibly coming from somewhere much smaller, it has a large and welcoming appearance as you turn in round the granite lighthouse on the pier to be embraced by its high wide wall on one side and the expanse of the New Quay on the other with the village rising up above the harbour. It can be crowded with big fishing boats, but there always seems to be a small colony of yachts rafted alongside the east pier below the quay. Once ashore, perhaps after climbing over a few decks and a couple of big trawlers, it is about fifty yards to the Waterford Harbour Sailing Club's shower rooms. At the end of the harbour there is a large building which looks like an hotel, which it was when the packet boats called at Dunmore in the last century before being transferred to the new artificial harbour at Rosslare. Since 1883 the building has been used as a convent by the Sisters of Mercy. From in front of the convent a path leads up to the pilot look-out station on Black Knob for a seaward view across the entrance to Waterford Harbour and the Hook Peninsula with its lighthouse. If you have been ashore for a while and sheltered from the weather in the harbour it is the point to go to for a look at the sea state.

Walking the other way the road bends uphill into the village which straggles for nearly a mile. It has very few shops, a tiny room in a house serves as the post office, and there are several old stone cottages with thatched roofs which have been a little too well renovated but have charm nonetheless. From the village street several paths run down the cliffs to very beautiful rocky coves which are the homes of many thousands of kittiwakes. Local dayboats lie to moorings just off the rocks, which are great fun for children to play amongst. It is unusual for kittiwakes to nest so close to human activity. The Haven Hotel, with a great bar whose windows overlook Hook Head and the Saltee Islands in the distance, has good cuisine using local produce, and their roast beef is exceptional. Six acres of lawns and woods offer a temporary retreat from boats and water. At the end of the village The Ship is a pub where young people sit talking to old men with insatiable thirsts. The little dining area is always crowded with people eating lobster salads and fresh strawberries and cream. In fact, the staff seem to spend as much time carrying bowls of whipped cream as they do pint glasses. I have the happiest memories of both the Haven and The Ship, having celebrated two birthdays in both of them – the first time it was by chance, the second time was by design.

If sailing westward from Dunmore it is as well to remember that the prevailing winds are westerly, and that advantage should be taken of any free wind which you are granted to press on as far west as possible and leave most of the short hops and stops for the easier run back. But before going on to Bantry Bay I must introduce the possibility of exploring the Hook Peninsula and the River Suir up to Waterford, or even taking a day sail to the Saltee Islands – about thirty-two miles there and back. For the latter you need a calm day so that a landing can be made by tender to see, during the nesting period, the tens of thousands of gulls, kittiwakes, puffins, razorbills, guillemots and cormorants. In June South Saltee Island is almost covered with eggs and the birds are aggressive, but by the end of July they will have gone to sea and so there is not much point in making the trip. The east side of the Hook Peninsula is not much favoured by cruising boats because it is wide open to the south and the south-east, and even when it gives good shelter in westerlies there can be a formidable race off Hook Head. Although when the westerlies are very strong small yachts do sometimes seek shelter in the lee of the peninsula on their way to Dunmore East or Cork.

If you have a tender with a small outboard a very interesting day can be spent in beautiful surroundings exploring Bannow Bay at the north-east end of the peninsula, an area of great historical significance with ruined castle and abbey, old silver mines and a lost town. For this purpose anchor just north of Ingard Point off the toytown harbour of Hillside in good holding sand. The harbour dries, but has about 5ft at half tide. However, it really is very small, the entrance not much wider than the beam of a 50ft trawler, and inside there is only room for about six fishing boats and no space to manoeuvre. From Hillside, which is the harbour for Fethard a mile inland up the creek, take the tender over to Bannow Island. Now joined to the mainland, it is a bumpy sandy little peninsula with the ruins of the thirteenth-century St Mary's Church very prominent and marking the site of a Norman town which has been covered by drifting sand since the seventeenth century. Approaching the beach someone may make that corny remark: 'I wonder if the natives are friendly?' It was a serious question in 1169 when 600 men led by Robert Fitzstephen and Maurice de Prendergast landed there – that was the start of the Norman invasion of Ireland. The answer that time was 'yes' because they were met by Dermot MacMurrough who had the permission of Henry II to recruit help from amongst the Normans in South Wales to retrieve his lost High Kingship of Leinster. The Earl of Pembroke, named Strongbow, had agreed to help in return for the hand of Dermot's daughter and, eventually, the succession to the Kingdom of Leinster. The 600 who landed at Bannow were an advance party. When I landed there I also had a friendly welcome, from a party of three nuns a'paddling!

Getting into Bannow Bay with a boat presents problems. The entrance has a bar with at times only a foot of water over it, and the bay is a landlocked lagoon 5 miles long, fed by two rivers, so when the ebb comes out waves over the bar stand up and look at you. It might be practical to port the tender a few hundred yards across the narrow isthmus below the church and launch it again inside the bay. Going up the bay the ruins of three castles can be seen a little way inland among the trees on sloping ground, and the tall chimney of a derelict lead mine. At the head of the bay, perhaps an hour by tender, is Wellingtonbridge Village, south-west of which on the water's edge are the tower and walls of a fourteenth-century Augustine church and the ruins of Black Castle, an early Norman fortress. Both buildings are surrounded by trees, and a number of small creeks give them the appearance of standing on islands. They make a pretty scene; an excellent place to stop for a picnic. Nearby is a small ruin called the Cowboy's Chapel because it was built by a cowherd who made his fortune. A little way south of the castle the remains of a harbour wall built of large stones can be seen at the water's edge with nearby a house incorporating a tower house (OS

Remains of the once-flourishing medieval town of Clonmines at the head of Bannow Bay

23.8413). The bits of wall are all that remain of the port of Clonmines which silted up about 1600. It was a flourishing medieval town dependent on the silver and lead mines around it which were worked until Elizabethan times. The town was given a charter by the Earl of Pembroke in the thirteenth century and, although it was scarcely inhabited in the seventeenth century, it continued to send members to Parliament up to 1800. The remains of several buildings can still be seen, particularly one of the old town gates, later converted into a lime kiln, a tower said to have been a part of the town hall, a two-storey castellated building which was the seat of an ecclesiastical court (one part of the ceiling is vaulted with ribbed arches and the other barrel vaulted), a curtain wall with a tower and a tower house. This extremely intriguing site is not signposted, it is on private property, and visitors are not encouraged. But since it is mentioned, albeit briefly, in the official Ireland Guide published by Bord Failte without mention of the private ground, no one can be blamed for going and taking a look.

Further down the west shore is Saltmills, a very small village at the entrance to a creek which once turned a tidal mill, hence the name. On the flood a dinghy can be taken up the creek to Tintern Abbey. If the name seems familiar but out of place, it is not. This Tintern Abbey was founded around 1200 and called after its famous counterpart in Wales, from which its first Cistercian monks came. The founder was William, Earl Marshal of England, following a vow made during a stormy crossing of the Irish Sea that, if he survived, he would found a church in Ireland. It is a strong squared edifice with a tower standing on a small hillslope above the water. Unfortunately it is now in a dangerous condition and there is no access to the interior, much of which was converted into living quarters over the centuries. But some restoration work has been started, and it will no doubt be open again very soon.

Baginbun Head, a mile south of Hillside, has a sheltered anchorage to the north of and inside the head with good holding, but watch out for salmon nets and lobster pots in the area. The head is marked by a Martello Tower which is now a private house. It was to Baginbun that Strongbow sent a second advance party of ten knights and seventy archers in 1170 before himself landing with an army at Passage East in Waterford Harbour three months later. The head had already been fortified by the Celts and was, therefore, easy to defend. The Normans built their own additional earthworks across the neck of the headland and were able to resist the attack of an army of Norse and Irish who arrived from Waterford to dislodge them. Cattle were rounded up and driven on to the headland, and then driven out against the Norse and the Irish; while they were busy dispersing before the frightened animals, the Normans attacked and routed them. Seventy Waterford citizens were captured, had their limbs broken so that they could not swim, and were then thrown over the cliffs. When Strongbow arrived on the scene the Normans moved to capture Waterford, and so began the modern history of Ireland. There is a rhyme which says:

> At the creeke of Baginbun
> Ireland was lost and won.

Traces of the Celtic fortifications and the Norman earthworks can be discerned, and by walking around this headland it is possible to visualise what happened in May 1170.

Slade, at the south-east end of the Hook Peninsula, has neither shop nor pub but the castle gives it a picturesque flavour

Slade near the end of the Hook Peninsula is ignored by the *Sailing Directions*, but it has a fairly big fishing harbour which dries. The walls are built so that boats have to go round a hairpin bend to get from the outer to the inner harbour. It is sheltered from the south and west round to the north. The village has nothing, neither shop nor pub, but Slade Castle right beside the harbour gives the place a picturesqueness. It was built in the late fifteenth or early sixteenth century, has a 56ft-high battlemented tower and illustrates the transition from fortified castle to castle-style stately home. Although very ruined, castle fanciers may scramble about inside by getting the key from Mr Rice who lives around the corner. One side of the harbour is flanked by cellar-like buildings with corbelled roofs which were used for the making of salt in the eighteenth century. From Slade it is about a mile walk along the cliffs over many stone walls, or two miles by road, to Hook Lighthouse. It is very distinctive: 80ft high, 40ft wide, white with two black bands with a shorter modern light tower on top of it. Such are the dry facts which do not make it seem much different from many other lights, but it is almost certainly the oldest in Europe. In the fifth century Dubhan, a pilgrim priest, arrived on the peninsula from South Wales and there founded a monastery. He then established a beacon light on the end of the peninsula as an act of practical Christianity, and the monks from the monastery looked after the light for the next thousand years. The tower which we see today was built by the monks some time between 1170 and 1182. The limestone walls vary from 12ft to 9ft in thickness, and through the thickness of the walls a stairway spirals round the tower to the summit. Several rooms are also built into the walls, the three largest being circular with vaulted ceilings. An incredible engineering feat for twelfth-century monks. On the cliff edge nearby are spectacular blow holes.

On the west side of the Hook Peninsula, Waterford Harbour, which is the estuary of the rivers Suir and Barrow, offers a day's sail through patches of very beautiful scenery. Both waterways are used by big shipping, and pilotage presents no problems. Normally it is not practical to continue under sail beyond Passage East where the Suir narrows and the wind becomes unpredictable. On my first visit to Cheekpoint to keep a luncheon appointment the crew was determined to keep sail up all the way. We got there after short tacking, but an hour late to find our host on the point of leaving in a huff. Even an easy-going Irishman thought we were foolish and a little impolite not to have used the engine. On the Hook shore the first site of interest is Duncannon, an unlovely fort on a rocky spur which was used by the Normans in the twelfth century, the English at the time of the Spanish Armada, the Irish Confederates in 1642, and was captured by Cromwell in 1649, after which it became a British garrison fort and then a prison. It has been connected with most of Ireland's troubles, and is now a summer camp for the Irish Army. Inside it is a hotch-potch of military architecture from Elizabethan to Georgian with contemporary bits added. The estuary narrows and the river proper begins at Passage East on the Waterford side and Ballyhack on the opposite shore. Ballyhack is a small fishing harbour with a steep village street and a castle tower, once a preceptor of the Knights Templar. A pretty place, but more interesting is the magnificent ruin of Dunbrody, a thirteenth-century Cistercian abbey beside a creek half a mile to the south (OS 23.7115). A key can be had from William Ryan who lives 150 yards away. It is a 195ft-long austere building and some of the domestic attachments survive, including the refectory and kitchen.

Passage East has quite a big drying harbour with three wide quays which form extensions to two large open squares, surrounded by neat and multi-coloured houses; very neat with a Continental flavour and a delightful little village to walk around. It was here that Strongbow landed to capture Waterford and claim his princess. The ground rises precipitously behind the village and there is a steep path leading to a now-disused village church from which you get a view of the harbour and across the Suir to Ballyhack. A mile south is the waterside village of Crooke which has no harbour and is of little interest, but, together with Hook on the other side of Waterford Harbour, it has achieved lasting fame in the expression, 'By Hook or by Crooke' which Oliver Cromwell is supposed to have said when discussing his plans to attack Waterford.

Cheekpoint, on the bend where the Suir and Barrow join, is, in my opinion, the best stopping place on the way to Waterford or New Ross and could be an alternative to Dunmore East as an overnight-berth stop. A half-mile walk up to the top of the point takes you to the Post Office-store and beyond to several viewpoints from which can be seen Waterford, the junction of the rivers, large

Passage East, where the estuary narrows on the way to Waterford. Ballyhack and its castle is on the other side of the River Suir

stretches of the estuary and the Wicklow Hills in the far north. The village is very small, one street, but it was once a thriving township when it was the port for the mail packets from England to Waterford. That was before the first pier was built at Dunmore East. The pier and quay at Cheekpoint are, as a result, substantial and provide secure berthing. The surge of the tide, however, makes well-adjusted breast ropes and springs essential. The place was renamed Bolton at one time by its benefactor, Cornelius Bolton, who established several manufactories there particularly for making hosiery. In Sleater's *Topography of Ireland* published in 1806 is the following reference: 'Bolton, formerly called Cheekpoint, cotton factory and hosiery, established by Mr Bolton. A most commodious Inn for passengers in the pacquets to and from Milford Haven in Pembrokeshire.' The Suir Inn by the quay is the same 'commodious Inn' and it was for a lunch there that we sailed in an hour late. And a memorable meal it was of baked scallops in a cheese-and-wine sauce accompanied by a cool dry white wine and followed by Gaelic coffee. Two years later I went out of my way to repeat the experience, but the landlord told me that they no longer served luncheon because the tourist trade had gone. If and when it came back, he said, they would start lunches again. Meanwhile they serve dinners with a seafood plate as a central item on the menu. The cottages on both sides of the street are all the same, single storey, each with a small portico and tiny walled-in front garden. They were erected in the eighteenth century as a model factory village.

There is navigation for large commercial ships up the Suir to Waterford or the Barrow to New Ross. The latter is the more scenic trip, but Waterford the more likely to be taken if only because of the lure of Waterford crystal. Visitors can go round the famous glass works, two miles out of town, but there are no bargains to be had there. To buy Waterford crystal you have to go to Knox's elegant shop in the town where you are likely to find yourself a stranger among Americans. To get a quick all-in-one-place lesson on Waterford's long history back to the eighth century when it was a Danish settlement, go to Reginald's Tower, 1,000 years old and now a museum. It stands near the river at the end of Parade Quay. There are, of course, many things of an historical nature to be found in Waterford, but finding them involves a lot of walking through some very dull parts of a commercial and industrial city. I may be doing it an injustice, but I could not be bothered. There are so many other places more charming and more compact for the traveller to spend time on.

Between Waterford Harbour and Crosshaven, the yachting centre for Cork, is the town of Youghal (pronounced 'yawl') just inside the narrow estuary of the River Blackwater. To go there involves a detour into Youghal Bay off the direct track clearing Ram Head and Knockadoon Head, but it is a detour worth making. The first time I sailed in there I was of the contrary opinion. The tide runs fast through the anchorage and about half an hour was spent laying out a kedge. By the time we had rowed ashore and ported the tender a few hundred yards upstream to have the tide with us for the row back, it was late in the evening and everything was shut except the pubs. We knew nothing about the town and obviously went through the wrong doors, for we had a boring evening talking among ourselves in almost empty bars and ended up with fish and chips. It was a chance meeting with a man in the Suir Inn at Cheekpoint on my later trip that led to my seeing Youghal in a better light. He told me that he was born and bred in the town and gave me a short list of people to whom I was to introduce myself as a friend of his. The result was that I was received more as a guest than a tourist when I went back there.

The N25 from Waterford crosses the Blackwater over a new road bridge at the head of the estuary two miles out of the town. It was built by an engineer from Wolverhampton, Ray Morris, who married a local girl, Nuala, and they now live in an old shooting lodge which belonged to the Duke of Devonshire. They have converted the stables and other outbuildings into a restaurant and wine bar called the Bush Courtyard. It is a 1¼-mile walk from the harbour, but there are two taxis in the town. It is a very good restaurant, intimate, candle-lit, with Irish and Continental cuisine, and the wine bar used by the natives as much as by diners is a good place for picking up local knowledge. The walls are covered with old photographs, dating from the end of the last century up to the 1950s, of the trading schooners which once filled the harbour and sailed up the Blackwater to load pit props for Wales. One of them, *Kathleen & May*, built at Connah's Quay in 1900 carried her last cargo in the coasting trade in 1960 – but not under sail – and is now preserved at St Katharine's Yacht Haven in London. Kathleen and May were the two daughters of Mr M. J. Fleming of Youghal, her owner between 1908 and 1931. The Flemings are an old seafaring family and it was a boat owned by them which found the *Mary Celeste* abandoned in mid-Atlantic on 5 December 1872 and towed her into Gibraltar. At that time at least one-hundred-and-fifty merchant ships had Youghal as their home port, and Youghal seamen had their own special way of whistling to announce their arrival to each other in ports all over the world.

Early in this century the river currents and tides built a sand barrier across the mouth of the estuary and closed the harbour to the steam ships which had replaced the schooners. Apart from being a port of call for yachts, the harbour is now a sea-angling centre and the river provides a rich harvest of salmon which are flown overnight from Cork to London and the Continent. It has of recent years earned the reputation for being a gastronomic town, not on a par with, or having the variety of, Dublin or Kinsale, but making it a place to call into for a good dinner ashore. The Bush Courtyard which I have mentioned is intimate and family-run, as also is Aherne's Seafood Bar in North Main Street which is possibly one of the best seafood places in the south of Ireland. Both restaurants have patio tables for warm evenings. A twenty-minute walk from the town centre is The Crow, a French restaurant and pub owned by a Frenchman who does the cooking himself. In the evenings it is often possible to buy fresh fish on the quayside and there are, despite my first experience, some interesting pubs. I should perhaps mention here that pubs in Ireland are quite happy to serve you with tea or coffee, and children are made welcome particularly in the country. For the company of local fishermen and longshoremen try Buttimers; it is by the Market Dock and has a mural on its outside wall showing a sailing ship passing between two lighthouses. Moby Dick is the pub which featured in the film of the same name and around the bar walls are lots of photographs of the filming and the stars. The Blackwater Inn is an old pub which has been in the same family for one hundred years, but has been 'done up' a bit inside to cater for younger tastes. They have ceilidh evenings, and hanging on the walls are several extraordinary extracts from the old Council Book of Youghal. This is one of them:

> 29th September, 1610. Whereas divers lewd and incontinent persons not regarding God or goodness do through their flatteries and practices labour and endeavour the abuse and overthrow of young and silly virgin maids to the great grief and discontent of the parents, and said young maids often utter undoing, it is therefore by this general Assembly provided that whosoever from henceforth shall abuse and deflower any such young maiden virgin being a mayor's daughter shall forfeit to the use of the maiden so deflowered 40 LI: an Alderman's daughter 30 LI; a Balive's daughter 20 LI or any freeman's daughter 10 LI, and a groom's daughter 5 LI to be levied by the mayor etc. aforesaid or the party so offending to marry the said maiden by him so deflowered.

The central feature of the town is the Clock Tower which spans the main street. It was built in the 1770s as a gaol and has an ugly history of beating, torturing and hanging rebels by the Protestant minority who ruled the town for two centuries. It now houses the Tourist Office, a museum and art gallery. A narrow flight of steps beside the tower leads to the remaining sections of the old town walls. They are as well preserved as any in Ireland, and there is a walk along the top of part of them. St Mary's Collegiate Church, now the Church of Ireland parish church, was founded in the thirteenth century and is considered a monument of national importance. The many objects of interest in it would take two or three hours to examine closely, but at least look at the monument designed and erected for himself by Richard Boyle, the first Earl of Cork. The sculpture shows the earl, his three wives and sixteen children. The colours of their dresses are only slightly faded and give a good idea of Elizabethan fashion. Next to the church is Myrtle Grove, a private house which can be glimpsed only by peering over the churchyard wall. It was the home of Sir Walter Raleigh for many years, the often-absentee Mayor of Youghal. They say that he planted the first potatoes in Europe in the garden of the house. The Presentation Convent at the top of the town has been famous for its lacemaking for over one hundred years.

Along the coast road going west is a permanent funfair and a large beach, around which the seaside resort of Youghal has grown up out of sight of the old part and is an ideal place to take the children for a break. The honorary Harbour Master, Theo Vastenhaut, is a ship's captain from Rotterdam who met an Irish girl and, after 34 years at sea, 'came ashore' at Youghal. He runs a very busy angling business, but when he is out with an angling party his boat *Ursce Beatha* (Red Boat) can be contacted on VHF, or you may pass her on the way in. The one time when Youghal should be avoided is when there is a south-westerly wind and an ebb tide, which produce a big swell with troughs of 4ft. The Blackwater is a pretty river for an expedition beyond the bridge in a tender, but between April and August great care has to be taken to avoid the salmon nets. The same applies all the way on down this coast. The salmon nets run out from near the shore for up to a mile, and it is often difficult to see the buoys from a distance.

Ballycotton on the way to Cork is a small artificial harbour with fishing boats inside. It is best to anchor off north-east of the breakwater sheltered by the offlying islands. To the north of the little village there is a four-mile flat sandy beach. Shark-fishing boats ply for hire from the harbour.

The Royal Cork Yacht Club founded in 1728 is the oldest yacht club in the world and for that, if for no other reason, a call in at Crosshaven should be arranged. It is the best yacht haven of Cork Harbour and the nearest to hand after passing through the entrance between Weaver Point and Roches Point, being on the port side just inside the Owenboy River. I have sailed with skippers who do not like the place because it has two marinas which are more expensive than fishing harbours, and because of the Royal Cork Yacht Club itself which, they say, gives it a tone more akin to a busy yachting centre on the Solent than a corner of Ireland. There is some truth in their assessment, but I have found the club to be most friendly and they do not put on any of the airs which they might, considering their age. One marina is operated by the Royal Cork on the town shore and is the berth to choose if you want to use the showers and other club facilities. The other marina nearer the entrance to the river is run by the Crosshaven Boat Yard, which has all the facilities of a very modern big yard. The *St Brendan* was built at Crosshaven Boat Yard and transported overland for launching in Brandon Creek, County Kerry. The staff there will never forget the appalling smell of the hides which pervaded the yard and polluted the air in the area for weeks during the building. Further up the Owenboy is Drake's Pool, a totally sheltered anchorage in a sylvan setting. Sir Francis Drake sailed into the river and hid in the pool on one occasion when he was being pursued by a superior Spanish fleet which then searched in vain for him all round Cork Harbour. To get away from the yachting scene for a while, take your dinghy or the ferry across the harbour to Curraghbinny Point on the north shore for a walk to the large prehistoric burial cairn on the summit. This is a Forest and Wild Life Reserve with trails through the forest and scenic views of Cork Harbour. Between the town and the boatyard is the Cobbles, a converted farmhouse restaurant which has long had a reputation for good simple food which you can eat in the garden in fine weather.

Cork City, about twelve miles away by bus, deserves a visit if you have time. Even better, if you have more time, is to sail there through Cork Harbour which

Murphy's pub at East Ferry, an anchorage in Cork Harbour. A very Irish pub

is itself an expansive sailing area if it should be blowing outside. The route is round Spike Island, past Cóbh (pronounced 'cove') and through Passage West. An alternative anchorage is East Ferry, a narrow passage east of Great Island. It is a most peaceful place. On the east shore there is a landing stage which gives immediate access to Murphy's pub. This is a typical country watering hole for boat people and was, until quite recently, pretty primitive. As one local yachtsman described it: 'They used to have a bucket in the bar for rinsing the glasses, and by the end of the evening you were drinking brown gin.' Well, they have running water now, but it remains very much an Irish pub. On the opposite bank is Butler's Marina, small and well thought out and tucked away below woods rising up from the water's edge. Visiting boats can lie alongside a pontoon for the day, and recently a clubhouse with a little restaurant and bar was starting to be built. At weekends the almost non-stop procession of yachts close tacking up and down East Ferry passage against the background of dark wooded slopes, the dropping and weighing of anchors, the movement of tenders going ashore to the pub, add animation and colour to the rustic scene. There is a pleasant walk on the beach and through the woods along the Great Island shore. Very few yachts go through the harbour and up the River Lee into Cork. 'Berths are available if desired, but before starting up river consult Port Operations Office, Cóbh, for permission' is all that the ICC *Sailing Directions* say about Cork. But I have it on the authority of no less a person than Bill Walsh, Admiral of the Royal Cork, that there are no formalities really. 'I have come up several times myself and no one has harrassed me. There is no mooring fee, and if you are in the way someone will tell you.' The two places to berth are Anderson's Quay, just before the Brian Boru Bridge and the bus station, or Albert Quay in sight of the City Hall. The berths are where you can find a hole between cargo ships. It is not very salubrious and there are no services. If you wanted water you would have to phone the Harbour Board and get them to come along and connect you to a dockside hydrant; a service for shipping rather than yachts. By Brian Boru Bridge there is a big yacht chandlers, Union Chandlery, much patronised by crews off French yachts which go up to Cork more than any others.

Cork is somewhat dominated by two conspicuous churches. St Finbarr's Cathedral, French Gothic style in white stone, and St Ann's, Shandon, with its tower on a hill and the best-known landmark in the city, are both Church of Ireland. Between them the two arms of the River Lee make an island of the old town which, in places, has a Dutch look about it. Until the late eighteenth century many of the streets were, in fact, canals, and merchants built their houses above waterside warehouses with steps leading up to front doors on the first floor. Many of the houses in South Mall still have their doorways above ground. The most popular picture-postcard view of Cork, and one which best illustrates its character, is seen from Father Mathew Quay looking west down the canalised south channel of the Lee, through the ballustraded arch of Parliament Bridge to the three tall thin white spires of St Finbarr's Cathedral in the distance. St Finbarr founded a monastic school on the site about 650, and the graveyard

You can take your boat right into the heart of Cork City but there are no facilities for yachts and you have to take pot luck among the commercial shipping

Cork has a character all its own. St Finbarr's Cathedral seen beyond Parliament Bridge from the promenade along Father Mathew Quay

became an honoured resting place for Gaelic and Norman chieftains. But the present cathedral is of the Victorian era, opened in 1870. Less imposing but more curious is St Ann's in Shandon, a run-down corner of the town to the north of the river. The church itself is rarely referred to; but its tower, known as Shandon Steeple, is to the people of Cork what Big Ben is to Londoners. It has a fine clock face on four sides and a pepperpot top. You can climb the stairs inside for a panoramic view of the city from a gallery all round the top. It is a stiff climb and for the last few feet you have to negotiate a wooden ladder in the belfry only inches from the bells. If you are on the ladder when they ring the sound is painful, and they almost certainly will for the amusing thing about a visit to Shandon Steeple is that the public are allowed, even encouraged, to ring a peal of bells. The almost continuous inexpert din during the summer months is accepted with great tolerance, if not a little pride, by the local people.

Shandon is, like many outwardly seedy-looking districts, a very neighbourly community with much exchange of views and gossip on the doorsteps and in the little pubs, of which there are many. An evening in any one would be most instructive if you could attune your ears to their particular dialect, quite different to that of downtown Cork. No guide book will tell you, and it may not be commonly known outside Shandon, but the locals are keen students of Shakespeare, and many of them are word-perfect in several parts. They were introduced to the Bard some years ago by the parish priest who started a Shakespeare street theatre which has become a part of their culture. Just below

Shandon Steeple is a round building which was the old Butter Exchange. It was there that the prosperity of Cork was created with a monopoly of salted butter exported to England, Europe and the West Indies which was controlled by the Committee of Merchants formed in 1769. The exchange only ceased operations after World War I. The building was twice gutted by fire in recent years, but is scheduled to be rebuilt to become the home of the Irish National Ballet which will almost certainly bring a lot of life back into the district. Professional ballet, amateur Shakespeare and tourist campanologists – no wonder the Cork Tourist Office and the Corporation have a plan to refurbish Shandon.

Shopping in Cork is a pleasure centred on Grand Parade and St Patrick's Street. Until 1800 both were canalised arms of the river, but are now wide thoroughfares joined together by narrow alleys. The undercover City Market off Grand Parade is the best place for meat, fish and vegetables and is interesting to walk round even if not buying. For shopping or browsing there are two large shopping arcades, Queen's Building in Grand Parade with an open-plan coffee bar as a centrepiece, and the Savoy which is a converted cinema in St Patrick's Street with Murph's Restaurant above it serving good middle-of-the-road food from hamburgers to T-bone steaks in spotlessly clean surroundings with a very pleasant staff. It is the ideal place for a quick meal and a glass of wine. Murph's was the first restaurant to win the Bord Failte Award for Excellence two years running in the 'less than £5 a head' category. In a little alley behind the City Market leading into St Patrick's Street is the Oyster Tavern, all old polished wood and brass – even a brass rail on top of the bar to keep your elbows dry – and a good restaurant much used for leisurely business lunches. Their food is very good and the service of an old-fashioned standard. For a Saturday night out with Irish ballads with your dinner there is the Black Rock Castle on a point sticking out into the river about two miles from the town centre. It is a castle and the castle atmosphere has been retained inside. The very best place to eat in Cork, possibly in Ireland, is the Arbutus Lodge Hotel. If you are in the mood to spend some money and time over your meal, you will have a memorable evening. The cooking, mostly French but with imaginative Irish dishes too, is internationally acknowledged, as is their wine cellar. There is a bar and patio where substantial dishes can be eaten, twenty bedrooms, hanging gardens and a high view over the river. Booking is essential, and there is no smoking while others are eating. Rob Roy in the centre of the city is a pub where yachtsmen tend to congregate, but for informed conversation and comfort try Le Chateau next door to the *Cork Examiner*, one of Ireland's four national newspapers, and of course it is an 'annexe' to the newsroom. It is on the corner of Academy and St Patrick's streets. Nearby up a narrow alley is Beechers, patronised by young executives and smart girls; they are good on lunches and bar snacks.

Three miles out of Cork is Blarney. I went there but did not see the stone, let alone kiss it. The coachloads of tourists turned me off before I got near the castle. There is actually no historical evidence that there ever was a Blarney Stone, but there are many different versions of why kissing it bestows the gift of eloquence. The more honest Irish will admit that it was probably a nineteenth-century invention thought up to amuse the gullible English tourists of the day. Anyway there is certainly a Blarney Stone now which thousands of tourists get themselves into a ridiculous upside-down position to kiss.

The route from Cork to Kinsale passes a succession of bays with some delightful names – Myrtleville, Ringabella, Carrigadda, Man of War Cove and Oyster Haven, the latter guarded by the Sovereign Islands, two of them, round and small; certain yachtsmen have a rude name for them. Kinsale is a natural harbour formed by the estuary of the Bandon River which bends in the shape of a back-to-front question mark. There is high ground on both shores, and the town itself is terraced above the actual harbour. It is a very pretty town, first seen from the water when rounding the bend in the question mark, and encircled by green hills. Alas, on my most recent visit modern holiday homes were sprouting on the lovely emerald hillside overlooking the harbour; yet more scars on the landscape were being inflicted by bulldozers preparing the foundations and access roads for a holiday-apartments complex being built by a Dutch consortium. The new marina may be a great convenience, but does give one that feeling of *déja vu* now so often experienced around yachting centres. One year we had anchored in a beautiful natural harbour; two years later we were on a pontoon, one boat among a hundred. In the north corner of the harbour off a small wooded promontory called Scilly there is a delightful backwater occupied by a few colourful local boats and the occasional fishing boat. Unfortunately it dries and, in the words of the Tourist Office official, 'exposes a horrible mud area'. So plans have been drawn up to have it dredged, and by the time this is read it will almost certainly have been made into a second marina.

As a town Kinsale is visually rewarding with its narrow streets full of architectural and historical surprises, but it is even more rewarding as a gastronomic centre, Ireland's best. It even has its own International Gastronomic Festival in October. There are no less than eight restaurants of the highest standard. I have not been fortunate enough to have tried them all, but to save the first-time visitor too much walking and hesitating I will mention three of the many. Skippers is nearest the Yacht Club, the Blue Haven Hotel has a very strong emphasis on sea food, and the Vintage Restaurant is for those who like menus which read like gourmet poetry. I quote:

> Breast of chicken: free-range chicken breast stuffed with fresh salmon and avocado, baked and served with a Pernod cream. Cantonese Roast Duck: uniquely this duck is filled with its spicy sauce, basted with honey and vinegar, hung overnight and then roasted. When boned it is cut into bite-size pieces and served with the sauce and rice.

On the other hand you can get most excellent fish and chips on the quayside, even beyond midnight. For evening drinking I would never bother with any other pub but Peter Barry's Greyhound Bar off Market Square. It is divided up into a small bar and four snugs, each no bigger than the accommodation on a decent cruising boat. It is just the place for crews to wash the salt out of their mouths while holding postmortems on the day's sail. Intimate, local, Irish and unchanging, it is the cosy little pub I always hope to find ashore.

Going west along the quay and turning up Denis Quay (a street which was formerly the fishing quay), there are some fine seventeenth-century houses in not too good a decorative state. At the end of the street a zigzag road leads up to Compass Hill which gives overall views of the harbour to the south including James's Fort on its promontory and Charles's Fort built in 1670 in the distance on the right. John Wesley preached on the Bowling Green in 1785, and there has been a Methodist community in Kinsale ever since. Along the Rampart above the town there are some interesting houses with slate-hung fronts, and St Joseph's Convent of Mercy where, in 1849, the Sisters started a school of Irish lace which brought fame to the town. In 1854 they sent a group of nursing nuns to the Crimea to work with Florence Nightingale. The Mall was the fashionable parade of the eighteenth century. A group of almshouses dating from 1682 has been sympathetically restored and is still serving its original purpose. Before descending to the town, have a look at the Norman church of St Multose through its medieval wrought-iron gates. The original building of 1200 has been subject to change but still exhibits many of its original features. The memorials and plaques inside give a fairly comprehensive précis of Kinsale's history and the families who shaped it. In the town proper the Church of St John the Baptist is a Classical building which replaced a small thatched building after the Catholic Emancipation in 1829. A notable feature inside is an elaborate candelabra in plaster executed by Italian craftsmen. In steep and narrow Cork Street are the small remains of Desmond Castle, a sixteenth-century Custom House and residence which has variously been used as a magazine by the Spanish commander during the 1601 siege, as a prison for French prisoners-of-war in the eighteenth century, and for American seamen captured during the War of Independence. For part of the last century it was the borough jail, and is now a National Monument. In the heart of the town is the 1600 Market House with its copper-covered turret and loggia-style ground floor, now the Kinsale Regional Museum. The old courthouse within it was the scene of the inquest on the victims of the *Lusitania*, torpedoed on 7 May 1915 off Old Head of Kinsale with the loss of 1,198 lives, many of them American. The sinking of the *Lusitania* was one of the factors which finally persuaded the USA to join the Allies against Germany.

A long but most pleasant walk is to Summer Cove on the north side of the estuary towards Charles's Fort. It is a one-street village with a stone jetty. The houses, all on one side of the street facing the water, are painted in muted colours and opposite the jetty is a popular pub. The cove is not suitable for yachts, but a boat can anchor off and the crew go ashore in a tender for a drink and possibly a walk to Charles's Fort on its headland. It is a monster octagonal structure which was garrisoned by the British until 1922, when much of it was burned down. It is now very much a tourist site with guided tours during the summer. On the other side of the water is James's Fort, a softer, moss-encrusted ruin and, at its feet, the architectural-prize-winning holiday village of Castlepark. If you are interested in geometric shapes clustered together out of which everyone is supposed to get a view of his own, it is there to study. Left over from the past is The Dock, a pub which turns its back on the alien houses and gives an uncluttered view of the river and Kinsale on the other side. That is the place to go to sit outside with your drink on a nice day and watch the yachts coming and going. It is a long walk up the river on one side, over the bridge and back again along the other side, but it is only a few minutes' row across the water from the marina.

Leaving Kinsale and sailing west the coast becomes heavily indented, backed by ever-more sparsely populated pastoral country. Five headlands – Tob Head, Cape Clear, Mizen Head, Sheeps Head and Dursey Head – ensure that there are no short cuts. They must all be sailed round to make progress westward, and between them are long bays which could delay the curious for days visiting their islands and innermost sheltered recesses. The number of yachts which penetrate this incised coastline is few enough to make the meeting of another boat in an anchorage a pleasant surprise. In the harbours along the way there will always be a few boats for company, but not so many that the people ashore have become commercial towards those who come in from the sea. The welcome is always there, not wide eyed and naive, but with the politeness of a warm-hearted people who know about the world. The farmers and fishing people who live in the coastal villages and on the little islands of the south-west and the west of Ireland have an old maritime tradition. For generations they have been seafarers, and have sailed the world as merchant officers and seamen. Most families will have at least one member who knows Buenos Aires and Calcutta as well as he knows Cork and Dublin. I have met many a man behind the bar in West Cork who was better read than I am, and young lobster fishermen with university degrees. The traveller who behaves as a guest among his peers will get friendly attention. The tourist who thinks he is looking at a slightly backward society will only receive the attention of those whose business it is to give him a bit of the blarney.

Six-and-a-half miles out of Kinsale Harbour is the Old Head of Kinsale pointing almost due south with a race extending about a mile off its end. This race runs south-east during an east-going tide, and south-west during a west-going tide. The Old Head should, therefore, be given a berth of about two miles when there is any wind blowing. Except for southerly winds the head can be rounded close to in good weather thus saving several miles of sailing. The clue is to see that there is no broken water extending to near the head. The end of Old Head is almost detached from the rest of the promontory, being joined by a thin strip of land almost eaten through by a bay on either side. On the highest point there is an old signal station designed to look like a castle and built during the Napoleonic wars. At the extreme tip is a lighthouse. Clonakilty round the fat

Going westwards, Glandore is the first port of call after Kinsale and it should not be missed

headland of Seven Heads is only approachable by small yachts which can take the ground. It was near this small market town that Michael Collins (1890–1922) was born. It is sometimes referred to as Clonakilty God Help Us!, a harrowing reminder of the potato famines of 1845 and 1848 which severely afflicted this town, as they did all of west Cork and Kerry.

Glandore to the west of Galley Head is the first port of call after Kinsale which should not be missed. I have the most pleasant memories of putting in there. The intention was to drop the anchor off the village at the end of the afternoon for a long evening ashore with local friends of our skipper. But tacking out and back round Galley Head put us three hours behind schedule, and as we sailed up the long estuary the June evening sun was low over our bows turning the still water into a cloth of gold. The little fishing village of Glandore is in the north corner of the estuary before it turns west to Union Hall and an alternative anchorage. Glandore, with its high curved stone pier, cluster of painted cottages and curtain of wooded hills behind, is a truly picture-postcard place. The Marine Hotel fronting the harbour usually has a sprinkling of yacht crews in the bar. People staying there have told me that the food is good, the service wonderful, and that nothing is too much trouble for the staff. Nextdoor is Peaceful Holidays Marine, a small chandler's shop. The Protestant Church sits on a ledge hewn out of the rock overlooking the harbour. The church gate is not at first apparent, being in a hole in the rock face beside the road and giving access by a sloping tunnel to the churchyard above. All along this coast it is the Church of Ireland churches which occupy the dominant positions in towns and villages, although some of them are only occasionally used for services. Their presence, and the siting of Catholic churches out in the countryside away from the communities they served, goes back to the days of the Ascendancy when this part of Ireland was colonised by the Protestant English planters. The morning after our arrival at Glandore we walked to Ross Carbery, a distance of just over four miles uphill through rather rocky farmland with dry-stone walls, a feature which starts in those parts and continues through the wilder country to the west. The centre of Ross Carbery is on a hill above its harbour in a drying estuary and is called the Place, a very Irish square of small shops full of things that farmers buy, two or three pubs, a butcher, baker and grocers where we did some revictualling. On the way back we bought large boxes of strawberries at a farm for a very small price. Strawberries are also sold at the Castle in Glandore; it is actually a house, a bit of which was once a castle. The village did have an abbey, but all that is left is the gateway.

Another walk from Glandore is to the Drombeg stone circle on a hill overlooking the sea at the entrance to Glandore Harbour (OS 24.2535). This is the best of a large number of circles in County Cork, and is thought to have been built around the time of Christ. There are seventeen standing stones and one lying flat, giving the appearance of a sacrificial altar. The cremated remains of a body were found in the centre of the site when it was excavated. Close by are the remains of two round stone huts joined together, and a stone-flagged pathway leading to a cooking place with a well, hearth and water trough. Experiments have demonstrated that hot stones dropped in the trough could have brought

The stone circle at Drombeg on a hill overlooking the sea. It was built about the time of Christ

water to the boil and kept it warm for at least two hours. The huts have been dated between the first and third centuries and the cooking place between the third and sixth, so evidently the whole site was used for possibly 600 years.

Surrounded by woods and greenery Glandore Harbour has, in fine weather, the placid appearance of a lake, and the boats at anchor just off the village look as if they could be in no safer place. But in a southerly gale it can be hell with a destructive swell coming like a bore up the estuary. One year a 100ft boat was taken inside the small harbour for repair work to be done on her, then a southerly gale came and she surged back and forth in the swell pulling away a bollard and a piece of the harbour wall. Her bow hit one wall and her stern the other until she broke up and sank. When southerlies are forecast it is better to anchor round the bend opposite Union Hall. There is a pier there used by quite large fishing boats, but it dries almost to the end where there may be three feet of water at low-water springs. The houses along the waterfront at Union Hall are all painted different colours, but because they face north-east it looks a rather grey place. Most yachts that anchor up towards Union Hall still take their tenders the half mile back to Glandore for a meal and a drink. Although it is barely three miles as the crow flies from Union Hall to Castlehaven and the village of Castletownshend, it takes a good two hours by sea clearing a small strung-out archipelago of islets before getting into the Haven. It is a place which should not be missed if you have any sense of history because for a long time it was the last bastion of the Ascendancy, the undisputed domain of three great Anglo-Irish families – the Townshends, the Somervilles and the Coghills – who for generations owned every big house and small cottage, every tree and blade of grass for miles around. Today there is one survivor of the Ascendancy in the village, Mrs Salter-Townshend, the present owner of Castletownshend – the castle itself, that is – now converted into a guest house and self-catering flats. The harbour is a long thin estuary beautifully sheltered, although in strong southerlies it is wise to anchor a bit above the village. There is a small quay and a slip, but all boats anchor off or pick up a mooring. It is an attractive, unspoilt village with several pleasant surprises. Going ashore at the slip it is a few yards' walk to the entrance gate to the castle at the bottom of the one street, which then goes steeply uphill and is lined by well-painted cottages and small elegant houses. Halfway up the roadway is almost completely blocked by two sycamore trees sitting in a stone 'flower pot'. No one knows by whom or why they were planted, but everything in the village is related to the Two Trees; you meet there, you live above them, or below them. Cars have to come almost to a stop to drive round them, and delivery vans sometimes have difficulty getting past. A few years ago a bad February rainstorm washed away a part of their stone wall. A young engineer, newly appointed by the council in Skibbereen and knowing nothing of local history and sentiment, decided the easiest thing to do was to have the trees cut down. The village was up in arms, a public meeting was called, and the local farmers surrounded the trees with tractors so that the council workmen could not get near them. Defeated, the council instructed forestry experts to vet the health of the trees, and they sent for a tree surgeon from Dublin to lop them a bit and then rebuilt the wall. In the shade of the sycamores is Mary Ann's Bar, a really very old pub and possibly the oldest in the country. Inside the oak-beamed bar visiting yachtsmen drink with local fishermen while waiting to be called to table on a half landing which can accommodate twenty people. The food is good, mostly lobster, crab, salmon, scallops, prawns, oysters and white fish, much of it straight out of the Haven. The yachtsmen who crowd the bar of a summer's evening will be talking in several languages, for Mary Ann's has an international reputation among sailing folk. It is, of course, futile to expect a meal unless you have telephoned 028 36146 in advance, preferably a day in advance. On good days there may by chance be a couple of places at one of the tables laid in the vine-covered patio or in the garden.

Castletownshend was the home of the writer Edith Somerville, and she and her friend Violet Martin (she wrote under the name Martin Ross), the joint authors of *Experiences of an Irish RM*, are buried beside each other in the graveyard of the Protestant church of St Barrahane. The entire church is a beautifully preserved, polished and dusted memorial to the three Ascendancy families. On stone and brass and in glowing stained glass are recorded the valiant lives of military and naval officers who went forth from Castletownshend to found an empire for the British Crown. Most monstrous of all the memorials is a marble triptych, three giant slabs recording in small compacted lettering, almost impossible to read without jumping lines, the Townshend family history from the Siege of Pendennis Castle, Cornwall, in 1646 by Colonel Richard Townsende (as then spelt) to the year 1903. The memorial was presented to the church by Geraldine Henrietta Townshend Mundy, Lady of the Manor of Bridgetown. An awful indulgence in genealogical pride, but something which needs to be seen to be believed – a terrible indictment of a closed society which thought itself better than the ancient culture it had driven out and even better than the English from whom they were so recently descended. Strangely, through all the 1921/22 Troubles when the houses of the Ascendancy were being burned down and their land taken from them, the families in Castletownshend continued to live in a vacuum, their property intact and unmolested. And so it remained almost until the present day. Talking to a local man I remarked on how well decorated all the houses were. He replied that most of them were now owned by foreigners: 'Ten years ago I knew everybody in every house, now I don't even know half their names.' As the old people died the young members of the families who were in professions and business elsewhere could not afford to come home to live or to maintain their ancestral properties as second homes. Instead they found that they were valuable and started to sell them, and it was foreigners who bought them. Mrs Salter-Townshend told me: 'There was a time when no house was ever sold, they just passed from one family to another. Now there are three owned by Americans, five by Germans and one by a French family. They were full of very beautiful things that the families had collected over the generations; now it has all gone. The new owners try to make them like Mediterranean villas inside.' I stayed at Bow Hall, a seventeenth-century house in the village once owned by one of her cousins. My hosts were Americans, the furniture was New England, and I had hot muffins with syrup for breakfast.

Before the Townshend family gave their name to the village in the seventeenth century, it was called Glen Barrahane after a local saint and was O'Driscoll country. They were a family of chieftains who held sway from Castlehaven westwards and maintained a fleet of small ships with which they exacted tribute from all shipping which passed along their coast. They had a castle perched on a small finger of rock further down the estuary, half-an-hour's walk from the village. There is little to see of it now save a few stones among bracken-covered mounds. After the Battle of Kinsale in 1601 the Spanish, who had occupied Castlehaven Castle, gave it up under the terms of the treaty made at Kinsale. It was reoccupied by the O'Driscolls who were, in turn, ejected by the combined efforts of the Spanish and English naval forces. The Battle of Kinsale finally established the English as the conquerors of Ireland, and from then on the settlers and adventurers poured in. Colonel Richard Townsend, an official of the Long Parliament, was granted large estates around the village and an English minister in Scotland, the Reverend William Somerville, having fallen out with the Scottish dissenters, crossed over to Ireland and eventually settled in the village, followed by his immediate descendants. The Coghill family arrived soon after. By the middle of the eighteenth century the families had prospered and become very genteel; they built nice houses and Castletownshend started to take on the appearance we see today. The 'h' in the Townshend name is pure snobbism. An early member of the family wrote in 1780 to a peer, Lord Townshend, who was no relation, asking permission to also use the 'h'. The peer apparently said that he was quite indifferent as to how a remote family in County Cork spelt its name.

Before the Ascendancy of the O'Driscolls, a pre-Christian community built Knockdrum Fort, a circular stone defensive settlement on a hill outside Castletownshend. It is well sited with commanding views of the approaches to Castlehaven, and overlooking Toe Head to the west and Galley Head to the east. On a clear day you can see inland to the Kerry mountains. The fort is a half-hour walk from the village along the Skibbereen road. A signposted footpath leads to a flight of stone steps laid on the hillside making for an easy ascent to the fort. It is 95ft in diameter and the walls, repaired some time before 1860, are as complete as when they were built. In the centre are the remains of a square dwelling, and in one corner of the circle a souterrain – an underground cavern used either for storage or for hiding the women and children in the event of the fort being attacked. Outside the entrance there is a large stone lying on the ground with cup-marks in it. Visible from the fort and a few hundred yards further along the road are three standing stones spread out like fingers on the summit of a smaller hill. Admiral Boyle Somerville, who was an amateur archaeologist, found that at a midsummer sunrise a gap in the stones aligned with the sun as it appeared above

Lough Hyne (also Ine) is one of the curiosities of the Irish coast. It is connected to the sea by a narrow channel about one third of a mile long and about twenty yards wide at its narrowest; but the fishing boat made its entry!

the horizon. There was a fourth 'finger', but some time in the last century one of the Mrs Townshend's had it removed to her rock garden. It is still lying somewhere in the castle grounds.

On the passage from Castlehaven to Baltimore you get a close-to view of the Stags off Toe Head. There are six of them and, seen from the east, they look like sharp serrated rock splinters, the tallest rising 66ft above the water. There is a good half-mile between them and the mainland free of hazards. En route from the Stags to Baltimore there is an anchorage called Barlogh Creek behind Bullock Island. Difficult to discern until close to and difficult of entry (it would be wise to go in and out under engine), this peaceful and secluded anchorage leads to

Lough Hyne, one of the curiosities of the Irish coast. The lough is connected to the sea by a narrow channel about one-third of a mile long and about twenty yards at its narrowest. At low tide it is a rocky defile with a broad stream running down the middle. At half tide it becomes a torrent of white water with rapids halfway through. Shooting the rapids has long been a popular sport for the local canoeists, but after three-quarter flood it can be negotiated by dinghy with an outboard although careful watch has to be kept for seaweed which can easily foul the propeller. The tidal race through the rapids exceeds 6 knots, and the water is only still for 2 or 3 minutes at the change of tide when the seaweed stands up and turns over. The time to enter the channel to go into the lough will have to be decided by observation, not by the state of the tide in the anchorage. The constriction caused by the rapids produces a delay in high and low water in the lough compared with that of the sea. It has an asymmetrical tidal cycle of approximately four hours of flood and eight-and-a-half hours of ebb. During the flood there is a heavy inrush of water causing a small whirlpool under the cliffs on the east side, and an anti-clockwise vortex occupies the whole of the south-eastern corner of the lough. When I was last there I saw a fishing boat of some 40ft length at anchor in the lough so it must be possible to take a yacht in, but I think all that seaweed would make it an extremely risky enterprise. If you are doubtful of your outboard pushing you through, it would be better to visit the lough on foot. The going is hard, up and down through chest-high bracken and brambles, but the effort is worthwhile both to get a close-up of the rapids and to see the lough itself, which is quite beautiful. Lough Hyne (or Ine as it is also spelt) is world-famous as a unique site for marine conservation. Unlike most sea lakes and fjords it is fully salt, no different from the adjoining coastal sea water, and it contains a fully marine flora and fauna. Although marine rapids exist elsewhere, no other is as accessible for investigation. The compact topography includes submarine cliffs, shallow mud and deep mud, a shingle spit and a sand beach, all providing a variety of habitats for marine life. A 'western trough' in the lough is over 130ft deep, and in summer the top half of water warms up while the bottom half remains cold and isolated, the oxygen in the water becomes depleted and the bottom flora and fauna disappear. In early winter the water mixes again and the bottom comes to life once more. This annual event occurs in many deep fresh-water lakes, but not in any sea lough anywhere else in the British Isles. Of special interest is the sea urchin *Paracentrotus*, the edible scallop *Pecten Maximus*, and its smaller relative *Chlamys Varia*. There is a 'forest' of 2yd-long brown seaweed in the rapids, below which there is an extraordinary wealth and diversity of marine life which is considered to be one of the richest in existence in temperate waters. The rapids reduce the vertical movement of the tide in the lough to about three feet, and there is little difference between spring and neap tides, in fact curiously the water falls slightly lower at neaps than at springs. There are three marine laboratories around the lough which are quite inconspicuous; they could be mistaken for three little cottages. From the west shore of the lough a path leads through the woods to the top of a hill, which gives a view over the lough and also Baltimore Harbour and Sherkin Island to the west. Back at the anchorage there is one more curiosity to visit before leaving the area. On the south-west side of Bullock Island a cave extends for just over 100 yards underground, and the far end of it can be reached in a small boat. The shores on both sides of the entrance into Barlogh Creek have several very fine rockpools with a rich variety of plant and animal life.

Baltimore, once a busy fishing harbour but now more a yachting centre, is the natural base for exploring the islands, creeks and harbours of Roaringwater Bay and Long Island Bay, an area also known as Carbery's Hundred Isles. This archipelago with its deeply indented mainland shore backed by rounded hills covers almost one hundred square miles, and could fully occupy a week of sailing to see it all. The entrance into Baltimore Harbour from the south between Sherkin Island and Beacon Point on the mainland is safe in all weathers, and the

No mistaking the beacon at the entrance to Baltimore Harbour! This entrance is safe in all weathers

anchorage opposite the village is between one and three fathoms deep and sheltered from all directions by Sherkin, Spanish and Ringarory Islands although subject to swell. The harbour pier is used by the ferry boats for Sherkin and Clear Islands, but yachts can lie alongside to take on water. The boatbuilding firm of Henry Skinner & Sons has a large yard with a patent slip and can undertake any work a visiting boat may need. Mr O'Driscoll in the village does repairs to marine engines. There are two good pubs, some small shops and a little French restaurant with 'continental' decor which looks misplaced in this little fishing village. On the outskirts of the village, all of five-minutes' walk, is Baltimore House Hotel set right on the water's edge with its own small pier. The dining room, and most of the bedrooms, look west over the sea and sometimes a spectacular sunset adds a glow to a good dinner, and there is always locally caught fish on the menu. Baltimore was founded by a Sir Thomas Crooke as an English settlement, and the most noticeable building is the Protestant church; the Catholic one is nearly three miles away in the countryside. Sir Thomas's settlers had a rude awakening on 20 June 1631 when two Algerian ships sailed into the harbour. The crews made short work of looting and burning all the houses in the one-street village and then rounded up 100 men, women and children, sailed off with them and sold them as slaves along the Barbary Coast. All but two of them were English settlers. So, scattered around North Africa there must now be several hundred people who are descended from those Anglo-Irish of Baltimore. Fifteen years after the event when the British Government sent a representative to Africa to ransom the victims at £30 a head, only two of them could be found.

The road north from Baltimore runs 8 miles to Skibbereen, for most of the The road north from Baltimore runs 8 miles to Skibbereen, for most of the way in sight of one channel of the River Ilen winding between the mainland and Ringarory and Inishbeg Islands. The main channel, which can be navigated on the flood almost to the edge of the town, runs on the west side of the islands. Just upstream of where the two branches of the river join together again there is the ruin of a castle called Old Court, and beside it a small boatyard where Pat Haggerty and his son still build wooden fishing boats. If you have the time it would be worthwhile motoring up the river to see the work of these traditional shipwrights in their old-world yard miles from anywhere on a picturesque bend of the river. Going out of Baltimore the other way the road climbs up to the high headland overlooking the harbour entrance between the mainland and Sherkin Island. On the summit is the white-painted sea-mark shaped like an artillery shell standing point upwards. On some maps it is named Lot's Wife. From up there you can see over to Clear Island, the most southerly bit of Ireland if you discount the Fastnet Rock 4½ miles further out to sea and just hidden from view by Cape Clear, most of Baltimore Harbour and many of the islands of Roaringwater Bay and Mount Gabriel beyond. Roaringwater Bay is a bit open to the south-west, but it gets its name not from its sea state but from the roar of the waterfalls of the two rivers which pour into it at Ballydehob. They flow for only a few miles but steeply from the hills. The old railway station on the water's edge just outside Baltimore has been taken over by a branch of the Centre Nautique des Glénans, the French sailing school founded in 1947 by ex-members of the French Resistance which is based on the Glénans, an archipelago 10 miles off Concarneau in south Brittany. They operate ten centres: five off the Brittany coast, two in the Mediterranean, and three in Ireland. The Irish ones are at Baltimore, on Bere Island in Bantry Bay, and at Clew Bay on the west coast. They run fortnightly sailing and cruising courses which involve long hours on the water, no-frills accommodation, and all the chores and cooking are done by the pupils. From the harbour Dermot Kennedy runs his Baltimore Sailing School with a fleet of dinghies and two yachts for coastal-cruising courses or charter.

In the sixteenth century, long before Guinness was invented, there was a flourishing sea trade between Spain and Ireland and wine was then the normal everyday drink of the Irish. Oliver Cromwell put a stop to that pleasant habit, as well as any further trade with the Papists. But the Spanish left behind one souvenir of their association with Ireland which can still be seen today. It is the Hooker, a tough, beamy, coastal-working sail boat which has a family resemblance to the Dutch botter. This is not surprising considering that Spain ruled the Low Countries at the time she was trading with Ireland. But the Hooker also has a fine entry forward with an accentuated sheer forming an upward sweep to the stemhead unlike the bluff bows of the Dutch sailing barge, which might have been borrowed from the sailing barges on the Tagus. Averaging 35–40ft overall, these boats were maids-of-all-work all round the Irish coast for some 200 years. Eventually they disappeared except on the west coast around Galway and Connemara where they were still working in the 1930s as fishing boats and in coastwise trade as cattle and turf carriers to the Aran Islands before the advent of bottled gas. Indeed, as recently as 1971 there were two solitary survivors plying between the mainland and Aran.

In the last century there were hundreds of Hookers sailing the west coast of Ireland; today there are less than twenty, all of them lovingly preserved by private owners and sailed in the old way for pleasure. 'In the old way' means by sheer muscle power without the aid of modern devices such as winches and, in most cases, without the comfort of soft manmade-fibre ropes. To sail a Hooker is to take a journey into the past, an experience as different from sailing a yacht as driving a horse and cart would be to driving a motor car. Until recently it was an unattainable experience unless you were a friend of one of the few owners of preserved Hookers. Now, however, Dermot Kennedy in Baltimore has completed the restoration of one of the best Hookers ever built. She is comparatively young, having been launched in 1920 for Merton Oliver who was known as the King of the Cladagh – an old and very Irish fishing area of Galway about which many songs have been written. Later she was owned by the poet Richard Murphy who wrote of her:

Horseshoe Harbour on Sherkin Island is almost landlocked. An idyllic anchorage but the usual landing place is a jetty on the east side below the ruined abbey

> In memory's hands this Hooker was restored,
> Old men my instructors.
> With all new gear may I handle her well
> Down tomorrow's sea road.

And for a while he did. She then came to be owned by an elderly lady who allowed her to fall into decline. Dermot Kennedy bought her in 1969 and has been restoring her ever since. 'She is ready to carry cattle again', he told me in 1981 when he started sailing her. He has now made her available for people who would like to join him and a local crew for day sailing out of Baltimore, but he is equally prepared to organise week-long cruises among the hundred isles of Long Island Sound and Roaringwater Bay, or round Mizen Head and Sheep's Head out of what the Irish call the Celtic Sea into the Atlantic and Bantry Bay. There is no accommodation on a Hooker, and cooking on board would be of the most rudimentary kind – a peat fire on a stone slab. Hookers do not sail close to the wind and need a fair breeze to get up any speed, so such a cruise would be leisurely with plenty of opportunity to walk and explore uninhabited islands and small fishing harbours with very much inhabited pubs! He will provide tents for sleeping ashore at night – yes, it would be that type of holiday.

The two most obvious and interesting expeditions from Baltimore are to Sherkin Island and Clear Island. There is no need to use up sailing time going over to them; there is a ferry which takes 10 minutes and 40 minutes respectively. The landing on Sherkin is at a jetty on the east side below the beautiful ruined abbey, and there is also an idyllic-looking anchorage in Horseshoe Harbour, an almost landlocked bay half a mile to the south round the headland on which the lighthouse stands. But the entrance is a bare 50 yards wide between rocks off the east side and the point on the south-west corner. Sherkin Abbey (as it is called, although it was a Franciscan friary) was built in the fifteenth century by one of the O'Driscolls, as was the castle nearby; both were destroyed in 1537 by the men of Waterford to stop the O'Driscolls' depredations on the ships sailing and fishing off that part of the coast. The O'Driscoll castle above the harbour in Baltimore was destroyed at the same time, and the ruin which can now be seen is a later building more in the form of a fortified house. There is a small Post Office-cum-shop on the island and a pub a few hundred yards from the jetty from which it is possible to watch for the ferry boat coming from Baltimore. This pub is not to be confused with the Sherkin Inn below it, an ugly slab-sided hotel built more recently to cater for the holiday trade. The island is rich in coves and sandy beaches on its east side, and the high ground at its southern tip looks over to Clear Island and most of Carbery's Hundred Isles.

Clear Island is a great deal more interesting. To start with it is a Gaelic-speaking area and, while the former inhabitants of all the neighbouring islands were little more than crofters and inshore fishermen who never went very far from home, the men of Clear Island have for centuries been deep-sea fishermen and great seafarers going into the merchant navy and, until very recently, the Royal Navy. They have a reputation for intelligence and an unusually high proportion have become doctors, surgeons and lawyers. Until the start of this century it was the Cape Clear pilots who took the sailing ships from America into Cork Harbour. These ships would sail as close as they could round Mizen

Sherkin Abbey was in fact a Franciscan friary, built by the O'Driscolls in the fifteenth century. It is above the ferry landing point from Baltimore

Head to save time, and then the pilots would board them off Cape Clear and take them to Queenstown, which is now Cóbh. The island population was then about two thousand, but it is now probably no more than two hundred although it is a prosperous community of hill farmers and fishermen. The whole island is hilly with bays on the west and sheer cliffs on the east side. Cape Clear points south-west directly at the Fastnet Rock and lighthouse. South Harbour is a bay which is a safe anchorage only in northerlies or as a temporary stop on a windless day with no swell running. North Harbour, an inlet into the heart of the gorse-carpeted cliffs, is where the post and ferry boat berths. The entrance is extremely narrow, 30 yards only, and it is most advisable to enter under engine as the high ground either side produces quite unpredictable air currents. The wind can be blowing from port or starboard one moment and, in an instant, back or veer 180°. In good weather it is possible to lie alongside the end of the outer pier, but if it blows up, especially from the south-west, it would be necessary to go into the inner harbour and take the ground. But if there is a very heavy swell running the entrance may be blocked by timber shuttering so that boats inside are literally locked in. During the great gales at the time of the 1979 Fastnet Race forty yachts found refuge in North Harbour, packed in like sardines in a tin and holding each other up. The population of Clear Island is fairly scattered, but there is a tiny village, Cummer, between North and South Harbours, with a small pub, a grocer's shop with a bar and a youth hostel. The bird life, particularly during times of migration, is regarded by ornithologists as of exceptional interest. Those interested in bird life should contact the warden at the Bird Observatory in North Harbour. Even more than Sherkin, Clear Island is for walking and talking with the locals. It is not yet too overrun by tourists because of the limited capacity of the ferry boat from Baltimore and another small one which brings day trippers over from Schull. But there is a Craft Centre where light refreshments and souvenirs can be bought in the summer months which I hope will not be the harbinger of further tourist development. Even the modest youth hostel is not altogether popular with many Clear Islanders who regard it as a threat to their Gaelic culture.

Only two of the other islands in the great bay between Cape Clear and Mizen Head are occupied; they are Hare Island and Long Island. The rest are used for grazing cattle. While in Baltimore you may be lucky enough to be able to watch cows being herded into open boats for shipment to one of the islands. This can be quite an hilarious sight for the spectator, although obviously not for the animals. The beasts are driven with much shouting and thwacking of sticks down the slipway and made to jump into a boat which, when it is getting full, means jumping on top of one of their own number. The fun comes, or did when I was watching, when a baulk of timber fixed alongside the gunwales to prevent the animals from jumping out of the boat becomes dislodged and floats off followed by half a dozen cows. Herding cattle on land is one thing; herding them from a boat while they swim around a harbour is quite another game. Having no sense of seamanship, the frightened animals swim in every direction except towards the slipway which is their only way back on to *terra firma*. I watched a boat with a single-cylinder diesel thumper, and the helmsman's ability to manoeuvre after the tiring animals was not improved by the fact that he had to leave the wheel and duck below decks every time he needed to change gear from ahead to astern and vice versa. The only other crew member, having recovered the missing baulk of timber, was desperately hanging on to one end while the other end, dragging in the water, acted as a wayward leeboard working in opposition to the boat's rudder. I doubt if it was a one-off occurrence because it attracted little attention from the locals.

Cruising among the islands requires very close attention to the chart and a good sense of distance because there are as many half-tide and submerged rocks as there are visible islands. But there is always shelter on one side or another of some island, whichever way the wind blows. The one time it would be foolish to attempt to sail through the islands is when visibility is poor. The first time I was in Baltimore the intention had been to leave by the north route round the top of Sherkin and Hare Islands and sail on to Crookhaven. But, when the time came to leave, a sea mist had brought visibility down to less than fifty yards and we crept out the way we had come in past Beacon Head, all eyes and ears straining for sight or sound of other craft or the sea slopping against rocks.

Later I was able to visit two places which I strongly recommend calling into: Rosbrin, which is not described in the ICC *Sailing Directions*, and Schull (pronounced, and sometimes spelt, Skull) north of Long Island Bay. Rosbrin is an inlet shaped like a wine glass, the base being the sea and the bowl an anchorage joined to the sea by the stem. Guarding the entrance is the ruin of an O'Mahony castle built in the early fourteenth century. The O'Mahonys were Irish chieftains who held sway westward of the territory held by the O'Driscolls. There is not a lot left of this castle although its tower looks romantically impressive from a distance, set on a rock on the edge of the water. Part of the tower collapsed early this century, and as recently as 1974 more of it was brought down in a storm. The most illustrious owner of Rosbrin Castle was Finnin O'Mahony who died in 1495. He was a great scholar of Latin and Greek as well as Irish and English. Although the castles of the Irish chieftains were no more than dark uncomfortable prison-like dwellings with hardly any furniture, rarely more than one window and rushes or straw on the floor for sleeping, their owners were not uncivilised. They used Latin as a common language when dealing with French and Spanish traders and pirates, and managed large fishing fleets and small navies of protection vessels. Rosbrin is an excellent anchorage, well sheltered from all directions with the bulk of Horse Island about half a mile long protecting its south-facing entrance. There are a few cottages and a single-track road along the head of the bay and, in summer, the whole area is ablaze with fuchsia. Incidentally, fuchsia proliferates around this area and becomes denser as you go west, positively dripping from the hedgerows. Andrew Stott from Liverpool, who retired from the Royal Navy in 1972 while still a young man, settled at Rosbrin with his Dublin wife Sheila. He decided to live there because, he says, it is the best bit of coast for yacht cruising in the whole of Europe. He has built himself a small slip opposite his house and a workshop in his garden and now runs a yacht-care-and-maintenance business with winter moorings. He also has a 1939 wooden Laurent Giles yacht for skipper charter and 35ft and 28ft yachts for bare-boat charter. He is quite happy to accept one- or two-day skipper charters from those who want to take a look round the Hundred Isles as part of a more conventional holiday. The Fastnet is only nine miles from his front door, and Baltimore, Clear Island, Schull and Crookhaven are all within an easy day's sail, but most of his one-day charterers prefer to go to one of the uninhabited islands. Horse Island on his doorstep is riddled with old copper workings and is a favourite picnic place with local boat owners. When I was last in Schull there had been a half-hearted protest meeting against a planning application by a German company to develop the island as a holiday village. Since the ferry service and all supplies to the island would be from Schull there seemed little hope of the protest succeeding.

Schull is a natural harbour nearly half a mile long and nearly as wide with a fishing port and village in its north-west corner. The fishing is still very active with a processing plant on the quay. The main street is a short walk up a hill and, once there, the harbour is out of sight. The place where the fishermen drink is Tommy Newman's, a very typical Irish pub of great character, as also is Tommy himself, a large florid man whose heavy West Cork accent requires some concentration to understand. He is an alderman and a fount of local knowledge when not too engrossed in conversation with his cronies. My last talk with him was not about Schull at all; his mind was still on London and the none-too-sober adventures he had had there during the week when a local Schull greyhound, Parktown Jet, had won the 1981 Spiller's English Derby at White City. The village has a fair assortment of small shops, and one very good eating place is The Courtyard where you will find local characters in the bar and excellent food in the dining room. Schull is dominated by the 1,339ft Mount Gabriel; round, steep and isolated, it looks much higher than it is. A tracking station near the summit does not prevent access, but a good three hours should be allowed to walk from the village to the top. Neolithic man covered the slopes with his forts, and he almost certainly worked the copper mines near the top which are still easy to find, as is an abandoned baryte mine on the north face. Copper was extracted by using fire to crack and break away the ore which was then pulverised with stone mauls. At one time these large egg-shaped stones, a perfect handful, could be found lying near the entrance to shafts, but archaeologists and souvenir hunters have probably cleared them all by now. Near the summit there is a small tarn, a black disc of water whose depths have never been plumbed. Given the right weather Mount Gabriel affords a panoramic view of most of West Cork with the cruising area between Cape Clear and Mizen Head laid out below like an embossed chart.

The morning we left Baltimore the mist lifted just as we sailed close in to the high cliffs rising to over 300ft along the east side of Clear Island where there is an unused, in fact never completed, lighthouse perched high on a ledge. Then we made a small diversion to sail round the Fastnet Rock. The lighthouse, although famous, is not very old. At one time a lighthouse on Cape Clear was the first and last mark for ships sailing from and to America, but it was ill placed and did not prevent a great number of ships foundering off the cape. In 1854 an iron tower was built on the Fastnet Rock which had eroded and collapsed by 1881. The present lighthouse, built of granite from Cornwall, was completed in 1903; its light is 158ft above sea level and visible for 17 miles.

Crookhaven, named after the same Crooke who founded Baltimore, was once a busy fishing harbour at the end of nowhere. It lies in a cul-de-sac of the sea behind Mizen Head. The haven is 2 miles long, only 1¼ cables wide at one point but opens out to ⅓ mile inside; steep-to on both shores, it is a calm and perfect shelter. Running inland almost due west, it usually requires a tedious succession of short tacks to get in. At the turn of the century Crookhaven was a busy mackerel port and lay-by for the windjammers from Australia who put in there to get final instructions by telegraph on which port to make for. When the fishing declined so did the village for, being the last in Ireland, it served no other useful purpose. Today it has brightened up with its houses turned into holiday homes and yachts using the harbour. We put in there en route for Bantry Bay because the Irish bus services and availability of a local taxi made it the most practical place in the vicinity at which to pick up a new crew member joining us from Lancaster. The nearest attraction, a mile walk west, is Barley Cove with its deep curved sandy beach, once a lonely beauty spot, but now having an hotel and a camp site. Above the cove on Brow Head are the remains of Marconi's radio station from which he sent his first signal to America – the letter 'S' in morse. All that is left is a small building with the wind blowing through it, but nonetheless of very great historical significance.

On Rock Island on the north side of the entrance into Crookhaven are the remains of the buildings which housed the workmen who put the Fastnet Light-house together – the cut stones from Cornwall were pre-assembled there to make sure they fitted together and then dismantled before being shipped over to the Fastnet Rock. The lighthouse on Rock Island is now automatic, and the row of white keepers' cottages is let to holidaymakers. The harbour is thick with weed so it is best to use a fisherman's anchor. The pier, which dries, has a slip big enough to take a 40ft fishing boat. The only shop in Crookhaven village is attached to O'Sullivans, the pub by the pier, a homely place. The other pub is the Crookhaven Inn. If stores are badly needed there are more shops in the bigger village of Goleen which is a ½-hour's walk from the north shore of Crookhaven. Or, in very calm weather, a boat can be taken up the coast and into Goleen creek which is little more than a cleft in the rocks which leads to a stone quay just outside the village. It is normally completely sheltered, but is unapproachable in a south-east wind. The quay dries but there is a pool below it in which to anchor; two anchors should be used as there is no room to swing. The area has several megalithic tombs and old copper workings. For a long walk, about five miles, there is Mizen Head, the Land's End of Ireland – spectacular, dramatic, red sandstone with pink and white strata, and abounding in sea birds and seals. To the north Three Castle Head, Sheep's Head and the great Bere Peninsula across Bantry Bay ending with Dursey Head make it a wonderful viewpoint. The south side of Mizen Head exhibits a superb example of folded strata.

The extremity of our cruise, and of my knowledge of the coast of West Cork, was Castletown (or Castletownbere) in Bere Haven, the first proper commercial port after leaving Cork. The little town with its small old-fashioned and very Irish shops looks today much as it did in 1900 postcards, but the harbour front, called Mainland Wharf, is now a huge concrete apron for the fish lorries. The new Harbour Master's office looks rather like the control tower of a provincial airport. Opposite the wharf Dinish Island, now joined to the mainland by a road bridge, has been developed as a fishing-industry complex. Yachts should berth at the west end of Mainland Wharf out of the way of the fishing fleet and then contact the Harbour Master or one of his two 'constables'. The fishing boats normally come in to unload on Tuesdays and Thursdays, but during June, July and August most of the fishing moves north up the coast so there is more room along the wharf. Outside those months the place gets crowded and it may be necessary to lie alongside a fisherman. There are spacious toilets underneath the Harbour Office, and by now two sets of hot showers should have been added. The Harbour Master, Michael Hogan, can be reached on VHF or telephone 220 128; any mail addressed c/o the Harbour Master will be delivered to you when you arrive.

He gave me this advice for coping with the hazards of the salmon nets which are laid in their dozens along the coast. Most of the salmon boats will be listening on VHF, so the yachtsman can call them up and ask where their nets are if visibility is poor. If a boat does find itself running into a net he says: 'For God's sake, don't put about; always try to take it at right angles. If you are on top of a net don't panic and turn hard to starboard or port; you will do less damage if you keep straight on. The buoyancy of a salmon net is such that, nine times out of ten, the keel will push it down and, before it can rise up and foul the prop, the boat will be over it. The fishing boat is usually on the outside of the net, so if you see a man in a boat you can be sure his net goes from his boat towards the shore.' There is always a limit to the help which a Harbour Master can normally give outside of his official duties, but Michael Hogan has extended the range of his services to yachtsmen through an agency run by his wife Tina from an office in the square. She will handle the domestic and logistic requirements which might

O'Shea's Bar del Marinero in Castletown, near the quay, is a perfect example of the Irish pub, unchanged since the 1930s

be needed by skippers and their crews; she will supply car transport, get tickets for bus, train or air, book accommodation, organise supplies of food and fuel, and arrange for boats to be looked after if for any reason they have to be left in the harbour.

O'Shea's Bar del Marinero in the town square is the perfect example of a little Irish pub where time has stood still since the 1930s. At least some of the showcards on the walls go back to those years, and the old lady who served me and has lived there all her life must certainly have served the fishermen coming ashore from sailing smacks. Just off the square is the Ivy Bar, a quiet pub where the quality of the Guinness is excellent. Nearby is Dermot Murphy's bicycle shop displaying the Raleigh Rent-a-Bike sign. Such shops are common all over Ireland, and bicycles can be hired by the day or the week quite cheaply. This is an excellent way of exploring the local countryside during a day ashore. There are certainly Rent-a-Bikes available all along the coast which I have covered at Arklow, Wicklow, Wexford, Waterford, Bantry, Cork, Crosshaven, Schull, Youghal and, of course, Dublin and Dun Laoghaire. For a seafood or steak dinner at a reasonable price I would suggest the Old Bank Restaurant in Bank Place. Dinner is between 7 and 10pm, lunches only on Sundays. From 11am until 4pm they serve cold dishes. The owner was formerly the manager of the South County Royal Hotel in Dublin. The building used to be a bank, and the vault is now the wine cellar. A place for a bit of lively entertainment is Waterfall Holiday Centre about two miles east on the mainland shore of Bere Haven. It has its own jetty where you can anchor off. Largely a permanent caravan site, it has a large bar and restaurant and, according to the Harbour Master's son, the best disco in that part of Ireland. There are, of course, all the usual facilities of a campsite including showers.

For a little solitude in an anchorage surrounded by trees and the ruins left by more troubled times, Dunboy Bay is an alternative to the industrialised scenery of Bere Haven harbour. It lies off the west side of Piper Sound at the entrance to Bere Haven. On the point are the inconspicuous remains of Dunboy Castle, and the anchorage is half a cable due north of those ruins. Anywhere else should be avoided because of dense seaweed. A short narrow creek runs west from the bay to a small landing stage opposite the ruined mansion of Dunboy House; there is a rudimentary beach and a pleasant walk among the surrounding trees. Dunboy House is a splendid ruin of a flamboyant Victorian pseudo-Gothic mansion, made all the more impressive for having been burnt out by the IRA in 1921. With the evening sun lighting up the empty sockets of the tall mullioned and transomed windows and silhouetting the tall chimneys and gables, the scene is much like the setting for a Hammer film. It was, in fact, the setting for Daphne du Maurier's book *Hungry Hill*, a fictionalised history based on the Puxley family from Wales who made their fortune from copper on the Bere Peninsula and started building the house in 1730 and went on adding to it until 1872. It was eventually sumptuously furnished and lived in, but never quite finished. Henry Puxley, the

Dunboy House, a flamboyant Victorian pseudo-Gothic ruin, was burnt by the IRA in 1921. It is seen here from the anchorage off the ruined castle in Dunboy Bay, an alternative to the industrial scenery of Bere Haven harbour

first member of the family to settle in Bere Haven around 1730, was in frequent dispute with Murtogh Oge O'Sullivan, a descendant of the O'Sullivan Beres, the Irish chieftains who were the earlier rulers of the peninsula and masters of Dunboy Castle. The disputes were largely over smuggling, which was the staple industry in those parts during the seventeenth and eighteenth centuries, and made fortunes for both the indigenous Irish chiefs and the English settler landlords. The castle was destroyed by the English in 1602, and nearly every one of its 143 defenders was either killed in the fighting or hanged afterwards. Today there is little left standing more than a few feet above the ground, but the layout of the walls and departments can be followed and, standing among the ruins, one can appreciate its commanding position over the narrow Piper Sound leading to the shelter and safety of Bere Haven.

Bantry Bay was once described as being large enough to shelter all the navies of Europe. From Castletown in Berehaven to Bantry at the head of the Bay is 20 miles and, with several tempting anchorages along the way, it could not be explored in detail in a mere 2-week cruise from Wales or England, but should you have more time it would be worth spending a couple of days sailing along its north shore.

Until 1938 Bere Island was garrisoned by the Royal Navy and the British Army, and for those who like looking at red-brick army barracks and gun emplacements it is an interesting place to wander round. Six miles long and mostly hilly, it supports a farming population of about two hundred. The anchorage is

The island of Garinish West in Bantry Bay where Patrick Moore (of 'Sky at Night' fame) has a
house

The ferry point to Garinish Island at Ellen's Rock in Glengariff Harbour. This beautiful, sheltered anchorage with its luxuriant trees and plant life is in marked contrast to most of the ports of call in southern Ireland

in Lawrence Cove on the north side near the eastern tip of the island. It leads to the little village of Rerrin with a couple of shops and Brendan Murphy's pub; he also runs the ferry. During the summer the village develops a youthful international character because of the Glénans Sailing School whose students are 50 per cent Irish and the rest a mix of nationalities. Adrigole Harbour is one of the loveliest of natural harbours lying at the foot of Hungry Hill, at 2,251ft much more a mountain than Mount Gabriel, and down its west flank in full view of the anchorage a waterfall cascades several hundred feet. The bay shoals in many places so the *Sailing Directions* need to be studied. There is a jetty and a slip on the east side, from which it is a half-hour's walk into the village. But if you turn right up the road which goes round Drumlave Point you soon come to two much-nearer pubs and a small shop.

Continuing along the bay towards Glengarriff the little island of Garinish West, a few yards offshore, is of passing interest as a home of Patrick Moore of 'The Sky at Night' fame. Glengarriff Harbour is an island-spattered bay surrounded by an amphitheatre of forested hills and from the water is a most delightful location. Best enjoy it from your boat though; Glengarriff Village is totally tourist orientated. Worst of all are the touts who harrass you to take one of the ferry boats over to Garinish Island, a lovely botanical garden with trees, shrubs and plants from every part of the world. If you can go in your own tender at a quiet time and wander around at your own pace it is well worth going, but you will not be popular with the local boatmen who are the greediest I have ever dealt with. For a 4-minute crossing and back in an open boat with 10 other

people under power of a 5hp outboard I was relieved of £1.50, which did not include the entrance fee to the garden. Behind Glengarriff is a 1,000-acre forest of giant oaks and ash lying in a valley at the foot of the mountains through which the Glengarriff river runs. They are the remains of the forest which once spread all over the area before the ancestors of Lord Bantry cut down the trees to make their fortunes smelting iron. There are forestry walks and an information centre.

Opposite Glengarriff is Whiddy Island with its tanker jetty where a tanker blew up in 1980. The oil-storage tanks are well camouflaged by landscaping and in that respect are unobjectionable. Behind the island is Bantry, which is of little interest to yachtsmen unless they need to do some heavy shopping. Bantry House, open to the public but somewhat run down for lack of funds, has a unique collection of magnificent French furniture and tapestries mostly of the Louis XV era; the second Earl of Bantry happened to be in Paris when the property of the guillotined royal family was being sold off. Bantry Harbour is mostly used by commercial craft from Whiddy Island, but there is a fleet of yachts belonging to Irish Atlantic Yacht Charters owned by Hugo du Plessis. His charter fleet is ideally placed for cruising round the south-west and west coasts up to the Shannon, to the Blasket and Aran Islands and the coast of Connemara, areas which few people would have the available time to reach in their own boat from the UK.

While in Ireland I was several times under great pressure from different people to visit the Kenmare River estuary which forms the next great bay beyond Bantry. I was told that it has a great air of beautiful loneliness with high mountains and many excellent little harbours, some almost totally enclosed by wooded islands. 'It would be a pity to ice seven-eighths of the cake and not the last bit', one man told me, but I never had time to get there so I can only pass on the recommendation to those who may have the time and opportunity.

The gardens on Garinish Island, Glengariff Harbour, Bantry Bay. There are trees and plants from many parts of the world

Ullapool was built all of a piece in 1788 as a
model village by the British Fisheries
Association. It is the terminal of the car ferry to
Stornoway

# 7 Ullapool to Loch Laxford

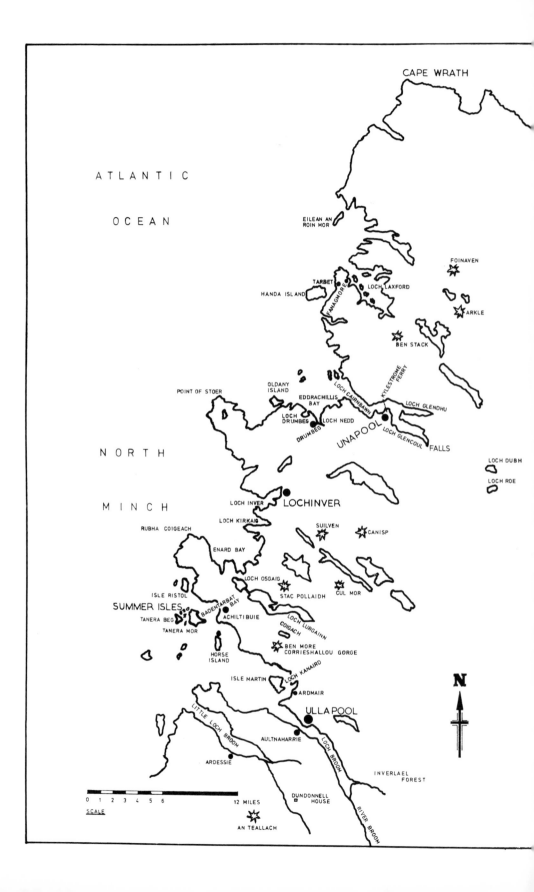

CAPE WRATH

ATLANTIC

OCEAN

EILEAN AN
ROIN MOR

FOINAVEN

TARBET
LOCH LAXFORD
HANDA ISLAND
FANAGMORE

ARKLE

BEN STACK

KYLESTROME
FERRY

OLDANY
ISLAND
LOCH CAIRNBAWN
LOCH GLENDHU
POINT OF STOER
EDDRACHILLIS
BAY
LOCH
DRUMBEG LOCH NEDD
UNAPOOL LOCH GLENCOUL FALLS
DRUMBEG

LOCH DUBH

LOCH ROE

NORTH

LOCH INVER LOCHINVER
LOCH KIRKAIG
MINCH
SUILVEN
RUBHA COIGEACH CANISP

ENARD BAY

CUL MOR
LOCH OSGAIG
ISLE RISTOL
STAC POLLAIDH
SUMMER ISLES BADENTARBAT
BAY
TANERA BEG ACHILTIBUIE
LOCH LURGAINN
TANERA MOR
COIGACH

HORSE
ISLAND
BEN MORE
CORRIESHALLOU GORGE

LOCH KANAIRD
ISLE MARTIN
ARDMAIR

N

ULLAPOOL

LITTLE LOCH BROOM
AULTNAHARRIE

LOCH BROOM
ARDESSIE
INVERLAEL
FOREST

0 1 2 3 4 5 6 12 MILES
SCALE

DUNDONNELL
HOUSE

RIVER BROOM

AN TEALLACH

The letter arrived on 20 April, by which date my diary was already filled with schedules from May to October with only a few, all too few, days free. Editors' deadlines were clearly marked like the hazards on a chart. There was going to be no way of changing course until the end of the season, no room for manoeuvre if something more interesting turned up along the way. The letter was an invitation from John Russell of Ardfern on Lochgilphead to join him at Ullapool on 31 May for a cruise up the coast towards Cape Wrath, across to Lewis and then out into the Atlantic for a visit to St Kilda. The temptation was enormous. John is not only a very fine skipper, he is the author of *Yachtmaster Offshore*, a classic in its field. His boat, *Haigri*, a Rival 38 would be a joy to sail in, and he knows the waters of the Highlands and Islands the way a blind man knows his own bathroom. He wrote: 'The reason for urging you to join us is that it should afford an opportunity to see and to photograph a spectacular and seldom visited area.' I knew it would be a memorable cruise, and so it was. Within a few days I had ruthlessly cancelled a trip through the Finnish archipelago, persuaded other people to alter plans, and written to John accepting.

Ullapool is a small neat town strung out in a shallow curve along one side of a snub-nosed little peninsula on the shore of Loch Broom. Apart from modern buildings surrounding it, some holiday flats and a caravan park, it looks as if it was built all of a piece, which it was, being established in 1788 as a model village by the British Fisheries Association. It is seen to its best advantage from across the loch a mile or so back along the A835. From there it can be viewed in its entirety with the waters lapping at the gravelly beach in front of the original fishermen's houses, now much modernised and painted white, and beyond to the scattered shapes of the Summer Isles. The fishing harbour is now dominated by the Caledonian MacBrayne car-ferry terminal for Stornoway, 3½ hours away across the Minch. Looking inland the view in every direction is of hills and mountains rising well above the rooftops. The main hotel, the Caledonian, has thirty rooms. There are also three smaller hotels, a youth hostel, a sufficiency of shops for most needs, thirteen places to eat, plenty of pubs and a local museum. To the east of the pier the wide bay in front of the town affords both good holding and good shelter with access to the pier in the middle of the town or to a broad slipway at its east end. I spent 24 hours at Ullapool before we sailed, but without doubt the place deserves a longer stay. Inland there are several low-level hill walks, mostly along old drovers' paths, leading to hill lochs all with brown trout, sheltered corries and windy spot heights, each with its own incomparable view. Depending on the season (low down in early spring, much higher up in summer), there is every chance of seeing a herd of deer or the odd lone stag statuesque on a ridge. On a summer evening the whirring of a snipe will often break the silence of seemingly infinite space. *Step into Space* is the title of a very detailed booklet published by the Wester Ross Tourist Organisation describing thirty-seven walks in the area, of which quite a few are within striking distance of a harbour or an anchorage.

The coast of Wester Ross from the entrance to Loch Broom. A good walk from Ullapool starts with a ten-minute ferry trip to the Altnaharrie Inn, a drovers' pub

A particularly interesting walk for crews visiting Ullapool starts by taking the 10-minute ferry across Loch Broom to the Aultnaharrie Inn on the other bank. It was a drovers' inn for centuries, and the walk is 700ft up the old drovers' road to Loch na h-Airbhe from where there is an extensive view of Little Loch Broom, 7½ miles long and otherwise known as 'The Loch of a Hundred Winds' because of its reputation for heavy squalls. An anchorage near the head of Little Loch Broom at Camusnagaul is a base for some good climbing on An Teallack (3,483ft), for the Ardessie Falls and Dundonnell House where the gardens and aviary are open to the public. Aultnaharrie Inn is a stone building which has been in existence longer than Ullapool, and claims to have one of the oldest licences in Scotland. It was modernised in the last century and again recently. The present owner, Fred Browne, who is the local vet, has made it into a holiday retreat, accessible only by water, for people who want to go hill and forest walking, bird watching or sailing. He has five boats for bare boat or skipper charter ranging from a Sabre 27 to a Slipper 42 and a few dinghies and rowing boats. If you despair of ever having the time to sail your own boat so far north, you can charter from Ullapool and even further north at Drumbeg, which I will come to later. Despite the remoteness of his inn, Fred Browne has managed to establish a cuisine which has earned him an entry in Egon Ronay; he serves genuine smorr-gesbrot at lunch time. 'My girlfriend is Norwegian so it is the real Scandinavian open sandwich. She also does a good dinner in the evening, but it has to be a limited menu because being so far north does present difficulties especially getting fresh vegetables, and then everything has to come across the water.' Fresh vegetables are rather rare throughout most of the Highlands and Islands.

When they are to be found the variety is very limited. The boating side of his business is aptly called Summer Isles Charter. A 2-hour sail from his little harbour will take you round Isle Martin in Loch Kanaird at the seaward end of Loch Broom and under the cliffs at the foot of the 2,500ft Coigach ridge for a miniature cruise. The shores of the island and the adjacent mainland cliffs teem with coastal wildlife: grey heron, black guillemot, Arctic tern, kittiwake, shag, eider duck, otter, porpoise and seal to name about half of the species which might be sighted. There is good fishing too for salmon and sea trout, pollock, mackerel, coalfish and bottom-feeding skate and dogfish. A day cruise could take in most of the twenty Summer Isles round which again there is an abundance of wild life with quite frequent sightings of whales. Beyond the Summer Isles the choice is to go north up to the seldom cruised and very wild Sutherland coast to Cape Wrath, or across to Lewis, or south down the more frequented Wester Ross coast.

A lazier way of seeing Isle Martin and the Summer Isles than piloting your own boat is to join one of the *Summer Queen* pleasure-steamer cruises out of Ullapool which take between two and four hours and have the advantage, for the uninitiated, of descriptive commentaries. Even if you want to do your own longer navigation of these islands, which you should do if you have the time, a *Summer Queen* cruise does provide a useful preliminary reconnaissance. For Isle Martin an alternative possibility is to go to the Ardmair Boat Centre 3½ miles up the A835 from Ullapool where you can hire a small self-drive motor boat or a rowing boat for a close inspection of the cliffs. Fishing tackle and bait are also available as well as waterproof clothing and lifejackets. If you go by water the Boat Centre have a stone quay against which it is possible to lie and dry out; they have a small chandlery shop, and specialise in outboard engines and glassfibre repairs. The bay to the east of the island is a good alternative anchorage to Ullapool; the bottom is mud and good holding.

If you want to find something a little different in Ullapool you need look no further than The Ceilidh Place, an hotel, restaurant, coffee shop and bookshop devised and run by the actor Robert Urquart. He started it as a place for ceilidhs which, he explains, are not Scottish hoolies but gatherings of people to talk, to tell tales, to sing, to hear some music and to drink a dram or two. To that he added a coffee shop, then some bedrooms, so it became also an hotel onto which was built a clubhouse with bunk rooms for those who wanted something cheaper than an hotel listed in the Good Food Guides. I can vouch for the coffee shop as an excellent place for salads, home-made pâtés, soups and cakes. He calls it peasant cooking. 'We have moussaka on the menu, but it is really a very good shepherd's pie.' In the restaurant prawns, clams, mussels, salmon trout and the best Scotch beef dominate the menu, but there are always three vegetarian dishes. The prawns they serve are the genuine langoustine, caught by the local fishing fleet. They should, correctly, be called Norwegian lobsters or *nethrops norwegicus*, the tails of which are pulled off and sold as scampi, that popular but completely nonexistent fish so well exploited by the catering trade. Your average scampi in pub and restaurant is, however, unlikely even to be the tail of the nethrop – those are mostly exported; it is usually skate tails or monk fish. Scampi, in fact, is a nickname invented by Young's from scampinello, the Italian name for a fresh-water shrimp. Among the activities which can be arranged at The Ceilidh Place are dinghy sailing with or without instruction, sea angling, water skiing, pony trekking and Land-Rover safaris into the hills. The Ceilidh Place is a brave effort to combine sophisticated comfort and good taste (in both senses of the word) with an indigenous ambience.

Local colour can be found at the Argyll Hotel, almost opposite the slipway towards the east end of the village. It is more pub than hotel, although you can have a room and a bath and eat in a small dining room or in the bar. The food is straightforward pub grills and fries plus black pudding or white pudding. The latter is black pudding without the blood, not unlike haggis. Mr Matheson, the landlord, welcomes yachtsmen, as do his locals who are mostly fishermen and he will take bookings for a bath and a meal on Ullapool 2422. An evening in his crowded bar can be educative if you are of a mind to listen to men who make their living from the sea.

Ullapool was once one of the big herring ports in Europe, on a par with Mallaig and Castlebay in Barra. Now the local boats only fish for prawns, while the big boats from Mallaig, Oban and the east coast go out to the Minch for mackerel and herring and sell to the Russian, Japanese, Korean, Bulgarian and Rumanian ships which anchor at the mouth of Loch Broom. At the head of Loch Broom, an easy trip in the tender, or a good 6-mile walk along the coast road past several good viewpoints, is Inverlael Forest, 1,000 acres in extent and one of the North Conservancy's oldest forests, dating back to 1929. Within the main forest is a 17-acre forest garden which has 150 species of tree and designated walks. Detailed leaflets are available from a dispenser at the entrance. At the eastern end of the plantations, a good five miles further on, is the Corrieshalloch Gorge, nearly 200ft deep and just under a mile long. The falls at one end drop 150ft into a rocky ravine and there are observation platforms above and below them. This is a dramatic sight when the River Broom is in spate, and a visit should be timed for the middle of the day so that the heavily wooded gorge is well lit.

We left Ullapool on a Sunday morning and as we sailed out of Loch Broom towards the Summer Isles we passed a Russian liner lying at anchor. A pinnace left her companionway filled with men and women all dressed in towny clothes for a visit ashore. We wondered what they would make of the place on the Sabbath when everything but the kirk is shut tight. When *Britannia* does her summer cruise to the west coast of Scotland she sometimes anchors in Badentarbat Bay between the only inhabited Summer Isle, Tanera Mor, and Achiltibuie on the mainland. The Royal Family then takes a launch round the point of Rubha Coigeach into Enard Bay for a picnic on their favourite beach, one of several along the south shore of the bay. For yachts the popular Summer

The Summer Isles looking towards the entrance of Loch Broom. The popular anchorage is in the eastern bay of Tanera Mor. This view shows a sheltered anchorage in the lagoon between Isle Ristol (right) and Old Dorney harbour on the mainland (left)

Isles anchorage is in the eastern bay of Tanera Mor, called The Anchorage. This is the biggest of the isles and once supported a fishing village with a school and a pub. Then the herrings left the local waters and for thirty years the place was deserted. Now a couple from the south are sheep farming on the island and they like to see yachts around and welcome crews going ashore. Inevitably some of the old houses have been renovated as holiday cottages. It is a grand little island for walking, being 1½ miles long and ½ mile wide at its narrowest. There are four lochans, some offlying islets, and cliffs which have been beautifully sculpted by the sea. Mostly covered by heather and bracken, there is no shortage of wild flowers too: foxglove, wild rose, forget-me-not and purple orchid. In the south corner of The Anchorage is a salmon farm. It is most important that boats keep well clear of the buoys supporting the nets, and any approach to the farm to watch should be done by tender.

A ferry boat is available from Achiltibuie to Tanera Mor by arrangement with the Summer Isles Estate (tel 085 482 281), and Ian McLeod at the Post Office runs a daily cruise round the Isles in his 40ft boat. The trip includes 2 hours ashore on Tanera Beg, the small neighbour of Tanera Mor, which is a completely deserted island surrounded at low tide by a fringe of pink coral sand. Between the two Isles are a dozen islets and outliers, the largest being Fada Mor. Among them are two good anchorages, well sheltered but requiring careful study of the *Sailing Directions* before going in. Once settled in, hours could be spent clambering around the islands from a tender. The Anchorage is within rowing distance of Achiltibuie which is connected to Ullapool by a daily minibus service. It means an early start as it leaves the village at 0725 for the 26-mile journey round the Coigach mountains, along the shore of four beautiful inland lochs and below the towering crags of Stac Poillaidh, arriving in Ullapool at 0840. It leaves for the return trip at 1410. For anyone with a love of mountains, Stac Poillaidh (or Stack Polly as it is more familiarly called) will be the prime objective of a day ashore. Using the minibus service from Achiltibuie, it is possible to spend over six hours on the mountain. From Ullapool it means hiring a taxi or getting a lift, which should be fairly easy in those parts. Although at 2,009ft it is not as high or as massive as its mighty neighbours Canisp (2,779ft) or Cul Mor (2,786ft), its relatively isolated position on the edge of Loch Lurgainn enhances its apparent height. From the south and south-east its pinnacled ridge takes on the appearance of a gigantic Ruritanian castle; when mist swirls between the pinnacles and black clouds hang overhead it looks more like the abode of some legendary giant. The face of the ridge, especially the western end, offers formidable climbing, but there is a well-beaten track from a car park off the road round the east end onto the shoulder round the mountain. The top of the ridge can also be reached from the same route, but requires at least good walking boots and a bit of scrambling. The stiff walk has its reward in the views across the 27,000-acre wilderness of Inverpolly National Nature Reserve with its ragged lochs, rocky hills, wooded glens and backdrop of mountains filling the whole northern sector. Westwards the Summer Isles are scattered over the surface of the sea, and to the south the view is blocked by the serpentine ridge of Coigach. From below, from above and from most points afar, Stack Polly is the most photogenic mountain in Scotland.

Achiltibuie village is a long string of low houses spread out along the road which goes nowhere except to the foot of Ben Mor Coigach. If it were not for that formidable massif the road could go on along the coast to be in Ullapool in about eight miles instead of having to go first north and then inland. A good excuse for stopping off at Achiltibuie is the Summer Isles Hotel, marked as an inn on the old charts. It is an hotel catering for people seeking remoteness and gentility with superb food. Dinner is on the stroke of 7.30 with a different menu every night. The restaurant can seat only thirty people, and they have twenty-eight residents when full, so it is essential to telephone at least the day before (085 482 282). It is somewhat regimented with its 'No smoking in the dining room please'. However it is a unique eating experience for the west coast of Scotland because everything is fresh. Mr Irvine, the patron, stood with me on the doorstep and, pointing to the bay below, said: 'Salmon come out of the sea down there, scallops from over there, prawns from the whole bay, lobsters and crabs from up the coast, venison from the hills behind us, and cucumbers, blueberries, black-currants and all our fruit and vegetables from down there.' Down below was a kitchen garden on the steep slope leading down to the shore. A path leads from the hotel to a small indent which provides a convenient temporary anchorage. If you are unable to book or do not want the formality of an hotel dinner, there is his Smokehouse Restaurant next door which caters for campers, people living in nearby holiday homes and passing tourists. A good meal can be had of smoked chicken, salmon, haddock, hams, venison and sausages, all of them prepared in

Culkein Drumbeg anchorage in Eddrachilles Bay

his own smokehouse. Mr Irvine has also built some showers especially for yachtsmen. He is a yachtsman himself, although now a frustrated one. For three years he kept his 39ft ketch anchored in the bay but found that converting a shambolic ruin with a tin roof into a comfortable hotel and gastronomic restaurant left him no time for sailing.

Our first day's sail out of Ullapool took us round the Point of Stoer, across the west part of Eddrachillis Bay and into Loch Nedd, a very pretty anchorage as safe as could be from anything but a howling northerly gale. A boat taking time off to sail around the Summer Isles would not get so far in a day and would most likely put into Loch Inver for the night. The Culag Hotel, large and well appointed, is useful for showers and a meal; the harbour is sheltered, the fish quay easy for landing, and the town of Lochinver has a sprinkling of shops for supplies but little of interest. If you are an angler there are 280 trout lochs in the parish, and salmon fishing in Loch Kirkaig with its famous falls is run by the Culag Hotel. Climbers, geologists and photographers might like to make a 5-mile expedition to the extraordinary 2,399ft Suilven sugarloaf which dominates the countryside. My preference is for Loch Roe, 2 miles beyond the entrance beacon to Loch Inver. The anchorage is in a little pool behind two tidal rocks at the entrance. The loch is rock-girt, but everywhere it is easy to scramble ashore for walks among a profusion of wild flowers and stunted trees. The east end of the loch, about a mile on, can be reached in a tender. Here the loch becomes a river for a few hundred yards, passing under a wooden bridge and then opening out into a second land-locked loch with islets and wooded shores. The wooden bridge leads to a short steep track up to Loch Dubh, a tree-fringed punchbowl full of fish. It is somewhat off the beaten track and you are unlikely to meet anyone else but the odd angler sitting on a rock. Less than a mile north of the anchorage is a sandy bay surrounded by crofts which is a campsite during the summer. There is a small

The entrance to Loch Roe, the wild but peaceful alternative to anchoring in Loch Inver, and more sheltered. The anchorage is in a little pool between two tidal rocks at the entrance

camp shop if you have need of milk or other basics.

Nedd village offers nothing more than a telephone kiosk, but a mile over the hill to the west is Drumbeg and the Drumbeg Hotel, a pub with six double rooms and a landlord, Andrew Mackay, who is himself a yachtsman. He has two aluminium 26ft Julian Everitt-designed mini-tonners available for charter. Although their accommodation is an improvement on boats used for racing, they are still spartan and are intended to appeal to those who wish, and are competent, to tour the Sutherland coast in a performance boat and so cover the maximum ground in the minimum time. The hotel serves meals, mostly local fish and venison, with lobster for those who 'want to cough up' as Mackay puts it. There is a visitors' mooring buoy in Loch Nedd, but with the good holding mud on the bottom it is not really needed. At the head of the loch is a small beach which is handy for drying out if you want to look at your bottom. Loch Drumbeg, to the west of Loch Nedd and about two miles east of the north point of Oldany Island, is another good anchorage sheltered among islets but a little exposed to the north-west. It is nearer the village, which is reached by taking the tender to the east corner of the anchorage, then walking up a hill path which comes out beside a craft shop and car park on the edge of the village.

A most interesting sail from Drumbeg is into Loch Cairnbawn and through the narrows at the Kylesku Ferry. The best anchorage is in South Ferry Bay where there is a small hotel. The loch divides past the narrows into Loch Glendhu and Loch Glencoul. The boat or tender should be taken up the latter through another narrows into Loch Beag. The good reason for the 5-mile trip up this blind alley is to go ashore at the head of Loch Beag and walk up the glen, steep and soggy most times, to the foot of the Eas a Chual Aluinn waterfall. Dropping over 500ft, it is acclaimed as the biggest or longest waterfall in Scotland. This is the subject of much argument because the water falls over three ledges but gives the impression of one single spill of white water. After exceptionally heavy rain the volume of water may be deep enough to clear two of the ledges and produce a free fall of at least 400ft. At any time it is a brave sight – the thundering water, massive rock scenery and the length of Loch Glencoul below. The approach by water is a classic example of the advantage of travelling by boat and tender. The overland route is a quite strenuous 5-mile walk over rock, bog and steep grass slopes, not to mention midges in high summer.

The afternoon of the second day found us anchored in Loch Laxford in the bay of Fanagmore village. What a wonderful loch! One could spend a day cruising round its twenty or more little islands and again as many islets and skerries. It is a complex geological structure of lewisian gneiss chiselled out by the most recent Ice Age and worn by millennia of Atlantic gales. Some thirty different species of bird can be counted in the loch, there is a small heronry on one of the islands, and colonies of both common and Atlantic grey seals. Sometimes porpoises and otters may be sighted as well as whales. I talked to a family who said that the day before we arrived they had been out with the local boatman and seen five whales. Apart

The remote tranquillity of Loch Dubh, a little row and a short walk from the anchorage in Loch Roe

Loch Laxford from the hills above Fanagmore. It has twenty or more little islands. The further-out boat is John Russell's *Haigri*

from where the A894 touches the head of the loch, the shoreline of Loch Laxford is a steep roadless wilderness with the prominent and distinctively shaped mountains of Ben Stack (2,364ft), Arkle (2,580ft) and Foinaven (2,980ft) rising into the sky to the south and east. From Fanagmore it is just a mile over the hill to Tarbet where the boatmen will ferry you across to Handa Island, a nature reserve with a bird population of staggering size and variety, second only in the British Isles to St Kilda. You do not need to know anything about sea birds or be particularly interested in them to be fascinated and astounded by the sight of them nesting in their tens of thousands on the cliffs and stacks, rows upon rows packed as tight as fans on a football terrace and making as much noise.

The boats from Tarbet land you on a sandy beach, and from there it is a short but leg-aching walk through the dunes to the bothy which is the home of the warden and where the Royal Society for the Protection of Birds, which manages the island, has a display and literature. Visitors must keep to the marked pathways to avoid disturbing nesting birds, particularly skuas. Below the bothy is Port an Eilean where terns, oyster catchers, ringed plovers and rock pipits breed and eider ducks and black guillemots can be seen feeding. That part of the island is alive with rabbits, some of them black, and the turf is the nesting ground for wheatears. A small plantation of lodgepole pine and alder has been established near the bothy which provides shelter for small birds. Port an Eilean is a good summer anchorage and, except for the beach where the ferry boats drop you off, is the only permitted landing place. The centre of the island is boggy and although duckboards and stepping stones have been laid down in places boots or wellies are in order. One of the commonest flowers is the spotted heath orchid, and in July and August the yellow bog asphodel covers the wetter areas. The path passes a group of ruined crofts which were cleared in 1848 and several little lochans before arriving at the cliff edge of Puffin Bay, which is really a misnomer. Very few puffins will be seen there, the cliffs being alive with herring gulls and fulmars, the latter recognisable by their still-winged flight. A needle stack in the bay supports guillemot and razorbill colonies with the occasional grey seal in the water below. The path then goes on to the Great Stack, a plug of rock rising 300ft out of the sea just off the cliffs which provide a viewing gallery around three sides of it. In summer up to 12,000 birds nest on the Stack, each species keeping to its own strata like humans of varying social condition occupying the stalls, the balcony and gallery of a theatre. The guillemots occupy the broader ledges, the kittiwakes which are small gulls with black wing tips and horrible screechy voices use the tiny projections, and near the top are the razorbills. At the very top which is grass covered are the burrowing puffins.

Continuing west about the path passes a black tarn and Poll Ghlup, a mighty blow hole well in from the cliff edge, and here the cliffs rise vertical for 400ft. It is razorbill territory with a few shags. The west side of the island is thick with gannets. Round the south shore divers, ducks and black guillemots can be spied on the water. The designated route is about three miles and, allowing for a few

The Great Stack on Handa Island, about one mile by sea from Tarbet. Some 12,000 birds nest on the Stack in summer

brief stops, it takes at least 2 hours. That is just long enough to be able to say that you have seen Handa Island. It is worth a longer stay and with binoculars and camera one could be absorbed for a whole day. On those rare days when there is almost no wind and certainly no swell it would be doubly interesting to take a small boat round Handa and see the cliffs and beaches not covered by the official path; you could even circumnavigate the Great Stack, but you might need an umbrella to shelter from the 'snowstorm' of bird droppings. If there is any Atlantic swell running such a trip would be ruled out.

Loch Laxford was our jumping-off point for the passage across the Minch to the Butt of Lewis and out into the Atlantic to St Kilda but that voyage went far beyond the range of the average cruising family; to do justice to those remote parts of Britain would require a whole book.

Motor cruisers are for hire at East Loch Tarbert.
Despite the long journey by road, this is a good
starting point for Tarbert itself is a safe, well-
sheltered fishing port

# 8 The Firth of Clyde and Loch Fyne

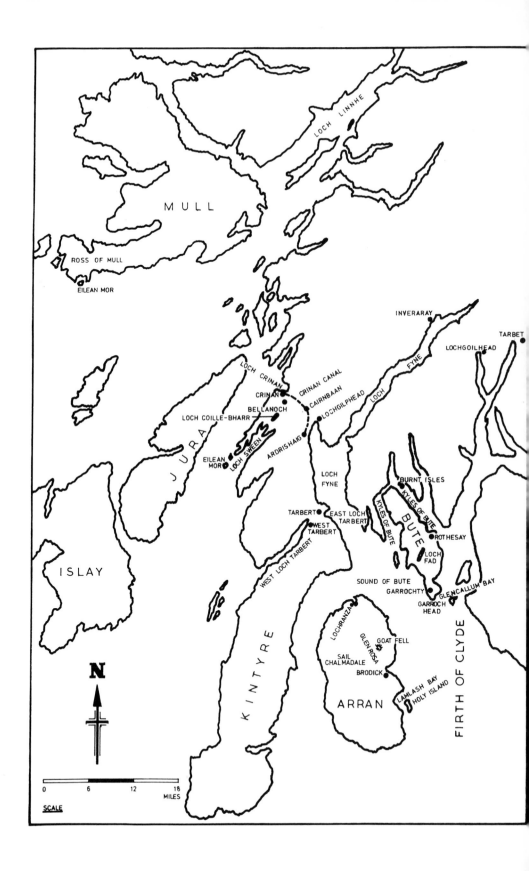

LOCH LINNHE

MULL

ROSS OF MULL

EILEAN MOR

INVERARAY

TARBET

LOCHGOILHEAD

LOCH CRINAN

CRINAN CANAL

CRINAN

CAIRNBAAN

BELLANOCH

LOCHGILPHEAD

LOCH COILLE-BHARR

LOCH
FYNE

JURA

EILEAN
MOR

LOCH SWEEN

ARDRISHAIG

BURNT ISLES

LOCH
FYNE

KYLES OF BUTE

BUTE

KYLES OF BUTE

ROTHESAY

TARBERT

EAST LOCH
TARBERT

LOCH
FAD

WEST
TARBERT

ISLAY

WEST LOCH TARBERT

SOUND OF BUTE

GARROCHTY

GLENCALLUM BAY

GARROCH
HEAD

LOCHRANZA

GLEN ROSA

GOAT FELL

KINTYRE

SAIL
CHALMADALE

BRODICK

LAMLASH BAY

HOLY ISLAND

FIRTH OF CLYDE

ARRAN

N

0    6    12    18
MILES

SCALE

If what I have written tempts you to go exploring the West Highland coast and islands, but the prospect seems a little daunting, I would suggest working towards the greater adventure by first spending a season or two cruising the sea lochs and islands of the Firth of Clyde. In those relatively sheltered waters the scenery is almost as grand as further north above Ardnamurchan Point, the point which is often said to sort out the cruising men from the boys; there are plenty of remote anchorages, remote from roads and trippers that is, but not remote in distance from proper harbours, town facilities and even one or two marinas. There are mountain summits, headlands and islets which are the stuff of navigation and pilotage round the Hebrides and along the Highland coast, but there is also a full complement of proper navigation marks everywhere. Although there are many towns there is also plenty of wild open country, moorland, hills, mountains and forests in between to satisfy the most energetic ashore.

Depending on how you use the area, whether you follow well-buoyed tracks, keep mostly inside the sea lochs and put into harbours at night, or whether you seek out your own anchorages, venture out to sea round Bute and Arran and so have to navigate a bit more and watch the weather, the Firth of Clyde can be a nursery or a testing cruising ground. It is also the ideal area in which to introduce an apprehensive family to Scottish cruising. It is far more accessible than the Highlands and Islands and there are numerous charter boats available. Whereas you have to give evidence of reasonable seagoing experience and seamanship to charter a yacht, several companies in the Firth of Clyde hire motor cruisers for which they demand no more experience than a week's holiday on the Thames or Broads. In fact if you want a holiday on the water and to see as much as possible in the time you have available, a motor cruiser which steams at about twelve knots is a very practical vehicle and non-sailing family and friends can make up the numbers and so reduce the cost. I have twice used a motor cruiser in those waters for a total of only 7 days but covered distances which would have taken 3 weeks under sail and still had time for extensive forays ashore.

East Loch Tarbert, where Loch Fyne Cruisers bases its hire fleet, is a good starting-off point, despite the rather lengthy road journey round the top of Loch Long and down most of the west shore of Loch Fyne to get there. Tarbert itself is a safe, well-sheltered fishing port which even the installation of pontoon berths for yachts has not spoilt. It has the statutory ruined castle – Bruce's Castle on a rock ledge above the harbour – and 2 miles up the road north towards Ardrishaig is a castle of a more comfortable sort. It is Stonefield Castle, now an hotel of baronial-hall dimensions and furnished in quiet luxury. It has a large garden full of rare trees and a great variety of rhododendrons, a swimming pool, tennis courts, sauna, solarium, children's playground and a yachtsmen's bathroom. You do not have to walk from Tarbert for a bath and a meal there. At the bottom of the garden is a little anchorage, called North Bay, behind Barmore Island, and the hotel has six visitors' moorings and a large slipway. It is just the place for a sybaritic break from the chores and claustrophobia of life on board, but it could

(*Opposite above*) The entrance to East Loch Tarbert from Loch Fyne; (*opposite below*) The fishing quay at Tarbert. Bruce's Castle can be seen above the houses; (*above*) The hamlet of Lochgair, on the west shore of Loch Fyne, is a good anchorage before the long haul to Inverary

be an expensive treat. The best rooms cost over £50 a night; it is that sort of place. In the garden there is a building of some curiosity – a coal house with weighbridge, now hidden among the rhododendrons, which is where the coal for the castle which came once a year by puffer from Glasgow was weighed. On passage from Glasgow the skipper would stop off once or twice for a trip to a pub where he would be offered a bottle of whisky for a sack of coal; without the weighbridge the deliveries could have been short.

Going up the loch towards Lochgilphead and keeping close to the west shore watch out for a small slipway marked by a perch 2 miles south of the pier and canal basin at Ardrishaig. Between mid-June and the end of August this is the point to drop your hook and row ashore to see if Forsyth Hamilton has any Loch Fyne kippers – if smoke is rising from his chimney you can be sure he has. His kippers are always local herrings, a species superior to the North Sea ones, most of them caught by local fishermen in the Firth, and when the ban on herring fishing in the Minch is lifted some will come from there. Whether you will be lucky depends on how the quota for the Clyde has been fixed and how his sales have gone just before you arrive. The quota for the Clyde dropped from 7,000 tons when the UK joined the EEC down to 2,000 tons between 1979 and 1981. There is no knowing what it will be when you read this. Mr Hamilton's kippers owe their flavour and rich colour to being oak-smoked for 24 hours. Later in September if he has enough fish he starts salting for the big winter trade in salt herrings. He explained to me that during the summer the herrings grow fat on the rich plankton in the water and their fat resists the salt so they would go bad. Only in September when the plankton has been reduced do they lose their fat and can be salted. Forsyth Hamilton's family has lived in Ardrishaig since 1800 and has always been in the herring-fishing business. They and their boats were the first customers of the Crinan Canal Company when the canal opened in 1801. He is a man who enjoys meeting and talking with people and, kippers apart, he is a mine of local information, ancient and modern.

The Crinan Canal which starts at Ardrishaig, runs north parallel to Loch Gilp for a while, and then turns west through forest country to Crinan on the Sound of Jura, is to many people just a convenient short cut from the Clyde to the Atlantic coast and the Hebrides. In fact it is a fascinating length of water which passes through beautiful walking country rich in local history. The canal is 9 statute miles long and the passage time is about four-and-a-half hours providing you have no hold-ups at the locks and swing bridges, but it would be well worth allowing yourself a day with two long stops for walks. Hire cruisers can do that, but they are not allowed to go out of the canal at the other end.

After passing through the sea lock at Ardrishaig into the basin there is a long reach of just over 4 miles to the start of Summit Reach at lock No 5 at Cairnbaan where the Old Coach Inn has been developed into the large Motor Inn stretching for about three-hundred yards along the canal bank. The bar and restaurant make it an obvious stopping place, and on the opposite side of the canal is the Forestry Office where local information on forest walks and loch fishing is available. From the canal side it is a little less than a three-mile uphill walk along the A816 going north to Dunadd, the hill where the kings of the ancient Scottish kingdom were crowned. Standing on its summit they could see all the counties over which they ruled. The hill was fortified in the sixth century as the capital of the Scots and tradition has it that the Stone of Destiny, now in Westminster Abbey, was used in the enthronement of those Dalriadic Kings. The remains of the fortification have been excavated and preserved. The surrounding area has as many archaeo-logical sites as anywhere in Scotland – Neolithic chambered cairns, cists and standing stones, ancient churches and ruined castles.

Starting from the south side of the canal is the Cairnbaan Forest Walk, a 2-mile circle. The path leads to the Ordnance Survey Triangulation Station (703ft) from which there are excellent views over the surrounding forest, the canal and Loch a Bharain beside it. The prettiest place to stop along the canal is Bellanoch Lagoon near the end of the journey where the canal runs beside the River Add which widens out into Loch Crinan. The two are separated by an earth dyke. In the lagoon you moor beside reed banks at the foot of a steep wooded hill. There are a few cottages and an hotel, and climbing up the hill the B8025 runs through Knapdale Forest on its way to the Sound of Jura at Keillbeg. About a mile up the hill an unclassified road leads to Loch Coille Bharr where two boats can be hired for fly fishing for brown trout from Mrs Robertson who

Fishing boats crammed into the basin inside the sea lock of the Crinan Canal at Crinan

You can moor beside the bank below wooded hills on the way through the Crinan Canal

lives by the road junction (tel 0546 2304). Nearby are two smaller lochs, Barnaluasgan and Linnhe: 'Smaller loch, smaller boat, smaller fish, smaller fees – ideal for the solitary or less energetic angler' say the Forestry people. There are two other little lochs reached by walking along forest roads where for £1 a day you can fish from the banks.

Loch Coille Bharr is also the start of the Oib Mhor Archaeological Walk, 6 miles long and taking about 3 hours. It features a prehistoric stone circle, a deserted village and holy well out of which crystal-clear water still flows. The well is marked by a stone with a cross on both faces and on one side a design of birds and geometric shapes. The date of the ruined village is not known, but the area was cleared in the nineteenth century. The name of the village, Kilmory Oib, means 'Chapel of Maelrudha', an eighth-century Celtic saint. Near the end of the loch is the Mill of Coille Bharr, an overshot mill fed by a conduit from the loch. Half a mile on are the remains of the steading at Oibmore which was inhabited within living memory. A track leads down to a landing place on the shore of Loch Sween which runs into the Sound of Jura. Another half mile on is a small early graveyard where a few carved stones can be seen. There were more of them, but they were removed to museums in 1928. The last site on the trail is Druim an Duin, an Iron Age fort which was excavated in 1903. It has two entrances with stone jambs and bar holes, and one entrance has a still partly roofed guardroom in the thickness of the wall.

Bellanoch Lagoon, the prettiest place to stop on the Crinan Canal. This is where the canal runs beside the River Add which widens into Loch Crinan

Brown trout are to be had in many of the freshwater lochs along the Crinan Canal

From Crinan at the end of the canal there are three more Forestry walks. A short one from the harbour goes along the sea shore for nearly a mile to the Sailor's Grave and then climbs to a 750ft viewpoint overlooking the Sound of Jura from where can be seen Jura, Scarba, Lunga, Mull, Luing and Craignish Point. The basin inside the sea lock at the Crinan end of the canal is an amazing sight on days when the fishing fleet is in. It is almost completely encircled by steep forest below which the boats lie packed tight like the proverbial sardines in a tin. In the pound above the first inland lock there is always an interesting variety of yachts and motor cruisers waiting for their owners to return another weekend. Crinan has a nice old lighthouse by the canal sea lock, an hotel and a boatyard and a well on the side of the basin, but there is also a tap by the Canal Store. The logical conclusion to a cruise up Loch Fyne would be to go ashore at Inveraray to visit the castle, but it is a 20-mile 'drive' to a dead end to join the tourist crowds. I never bothered, but it is usually the first place that hire-cruiser crews make for.

If, after leaving East Loch Tarbert and making south down the Mull of Kintyre to the Sound of Bute it should blow up from the south-east, there is tempting shelter in Loch Ranza on the north tip of Arran. Since it faces north-west it looks a likely place. That is where we went in just those circumstances and spent a very uncomfortable night on anchor watch with white horses racing past our hull. What we had not noticed, but which the Ordnance Survey map and chart clearly show, is that Glen Chalmadale at the head of the loch runs south-east between steep hills and when there is a fresh south-easterly a veritable gale funnels through the glen and straight down the loch. We should have read our CCC *Sailing Directions* which mentions it and run for shelter in the Kyles of Bute, but running in a motor cruiser is not much fun – especially when the owners have governed the engines and made it difficult to adjust speeds to a following sea.

If you want a gentle cruising holiday spending as much time exploring ashore as sailing, take a day or two to circumnavigate Bute. It is only 15½ miles long and varies from 1¼ to 5¼ miles across, so you can make a really detailed study of it and sail through the very beautiful scenery of the west and east Kyles of Bute. One or the other is bound to be sheltered unless the wind is strong from the south, and then you can either hide in the lee of the north of the island where the Kyles join or run into Rothesay and spend the day in a genuine Victorian seaside resort. Rothesay was where I picked up a small motor cruiser with a single engine from Scotia Islands Chartering but, because it was a single-screw boat with no other means of propulsion, I did not consider it wise to go far afield, round Arran and to the limit of the Kintyre peninsula for instance. So a friend and I contented ourselves with a leisurely 5 days discovering Bute. Arriving from the mainland by the Wemyss Bay to Rothesay ferry, my first discovery was the men's lavatory on the harbour wall. It is a wonderful example of a Victorian civic building, the urinals in black marble, the pipes and fittings in brass and copper all kept shining bright, and the cisterns made of glass and brass bound with their ball cocks, plungers and siphons all visible. The WCs are like thrones on raised daises with massive wooden seats and grafitti, painstakingly carved with penknives, dating from the turn of the century. The town is fronted by a promenade with flower beds, ornamental street lamps, a bandstand, Chinese-style winter gardens with a funfair, and palm trees. The shops, pubs and hotels are adorned with much 'tortured' ironwork and barleysugar drainpipes, and a moment's walk from the sea is a fine castle ruin. Rothesay Castle, open to the public, is a circular fortress built on a mound and was prominent in Scottish history from the twelfth to the seventeenth century. It was the home of the Bute family until it was destroyed in 1685 by the Earl of Argyll's troops during the Rebellion. In Stuart Street behind the castle is a very good natural-history museum which goes beyond the usual Bronze Age remains and stuffed birds. A large collection of old photographs of the Clyde pleasure steamers, yacht regattas, trams and the streets and buildings around the turn of the century brings back to life the period when Bute was the holiday Mecca of Glaswegians. In the nineteenth century the Glasgow merchants and industrialists built themselves grand houses there; they were followed by successful tradesmen who took seaside villas, and then came the masses on day trips away from the sweat shops and clanking sooty factories. From about 1880 until the outbreak of World War I up to forty paddle steamers a day made the crossing to Rothesay or cruised through the Kyles of Bute with German bands playing on board. In 1901 the Berlin Philharmonic was engaged to play on a cruise through the Kyles. Rothesay remained the Number One holiday centre in the Clyde between the wars, but since the last war has declined into a slightly seedy shadow of its former self deserted by the latter-day Glaswegians, first for the Costa Brava and now for

The narrow entrance into the inner harbour at Rothesay, a genuine Victorian seaside resort

Disneyland. But it can still get crowded with day trippers in July and August, and with the coming of the roll-on roll-off car ferry it is given a quick look-see by motorists and coach parties along with Loch Lomond and Inveraray Castle. It is a popular stopping place for cruising yachts, and when there is more than a ruffle on the sea outside the harbour will be crowded with hire cruisers.

The Great Highland Fault, which produced the Great Glen through which the Caledonian Canal passes, cuts Bute in half giving the island three distinctive topographical and geological divisions. In the north moorland, bog and rock rise to around 900ft, a valley with Loch Fad almost cuts the island in two, and the smaller southern part is a plateau with steep escarpments. The northern part is a miniature Highlands with igneous rock and metamorphic schists largely heather covered. In the south are sedimentary rocks, slates and red sandstone with some sandstone lavas, and the plateau with rounded hills is grass covered and fertile.

The first day of our Bute cruise was down the east coast to Glencallum Bay or Callum's Hole, a small bay on the south-east tip of the island marked on its north point by a red flashing beacon. I had long wanted to go into that bay because, although it is miles from any road and backed by steep hills, there are the ruins of

(*Above*) The lighthouse on the eastern side of the entrance to Glencallum Bay; (*opposite above*) Glencallum Bay at the southern end of the Isle of Bute. It is miles from anywhere and there are the ruins of a pub just off the beach. This is where trading ships out of Glasgow waited for a fair wind to cross the Atlantic. Little Cumbrae is in the middle distance; (*right*) the mountains of Arran seen from Garroch Head at the southern tip of the Isle of Bute

a pub just off the beach. The *Sailing Directions* say that it is only a temporary anchorage exposed to southerly winds, but it was once used by sailing ships out of Glasgow waiting for a fair wind to take them across the Atlantic, and the pub was built to keep their crews happy while they waited. We went in keeping near the south side to avoid the rocks which lie about the centre of the bay and cover at high water, and anchored about two-thirds of the way in towards the beach. The bottom is thick with kelp and it took several goes to get the anchor to hold, so we put a kedge out as we expected to be ashore for some time. The pub, about two hundred yards from the water's edge, is now reduced to walls about three feet high but the shapes of the rooms are clearly defined. In front of the building there is a well which has filled with stone and earth to within a few feet of the top. About a third of a mile up Glen Callum is a ruined croft with its corn-drying kiln. Returning to the bay we struck off west along a path, little more than a sheep track with here and there a bit of scrambling, along the ridge above Garroch Head, the southern tip of the island. From the ridge we looked across to Goat Fell and its associated peaks on Arran and down its east coast as far as Holy

Island just over from Lamlash Bay. The sun was in the south-west and the sky heavy which made Arran look dark and foreboding. Passing a small cave where the basalt sill lies on top of old red sandstone, the track drops down the north side of the ridge and there below us lay Loch-na-Leigh, 'the Pool of Healing', as pretty a piece of water as you could wish for. The edges are broadly rimmed with bullrushes, and yellow water lilies cover most of the surface. The rest was white with thousands of floating birds. We approached down the steep track as quietly as we could after our first exclamations of wonder, but we must have made more noise than we thought because while still several hundred yards off the birds all rose together like a billowing sheet off the water and flew high and away from us. Loch-na-Leigh is a lovely little wild-life sanctuary. Sedge warblers occupy an island which is actually a floating mass of willow roots, and teal and tufted duck nest in the bullrushes. Stonechats, whinchats, pipits and wheatears can be seen on the rocks and among the surrounding bracken. And of course at times, as when we arrived, it is crowded with sea birds, and occasionally a kestrel or buzzard can be spotted hovering overhead. The east side of the loch is boggy and virtually impassable, but along its west side there is a long thin ridge about fifty feet high from which one gets an oblique view over the water. If you have time to, lie still on the ridge until the birds have settled again; it is a perfect hide.

At the north end of the ridge the track goes down to flat waterlogged ground leading to Plan Farm where it divides, one way leading to the farmhouse and the other round the outside of a sheepfold. We took the latter track towards our destination, St Blane's Chapel half hidden among trees at the top of a gentle slope. St Blane's is many things, but what one remembers most is its enchanting setting. The remains of the Celtic monastery founded by St Blane in 570, and the small Norman church built among its ruins 300 years after it had been sacked by the Vikings in 790, occupy a hollow backed by a rock escarpment. Ash and elm trees growing around and within the walls give the site a sylvan air. Looking south the way we had come the ground slopes away, a green corridor to the sea, the view bisected at the last moment by the high ground above Garroch Head. The present ruins are largely twelfth century with a fine example of a Norman arch, but there are numerous signs of earlier buildings belonging to the original monastery. Three walls remain, one enclosing the site of a primitive building below the escarpment, one enclosing the church and two burial grounds, and parts of the outer wall encircling the monastic land. Beyond the outer wall are the remains of an even more ancient hut circle and the Devil's Cauldron, a massive stone circular enclosure the purpose of which is not known. It may be the lower remains of a tower similar to those found in Ireland but pre-dating the Celtic era. Maybe it was only a round store house, but the stones are unnecessarily massive. If time is spent many traces of the religious community life can be discovered; a hollow which was a corn-drying kiln, a stone basin where pilgrims washed their feet as part of the rites of the Celtic church, a well, and a long tombstone near the doorway to the burial ground traditionally believed to

St Blane's Chapel, part of a Celtic monastery founded in 570. A small Norman church was built among the ruins after it had been sacked by the Vikings in 790

be St Blane's. A large fuchsia bush gives an indication of the mildness of Bute winters, and for the naturalist there is a great variety of lichens covering the ruins.

From St Blane's we walked to Dunagoil Bay and climbed up a rocky crag overlooking it to the vitrified fort on the summit. There is little to see, but a careful search will reveal lumps of half-melted vitreous stone looking not unlike slag from a firebox or furnace. The commanding but horribly windy location makes it an obvious defensive site. The panorama takes in Holy Island, the mountains of Arran, Skipness on the Mull of Kintyre, the entrance to Loch Fyne and much of the west coast of Bute with its succession of bays. Due south on the side of St Blane's Hill is Garrochty, the house of the late William Macewen, the Bute-born surgeon who was the first in this country to operate on the brain. Below the fort, caves, trap dykes of basalt thrusting through old red sandstone, columnar basalt cliffs and pillow lava with its steam cavities making it look like petrified sponge, are all there to delight the geologist and all within a few minutes' walk. There are also foundations of a Norse longhouse, which I failed to identify, and several cup stones. After looking at so much we found we had been ashore for several hours and started to worry about the boat in its 'temporary' anchorage. When we got back it was still there and the anchors holding. There was no wind when we left Glencallum Bay, the sea was flat and the evening light quite golden. We had intended to go back to Rothesay and look at the Kyles the next day, but with a maximum speed of 12 knots we decided to play truant from Bute and make a dash across to Brodick on Arran and go to the top of Goat Fell instead. You can make that sort of impulsive decision

(*Left*) 'Our crew plodding the squelchy boggy slopes of Glen Rosa to tackle Goat Fell on Arran'; (*right*) The Burnt Isles in the narrows of the Kyles of Bute. The anchorages in the East and West Kyles provide good shelter if the wind is not strong from the south

with a power cruiser. Brodick really is a depressing place to stay the night tucked in behind the ferry pier with nothing to look at but its weed- and mussel-covered timbers.

The next morning we set off for the long walk up Glen Rosa to tackle Goat Fell from behind. The going was very heavy and we gave up before the summit when the clouds came down and we realised there would be nothing to see if we went on, but when we set off back to Bute in the afternoon we felt we had added another experience to the week and taken some very therapeutic exercise. In the morning we took the short run up to Burnt Isles at the top of the Kyles. Anchoring in Balnacailly Bay to the south of Eilean Mor we rowed ashore for a cross-country walk to Bull Loch, a remote patch of water up in the hills. In the woods near the shore we came across a widespread colony of anthills standing some 2ft high. Here and there between the trees one got delightful views of the Burnt Isles and yachts sailing between them. As well as anthills we found numerous insectivorous blue butterworts. The woods are full of tussocks of soft pale-green sphagnum moss and also hair moss which the Girl Guides of Bute collect and send to the Haig Poppy factory in Edinburgh to be used as the backing for poppy wreaths. Coming out of the woods at about three hundred feet we came across the deserted settlement of Balnakailly. No one knows for certain when it was deserted, but the last child was born there in 1865. It was for a time the home of Marconi's grandmother before her parents moved to Ireland. From there on it was an hour's walk to cover the mile or so up and down over soggy ground through heather and cotton grass to the top of the ridge above the loch. The loch is covered with water lilies and otters live there, although we did not see any. A herd of wild goats roams the north end of Bute and can be spotted occasionally near here. I later learned that the anthills we had come across are the huge nests of the Wood Ant, and that their tracks along the forest floor run for up to eighty yards. Each hill houses about 100,000 ants, contains hundreds of passages and inter-communicating chambers, and also underground cells reached by tunnels. At night gateways into the conical hills are closed off with sticks by worker ants and then guarded by sentry ants. Each community has several queens with life spans of fifteen years, while the worker ants live about six years. Such longevity compared with, say, the three-week-long life of the honey bee allows for a very successful and stable social structure among these insects.

Those who cruise from marina to marina and never use their legs miss the opportunity of seeing and learning some amazing things.

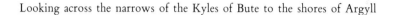

Looking across the narrows of the Kyles of Bute to the shores of Argyll

The quay at Snape where you can leave your boat
while you enjoy a concert at the Maltings. The
concert hall is just beyond the trees

# 9 The Rivers of East Anglia

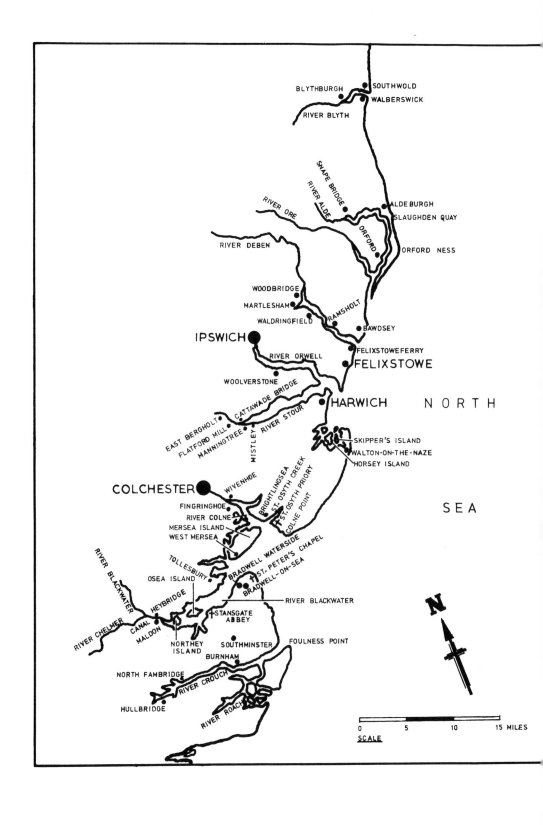

BLYTHBURGH
SOUTHWOLD
WALBERSWICK
RIVER BLYTH

SNAPE BRIDGE
RIVER ALDE
RIVER ORE
ALDEBURGH
SLAUGHDEN QUAY
ORFORD
RIVER DEBEN
ORFORD NESS

WOODBRIDGE
MARTLESHAM
RAMSHOLT
WALDRINGFIELD
BAWDSEY
IPSWICH
FELIXSTOWE FERRY
RIVER ORWELL
FELIXSTOWE
WOOLVERSTONE
CATTAWADE BRIDGE
HARWICH
NORTH

EAST BERGHOLT
FLATFORD MILL
MANNINGTREE
MISTLEY
RIVER STOUR
SKIPPER'S ISLAND
WALTON-ON-THE-NAZE
HORSEY ISLAND

COLCHESTER
WIVENHOE
BRIGHTLINGSEA
ST. OSYTH CREEK
ST. OSYTH PRIORY
COLNE POINT
SEA
FINGRINGHOE
RIVER COLNE
MERSEA ISLAND
WEST MERSEA

RIVER BLACKWATER
TOLLESBURY
BRADWELL WATERSIDE
ST. PETER'S CHAPEL
OSEA ISLAND
BRADWELL-ON-SEA
HEYBRIDGE
RIVER BLACKWATER
RIVER CHELMER
CANAL
STANSGATE ABBEY
MALDON
NORTHEY ISLAND
SOUTHMINSTER
FOULNESS POINT
BURNHAM
NORTH FAMBRIDGE
RIVER CROUCH
HULLBRIDGE
RIVER ROACH

N

0   5   10   15 MILES
SCALE

As a Londoner the East Coast has always been on my doorstep and was the first one I came to know. Long before I became interested in boats but was old enough to have a motor car, the villages and creeks of Essex and Suffolk were the preferred weekend destinations to the South Coast seaside towns with very little countryside between them. By car or by boat it is ideal weekend country because you can take in one estuary and river at a time. Most of my boating on the East Coast has been like that – going out of Burnham to follow the racing, or a Barge Match out of the Blackwater, a weekend on an old gaffer in the Walton Backwaters or on a barge from Ipswich to Woodbridge. The only extended cruise down the coast which I have done was in 1976 from Woodbridge to London on board *Light Barque*, a 30ft Nelson pilotboat-type motor cruiser which had a maximum speed of 17 knots. My hosts were Steve Williamson and his wife Tiny who were then both nudging seventy. Steve had spent the previous few years charting the East Coast rivers for Imray, Laurie, Norie & Wilson which made him a very informative guide. This chapter follows the route of that trip with additions about places I have been to at other times on board different boats. For all its potential speed *Light Barque* was not able to visit more than a fraction of the rivers and creeks in the week available, and they are what make this coast so worthwhile; because the land is so low-lying a coastal passage can be visually monotonous.

There are ten rivers with 300 miles of navigable waters flowing into the North Sea between the Alde in Suffolk and the Swale in Kent – a distance of only 45 miles as the crow flies. These rivers provide a unique cruising area which requires the skills of both the river pilot and the coastal navigator. Sand flats and gravel banks protruding into the North Sea like fingers make an inshore passage between some estuaries difficult, if not impossible, without good local knowledge. To explore the best of these rivers a shallow-draught boat which can take the ground is most practical, and for power craft a stern drive is best because, as most of the harbours and estuaries dry, the visitor is bound at some point or other to have to take the ground and without intimate local knowledge he may well run out of water up some of the rivers. A shallow-draught inland-water-type cruiser is no use; it must be a boat which will take the short steep seas which are more often than not encountered round the coast. Buoys and lights are prolific, so a sharp eye is as useful as a compass. Detailed charts are available for the rivers, and even the most tortuous channels are, during the season, well marked with leading lights, beacons and withies. But there are many reaches which dry out to a 6-inch trickle at low-water springs, and there are shingle bars at the entrance to most of the rivers. So it is necessary to keep an eye on the wind direction and to study the tidal streams and tidal constants for all the places to be visited. All the information that anyone could ask for on pilotage is contained in the *Yachting Monthly Pilot for East Coast Rivers.* With that publication on board, together with the relevant charts, you should be able to explore this area without having to sit out a tide on the ground too often.

Much of East Anglia remains unchanged from Constable's day: the approach to the Maltings at Snape, River Alde

Why go cruising along a coast which involves more ditch crawling than passage making, and where waiting for the tide will occupy a lot of your time? Because it is, with the exception of the more rugged and almost uninhabited parts of Scotland and North Wales, the least changed part of Britain. Much of it is Constable country, and there are still parts where the landscape looks very much as it did when he painted it. It was hardly touched by the Industrial Revolution so there are no big industrial centres once away from the Thames, and the countryside is almost entirely agricultural. There are dozens of beautiful villages and more medieval and Tudor houses, farms and churches than in any other comparable area of Britain. Because of the coastal topography most waterside villages are remote from main road or railway, and are served for the most part by dead-end lanes. This has saved them from being totally taken over by commuters. They are still communities with their cultural roots going back centuries. Apart from the obvious seaside resorts, like Clacton and Felixstowe, the shorelines have not been obliterated by holiday developments, and most of the time you sail past fields or woods fronted by beaches, reed beds or mud flats. For a coast so near London and containing three large commercial ports, it remains remarkably natural and unspoilt. There are a few marinas which are useful, but they have no ugly onshore complexes and blend into the landscape. I would hazard a guess that a majority of local boats on the Essex and Suffolk coasts still live on swinging moorings, in mud berths lining the fairways, or in snug little holes in the saltings. The tides rule every activity, and once in from the sea and into the rivers there is for part of every day more mud to be seen than water. The pace is, perforce, more philosophical than it is in the more fashionable yachting centres. The East Coast yachtsman tends to be a traditionalist; old gaffers, tan sails, clinker hulls, bowsprits and spritsails are as numerous as modern boats. One often glimpses a scene where time seems to have stood still for half a century.

It is the sailing barges with their high, peaked sprits, great expanse of tan sail and bluff bowed, straight high-sided hulls which make these waters so unique. On the days of Barge Matches they take over again for a while their lordship of the swatchways. Those who have grown up in the postwar years may wonder how these craft have managed to survive and are still sailing. Part of the answer is that they are not as ancient as they appear, although as a type they go back nearly 200 years. Most of the barges seen sailing today were built around the turn of the century and on into the mid-1920s. In 1900 there were 2,000 of these utilitarian but beautiful sailing ships in trade, and one of their jobs was carrying the horse droppings from London's streets to the farms of Kent, Essex, Suffolk and Norfolk, and supplying the stables of London with straw and hay from those same farms. A handful continued trading up until the end of the 1960s. Today there are about fifty of them to be seen under sail, most of them doing charter work to defray the enormous costs of maintaining them. And wherever a barge is seen it is more often than not attended by one or more old gaffers, former East

The hard at Pin Mill, River Orwell

(*Left*) The Tide Mill at Woodbridge has been beautifully restored; (*right*) The Shire Hall, Woodbridge

Coast smacks and bawleys, lovingly preserved and sailed by private owners. Old yachts and converted fishing boats which might be scorned in the smart marinas of the Hamble or Cowes are appreciated and accepted on the East Coast; also nowhere else round the British coast are you so likely to see a puff of steam or a trail of smoke on the horizon. Nearly every harbour, and Maldon most particularly, has its steam buffs and often when barges and old gaffers race steam tugs, box-shaped puffers and launches go out as committee and spectator boats. A cruise round here is still in part a voyage of discovery into the past, and a chance in the remoter creeks and backwaters to commune with nature. But progress is on the rampage and developers on the march; it is a cruise which should be made before it is too late.

Woodbridge at the head of navigation on the Deben is not the easiest place to get to by water. A frequently shifting bar at the entrance to the river requires careful pilotage and attention to the *Sailing Directions*. It is impossible to enter against the ebb unless you can motor at more than 5 knots. The last 2 or 3 miles before the town, especially the aptly named Troublesome Reach, virtually dries out between half ebb and half flood. Unless arriving and leaving on a tide, you must expect to take the ground for a while. The town, with its restored tidal mill surrounded by a forest of masts, rising from the waterfront looks very inviting when approached by water. My first approach was alongside the water on the local one-carriage train from Ipswich which stops right by the Ferry Dock. You hand in your ticket, cross a bridge over the line, and are immediately by the water's edge looking at a motley collection of boats sitting on the mud and reached by rickety staging. It is one of those little corners which are delightful to look round, largely occupied by old boats and half-finished conversions whose owners often have more optimism than money. The modern yachts and motor cruisers lie in a horseshoe-shaped marina made out of the mill pond. It has a sill which allows a boat drawing 3ft to enter and leave from 3 hours before to 2 hours after high-water neaps. On springs there is a good 6ft over the sill. The Tide Mill itself has been beautifully restored with white-painted weatherboarding and is open to the public. There has been a mill on the same site since 1170, and the present one was working until 1957 when its main shaft broke. For 10 years it stood derelict and rotting until a private trust fund was set up and restoration began. The machinery was put into working order – but not by water any longer – and a new water wheel installed. The wheel was turned by the ebb tide, and when that fell below the wheel the miller released water which had been trapped in the pond at high water. His working hours were therefore dictated by the tides so he had to work as often at night as by day. Four pairs of stones ground corn, maize and beans for cattle food. The mill is part of Whisstock's Boat Yard and in 1976 Claud Whisstock, then seventy years old, was still building wooden yachts, most of them for American customers. As a boy he earned his first pocket money helping the miller.

Beside the railway station is the Woodbridge Electric Theatre built in 1915 which, when I was last there in 1981, was still showing films but there was talk of it closing. Quay Street leads up into the town and at its lower end is The Captain's Table, a restaurant with a nautical flavour, a reputation for sea food and a patio for al-fresco eating in summer. In February 1982 natural history was made at The Captain's Table when a female lobster in their aquarium waiting for a customer to buy her for his dinner gave birth to several hundred offspring, smaller than tadpoles and translucent. The World Wildlife Fund said that it was an event so rare as to be unheard of. In the Middle Ages a fair was held on Market Hill in the square in the centre of town on St Audrey's Day, 23 October, and it was souvenirs of the saint which were sold which gave the word 'tawdry' to the English language. There is now an open-air market held on Thursdays. The Shire Hall in the centre of the square was built in 1575 in the Flemish style as the Sessions House. It is a three-storey building with a Dutch gable and a double stone stairway to the front door on the first floor. The ground floor was used as a corn market until the late 1930s and has a lock-up on the south side. The building is still in use as a magistrate's and juvenile court. In front of the Shire Hall is a delightful Gothic-style pump worked by a large hand-wheel and a drinking trough. On the west side of the square is a terrace of cottages with higgledy-piggledy gables, crooked tiled roofs and eighteenth-century shop fronts. Among them is a restaurant, La Provencale, which would not look out of place in a side street in St Tropez. The food must be good because even after several attempts over the years I have never been able to book a table. My favourite pub and bed-and-breakfast place is The Mariner's Arms at the lower end of New Street.

(*Above*) Well-restored houses with Georgian shop fronts at Woodbridge; (*right*) the Bell and Steel Yard, Woodbridge. The steel yard, projecting from the building, weighed wagons on their way to and from market

Unpretentious from the outside, the bar is low-ceilinged and cosy with a large photo mural of Woodbridge in the days of sail. Your hosts are Carol Wood, a fun lady from the USA, and her talkative parrot. She serves good meals in a small restaurant behind the bar, and if you stay the night you can have breakfast in the garden. In a typically American manner Carol is quick to introduce you to all and sundry in the bar, so going to The Mariner's can be like going to a party.

At the top of New Street is the Bell and Steel Yard, a two-storey Tudor building with eighteenth-century casements, which sells very good beer in an oak-beamed bar. The steel yard which still projects from the front of the building was used for weighing wagons on their way to the market. Chains were passed under the wagon, and the yard was hauled up by tackles until the chain slings became taut. A 108lb lead weight was pushed along the yard until leverage lifted the wagon wheels off the ground. On its return from market the wagon was again weighed and thus, by simple arithmetic, its original load and therefore market dues payable were calculated. This simple contrivance was capable of lifting 2½ tons, and was last used in 1880. For a 'posh' evening ashore there is Seckford Hall, a well-preserved Elizabethan mansion just over a mile out of the town on the other side of the A12. It is listed in the guide books as a splendid hotel with beautiful grounds and lake. Theatre Street, leading out of the top of Market Hill, is named after the theatre which opened in 1814 and closed in 1860 to become a school. Further along this street is one of Suffolk's few remaining windmills. Buttrum's tower mill was built in 1816, was in operation until 1928, and in 1954 it was restored by the East Suffolk County Council and the Pilgrim Trust. Although privately owned, anyone seriously interested can usually get

permission to look round from the owner of Mill House. It will probably surprise most people that as late as 1933 Suffolk still had 64 mills working, 29 of them by water and 35 by wind. One of the reasons that these mills went out of business was that they could not produce white flour. Now, too late, there is a growing demand for bread made with stone-ground flour.

There are some good walks to be made from Woodbridge and perhaps the most popular is to Sutton Hoo, up the west side of the river to Wilford Bridge and down the other side. But most people are not impressed when they get there. All that is left of one of the most exciting archaeological finds in Britain are a few humps and a notice board. In 1937 the impression of an 80ft Anglo-Saxon burial ship was excavated there; the timbers had disintegrated, but the personal possessions, armour and regalia of a pagan king were largely intact. Gold coins found dated the burial as AD 625. Although all you can see is where the excavations have been filled in, the treasure itself is in the British Museum. The area does, however, provide excellent views of Woodbridge and the tide mill. For a walk into the recent past go south from Woodbridge a mile to Martlesham Creek. You can get there by boat but with difficulty because it dries to a mud bath, so it is better to go on foot. On the south side of the creek below the church is a little quay reached through a wood where boats lie in the mud, or against spindly staging when the tide is in. It is a scene which was common until the end of the 1950s when the yachting boom started and the proliferation of plastic boats made yacht harbours and marinas both necessary and viable. On a Sunday morning several members of the congregation can be seen after morning service making their way through the wood to work on their boats. Their attendance at church is a politic thing to do since the access to the water is owned by the parson. The local pub is the Red Lion with a sign made from a ship's figurehead salvaged from a wreck in 1672. Waldringfield, 3 miles down river from Woodbridge on the west bank, is known for the Maybush Inn with its rose garden by the river where you can sit with your beer and watch the Waldringfield Sailing Club dinghies racing to and fro like butterflies. There are two rows of moorings off the beach with a gap left for visiting boats to drop their hooks. There is easy landing on the firm beach for tenders. The Maybush has a reputation for keeping good Tolly ales and pub food. The window in the Gents is said to give the finest loo view in Suffolk. One of the regulars is Giles, the cartoonist, who keeps his boat at Waldringfield. Up the road the village store has a stock of good wines.

The last stop on the Deben is further down on the east shore at Ramsholt, an old ferry point with a barge quay which is still useful for lying against for scrubbing. The Ramsholt Arms was once the ferry house with one room used as a bar, an oil-lit snug run by Mrs Nunn, who sent customers down to the cellar to draw their own pints from the barrel. It was then a much beloved rendezvous of East Coast yachtsmen, and there would often be a crowd of half a dozen yachts calling in of a summer evening. She died in 1957 and it has since been enlarged

You can sit in the Maybush Inn at Waldringfield and watch the dinghies racing by like butterflies

into a proper pub. There are now over 200 swinging moorings, so visitors usually have to anchor mid-channel. Old timers talk about Ramsholt with an enormous nostalgia which has rubbed off on subsequent generations of yachtsmen, so the place is often overcrowded. There are two bars in the Ramsholt Arms; in one you can pick up local knowledge from sailors, in the other you can learn about the art of the poacher from the local gamekeepers and estate workers who line the bar drinking with their cloth caps on. But do not be deceived; they have a philosophy and knowledge of the land not too often met with these days. The pub is the only building, and the foreshore is hard. Like many similar places around the coast it was once in the smuggling business – casks of wine and brandy in Napoleon's day, wool, silk and tobacco for many generations before then. On moonless nights horsedrawn wagons, their wheels muffled with sacks, would use the steep cart track down to the beach to load up with contraband. The track is now a road lined with cars during summer-weekend opening hours. Ramsholt Church which stands on a hill with no village to serve (the last cottages round the church disappeared in 1964) has a tower, almost certainly built as a look-out, which appears to be oval, an optical illusion created by the buttresses which run to its top. It has interesting nineteenth-century box pews and a carved screen at one end to provide a 'windbreak' for the congregation. Felixstowe Ferry, at the entrance to the Deben opposite Bawdsey Manor on the east shore, is a collection of holiday bungalows and a pub fronted by a steep shingle beach. It is not a good place to anchor because of the strong tide, especially the ebb, flowing through the narrow entrance, and there is little of interest to go ashore for unless you want to take a bus into Felixstowe. South of the Ferry are two good specimens of Martello Towers, but they are common in these parts.

The Ore and the Alde, a single river with two names, 7 miles up the coast from the Deben is equally if not more difficult to enter. The Ore, which is the first part of the river, runs for 10 miles behind a shingle spit which is a bare 50 yards wide in places and no more than 400 for most of its length. This, of course, means that there is a shingle bar and banks at the entrance which shift around as the tide continually washes away the end of the bank and then builds it up again. The *East Coast Pilot* should be read carefully before attempting this entry. There is no other river in the British Isles quite like it; the nearest to this phenomenon would be the Chesil Bank in Dorset, but the water behind that shingle spit is a lagoon, not a river. It has the smallest rise and fall of any river on the east and south-east coasts, the range being from 6½ft at neaps to 7½ft at springs. At the same time it is the fastest-flowing river with a 7-knot current at the entrance on the ebb. It changes its name above Orford to Alde, and at Slaughden Quay it comes within a few yards of breaking through its retaining spit before turning west to wind its way at low water through thousands of acres of mud to Snape Bridge which is the limit of navigation. It must at some time in the past have emptied into the sea at Slaughden where one can kick a stone into the river on one side and into the sea on the other at high tide while standing only about 3ft above the water. What fun it would be to borrow a bulldozer for an hour or two and dig a channel to let the Alde flow straight into the sea again. No doubt it would only take a couple of tides to repair the damage. Two miles above the entrance the river divides round Havergate Island, which is a nature reserve under the management of the Royal Society for the Protection of Birds. Landing is therefore restricted to those who have obtained special permission from the society at The Lodge, Sandy, Bedfordshire. Such permission to visit the island on your own will depend on your bona fides as a naturalist or membership of the society. Lesser enthusiasts can join an organised party in charge of the Warden, Mr Partridge, leaving by motor boat from Orford Quay. For details of times and bookings ring Orford 222. Another way to study the bird life is to anchor your boat in the river and haul yourself a little way up the mast in your bosun's chair, or stand on the wheelhouse roof, if you have that kind of boat, and use your binoculars. You may very likely see a pair of avocets swooping around, up to six types of tern, sandpipers, godwits and curlews.

Orford Quay just north of the island is *the* stopping place on this river. Anchor below or above the Quay and land on the shingle beach. The slipway is likely to be in continual use at weekends by people launching and recovering dinghies and runabouts, and it is also used by the landing craft which runs to and from the Atomic Weapons Research Station on the other side of the river where landing is

The Jolly Sailor in Quay Street, Orford, was once on the waterside

THE
JOLLY SAILOR

ADNAMS ALES

· Patrick John Buckner ·

Licensed to Sell Beer, Wines, Spirits & Tobacco

ADNAMS

·ENTRANCE to BARS·

·STEPS DOWN·

very strictly forbidden. First there is the old quayside pub, The Jolly Sailor, which is no longer alongside the water but 500 yards up Quay Street which ships once sailed up. Records show that in 1530 the entrance to the river was opposite Orford Castle, since when the spit has grown and its tip at the present entrance is now 4½ miles south-west of the castle. The Jolly Sailor looks quite undistinguished from the outside – a flat-fronted two-storey red-brick building with white-painted sash windows and a modern pantile roof (the old roof was blown off in a local 'hurricane' in 1963), but it has an interior which fascinates. The tap room, called the kitchen, is furnished with high-back settles, an iron stove, a rough-hewn table and shove ha'penny board. The structure behind the more recent brick is of old ships' timbers and the fireplaces are Tudor. In an upstairs room a mural of a ship was found when fourteen layers of wallpaper were stripped off. It has had a long run in the *Good Beer Guide*, bed and breakfast can be had, and the usual pub snacks. Quay Street leads up the hill to the village proper past a large car park of about two acres. Its size is a sure warning that Orford is to be avoided on high days and holidays. Further up the street is flanked by a long green backed by a row of pretty cottages and houses too beautifully pointed and painted to be owned by their original families. The centre of the village is the Market Square, no longer serving its original function and desecrated by a chequerboard of white lines indicating parking spaces, but the buildings surrounding it are delightful. The King's Head has its roots, or foundations, in the twelfth century and the cellar entrance is in the churchyard. Opposite is the Butley and Orford Oysterage which provides one of the best reasons for stopping at Orford – oysters and smoked salmon, cod's roe and mackerel cured over charcoal from oak chips. The patron, Mr Pinney, who does his own smoking, also breeds the oysters and keeps quite a good cellar including local English wines which I found delightfully light and refreshing when my wife treated me to a July birthday lunch there a few years back. St Bartholomew's Church dating back to the twelfth century is extraordinarily large for a small village and is full of interesting things – eleven brasses, old bells, an ornately carved font c1400 and the village stocks which were last used in 1864. The massive 90ft-high tower with its medieval staircase provides excellent views of the village, the river and across to Orford Ness. The view that most people go for is that from the top of Orford Castle which, being further inland, is not quite so good. The castle was built for Henry II and was started in 1165, garrisoned in 1171 and completed in 1173. It was of advanced military design for the time, the only one in East Anglia, and the earliest castle for which records still exist of its building and cost, £1,407 9s. 2d. For the first hundred years of its existence it changed hands many times, being alternately in the possession of the king and rebellious barons. For a short period after the death of King John it was held by King Louis of France. Today only the keep stands, but foundations of the outer buildings and curtain walls can be traced by the earth mounds which surround it. The interior has two floors and a basement or dungeon, in the centre of which is

The Moot Hall, Aldeburgh, featured in Benjamin Britten's opera, *Peter Grimes*

a well. A staircase leads to the 100ft-high battlements.

Upstream from Orford the river runs deep, around 20ft, with a wide channel for the 5 miles to Slaughden Quay where the best anchorage will be found between the Martello Tower and the Aldeburgh Yacht Club. Clean landing can be made on the shingle or at the quay at all states ·of the tide. Apart from requiring help from the yard or something from the chandlers there is little of interest here, but if you have a taste for fresh fish you can buy it off the beach at Aldeburgh, a mile's walk away. In Elizabethan times Aldeburgh was a large port with a river mouth. A fine moot hall was built at the back of the town, a jewel of Tudor craftsmanship in timber, flint and red brick and, although it has not been moved, it now stands beside the shingle beach, a stone's throw from the sea which, in onshore gales, throws stones against its walls. What happened at Dunwich has happened here and the houses, streets and quays of the Tudor town have long since disappeared beneath the waves. The beach above the high-water line is lined with tarred fishermen's huts from which winch cables flake down to the water to haul up their beach boats. The boats come in about nine or ten in the

At Aldeburgh the fishing boats are hauled up the shingle beach and the catch is put on sale

morning and, according to the season, land lobster, plaice, sole, longshore herring and sprats, which are then sold from the huts. The town has become famous for its Festival of Music and the Arts, founded in 1948 by Benjamin Britten, a Lowestoft man, which has made a smart Victorian seaside resort even smarter. The main street is wide and a mile long with several hotels, and the shops include a health-food store, a tea shop serving home-made cakes and scones, and an off-licence where you can buy Nut Brown Ale, known locally as Southwold Jack, and English wine from the nearby Kelsale vineyard.

What is worth doing is to go on from Slaughden Quay up the Alde to the Maltings at Snape Bridge, but it needs very careful attention to the withies and you have to get the tides absolutely right. It is a difficult trip when the early flood coincides with the sun in the west as the withies can then be difficult to see. There are 40 of them, closely but irregularly spaced along the 6-mile channel which in places is only about 16ft wide at low water. If a mark is missed the boat will almost certainly run deep into soft mud. At Snape there is a quay alongside the Maltings which can be reached by boats drawing up to 6½ft. If the tides serve it would be quite feasible to go up there on the flood one day, go to a concert that evening, enjoy dinner ashore, and go back the next day. Concert lovers should arm themselves with the Snape Maltings Summer and Autumn Concert Calendar annotated with the times of high water. Another way of getting to Snape Bridge from Aldeburgh is along the lonely, somewhat haunting, Sailors' Walk, a footpath across a mixture of marsh and arable land with the serpentine river and saltings always on one hand. It is an 8-mile walk and will take over 3 hours. The way back by road from Snape village is faster and easier going, and only 5 miles.

Even if there is no concert to go to the Maltings, with their ivy-clad walls, roofs like dry-ski slopes topped with beehive structures, and fronted by lawns on the edge of the saltings, are a surprising sight. They were working up until 1965 converting barley into malt for export to London and the Continent. In the last century and for most of the first half of this century, barley was delivered and malt taken away by sailing barges, more recently motor barges, the only commercial craft which could float fully laden in the shallow tortuous channel. Barges still come but now they carry charter crews and holidaymakers. The buildings were converted by the Swedish firm of Ore Aarup, and although their architectural form is of nineteenth-century Suffolk origin, when seen from the water they have an uncanny resemblance to modern Swedish architecture and, under a covering of snow, would present a true Scandinavian aspect. At almost all times of the day and evening between April and October the sounds of music can be heard coming from one building or another. Master classes for singers and string players, practices and rehearsals, performances in the Recital Room and the great Concert Hall itself ensure that the Maltings are rarely silent. At the same time there is a full calendar of other cultural and folksy events from an Antiques Fair to demonstrations of traditional English smocking, and weekend courses on landscape painting and caring for antiques. The tyro naturalist who wants to add another dimension to cruising the East Coast might consider a weekend course on 'Birds of the Suffolk Coast' or 'Suffolk Rambles'. The Aldeburgh Festival, the highlight of the season and on a par with Glyndebourne, takes place in June.

From the original concert-hall concept the complex has been developed around its periphery into another 'place to visit' with craft shop, picture gallery, countrywear shop and the mandatory granary tea shop with salad buffet which has a mention in Egon Ronay's *Just a Bite*. On my last visit a Dutch botter was waiting for the tide to take trippers on an evening cruise down river to Aldeburgh. After looking at the prices in the wine bar I retreated to The Plough and Sail nearby which sells real ale and smoked-fish lunches. They have bar billiards in an otherwise empty room if you want to get out of the weekend crush in the bar, and around the billiard table are some most interesting photographs of old barges loading and discharging at the quay. The captions are informative: in 1895 the cost of shipping malt from Snape to Harwich was 5s. 10d. a quarter, and from Harwich to Rotterdam 5s. Among the sailing barges were two 100-ton steam barges, *Catherine* and *Gladys*. *Gladys* is seen moored by the engineers' workshop which is now the Craft Shop. Other photographs are of the local fire brigade. In 1922 the Snape Maltings bought a hand-pumping appliance for £55 which was pulled and worked by eight men. In 1939 a 100hp Dennis fire engine was bought secondhand from the London Fire Brigade for £154, the pumpers were paid off and a new, presumably more mechanically minded, crew of ten men was taken on. They look splendid posing on the fire engine in their brass helmets.

A little north of Snape Bridge is the oldest dated windmill in Suffolk, 1668, converted into a home where Benjamin Britten lived and wrote his opera *Peter Grimes*.

Sailing back down the Alde (it may have to be motoring because there is little room to tack) or on your way up, look out for the little beach at Iken, a popular anchorage among those who venture that far up river, and above it St Botolph's Church with its black-flint fifteenth-century tower. There is no access by road to this place where St Botolph established a monastery in the seventh century. It can only be reached on foot steering a course past 'No Trespassing' notices. Even a funeral cortège has been halted by the local landowner. At least that is how things stood when I was there.

Before making further progress north to Southwold, one has to go 10 miles south from Aldeburgh and then 10 miles north outside the spit. Although Southwold's lighthouse is in the middle of the town above the roofs of houses, which photographers find very photogenic, the harbour is about a mile south, being the entrance of the River Blyth extended out to sea by two piers 40 yards apart. The ebb flushes out at about six knots so it is really only feasible to enter on the flood, and if there is a bit of a swell running it is rather like threading the eye of a needle. It is quite instructive to stand at the inshore end of the north pier and watch flat-transomed, planing-hull motor cruisers slewing about as they come in. When they reach the calm of the river itself you can almost hear the 'phews'. The banks are lined with stagings used by a variety of local boats and fishing craft. A visitors' pontoon is conveniently moored by the Harbour Inn.

The village of Walberswick which comes down to the south bank was once some way inland on a bend in the river where it turned south to enter the sea at Dunwich, a big town in the Middle Ages, now under the sea. The railway bridge about a mile up the river ends the navigation, but it would be possible to take a tender on the flood beyond that across the tidal marshes three miles to Blythburgh with its Dutch-gabled White Horse Inn. It has a huge church for its size with some most amusing carvings on its benches depicting the Deadly Sins. Blythburgh is now a small village, but it was a busy port until ships got larger and their draughts deeper and the river started silting up.

Many people would say that Southwold's claim to fame is that it is the place where Adnam's beer is brewed, and the locals and those who sail round the East Coast have always said it is the best beer in England and I think they may be right. The town is set on a hill with cliffs along the sea front, but it is geographically an island surrounded by the River Blyth on the south and Buss Creek to the west and north. The creek no longer quite breaks through to the sea, but that is a man-made modification. Much of the town is Georgian with Victorian seaside resort additions and lots of greens, making it a pleasant little place. It has an air of gentility with plenty of shops, a local museum with an emphasis on things nautical, and the Sailor's Reading Room. In the latter there is a model of the *Bittern*, a 49ft beach yawl built in 1890 for one of the sea-salvage

(*Left*) Adnam's brewery is hard by the lighthouse in Southwold; (*right*) the Cat House at Woolverstone; although the cat is fake now, it is mentioned in Pevsner's guide to the buildings of Suffolk

beach companies that operated at a profit along this coast before the establishment of the RNLI. The beach yawls were sailed or rowed by large crews using sacks full of pebbles as moveable ballast. Speed was the essence of the business; first to arrive got the salvage money. The *Bittern* had the temerity to challenge the *America* of America's Cup fame to a race, but the American captain avoided the contest by demanding a prohibitive sum as prize money. Local people say that in heavy weather the *Bittern* might well have won.

After leaving the Ore on *Light Barque* we gave Southwold a miss and instead took a long sweep out to sea round the Cork Light to get some wind on our faces after so much ditch crawling, and then entered the busy shipping lane into the entrance to the Orwell between Harwich and Felixstowe. Our destination was Pin Mill, halfway up the river towards Ipswich, to be in position to watch the start of the Barge Match the next day. This anchorage is the setting of *Ordinary Families* by E. Arnot Robertson which has been fairly described as 'the classic sailing novel'. The trouble with Pin Mill is that one may not always be able to pick up a mooring and, if not, will have to anchor below the moorings. Either way it will mean a fairly long haul in the tender to the hard which, when the tide is out, is about a quarter-of-a-mile long and very muddy. If the tide is flooding the tender will have to be pulled along the gully beside the hard so that it is waiting for you on dry land when you come out of the Butt and Oyster later on. Rejoining your boat at the bottom of the tide at night can be a bit chaotic. There will be several other crews trying to find and get into their tenders in the dark from the very slippery end of the hard and somebody usually ends up in the mud. At low water a tender has to be 'paddled' over a long stretch of mud before there is enough depth to put an outboard down or to row. It is all good fun for the young and fit, but my hosts opted for the facilities of Woolverstone Marina opposite Cathouse Point a mile up river, and the hospitality of the Royal Harwich Yacht Club next door – they keep open house for visiting yachtsmen and offer showers, meals and a bar. The marina and club are in a lovely setting with boat sheds, a chandlery and dry-standing for boats all concealed in woods where, during the war, tanks were hidden before being loaded onto landing craft for D-Day from a hard which is now part of the marina. By the water's edge is a Georgian Gothic cottage called Cat House with a painting of a cat occupying one of its window panes. It is reputed to have been used as a signal station for smugglers; when the coast was clear a cat was put in the window.

From the yacht club at Woolverstone there is a most beautiful walk of a mile along the river bank under a canopy of gnarled oaks to Pin Mill and the sixteenth-century Butt and Oyster Inn where, from a window seat, you can look out over the sailing barges sitting on their flat bottoms like stranded sea monsters waiting for the tide, their tan sails braided up on their sprits reflecting a rusty glow onto the wet mud. At high tide a dinghy can be rowed to the window where in less busy times many a pint was served. The bar is quite unspoilt; rough wooden floors, barrels with taps and dark woodwork everywhere against which the colours of sailing gear positively glow. It is one of the best-known yacht pubs in the country where the talk is all of passages made or being planned, of sagas big and small. Mingling with the yacht crews are the men and women off the barges – a patient, optimistic breed who, in the Herculean task of maintaining their wooden leviathans, are dedicated to work which will never end. They can usually be recognised by their unfashionable well-worn overalls and holey sweaters, roughened hands and beards. Not that the yachting types at Pin Mill are all that smart; they do not have the chance anyway in a place where they have to come to terms with the mud, and row to and from their boats whatever the tide and wind are doing. The majority of crews coming into the Orwell go to one of the three marinas where they can get ashore dry-footed and so, providing no developer ever gets his hands on the place, Pin Mill will remain a picturesque backwater with an old-world atmosphere. An almost total lack of car-parking space means that the lane down to the water is lined with cars at weekends and unwitting visitors can spend a lot of time and energy extracting themselves from this narrow cul-de-sac. There is just one modern development down by the hard of which I strongly

Pin Mill as seen on the walk through oak trees from Woolverstone. The famous Butt and Oyster pub is the pink-roofed building, centre

approve – a super set of public loos. There are still plenty of people who prefer their boating 'au natur' and the waiting list for permanent moorings is so long that you need to put your name down at birth. For a temporary mooring speak to Jack Ward at the chandlers shop; with luck he may have a spare one within a half mile of the hard.

The night before the Match the Pin Mill Sailing Club was full of old barge skippers and hands come out of retirement for the morrow, and their young amateur crews buying them pints and hanging on their every word. The next morning eighteen barges lined up for the start and drifted raggedly over the line in airs too light to fill their sails. After a while a little breeze sprang up and across the water came the sound of clanking leeboard chains and creaking ropes, and the bang of sheet blocks the size of a man's head hitting decks as they tacked down towards the sea. The oldest barge sailing that day had been built in 1881, the youngest in 1923. At the entrance to Harwich they were overhauled by the fleet of ocean racers setting out on the RORC Harwich–Hook of Holland race. Each fleet had its attendant pack of spectator boats, a coaster making its way up river to Ipswich threaded its way through the crowd of sail, car ferries to and from

Scandinavia came and went like floating grandstands, and a container ship nudging its way into Felixstowe towered over us, its superstructure the height of a city block. This visual feast of craft ancient and modern, commercial and leisure, can be enjoyed quite often during the season. It brings home the fact that the Orwell, especially at its mouth, is a very commercial river and those who sail for pleasure must be mindful of the fact and behave accordingly. The traffic up to Ipswich does provide one bonus – a well-dredged channel for the whole 9 miles although it becomes rather narrow above Pin Mill and there is never any chance of power giving way to sail. So it is best to make up the last half of the river when the tide has well covered the mud flats either side of the channel.

The Suffolk Yacht Harbour 2 miles up river on the north side is a useful stopping place if only using the river for shelter or waiting to make a North Sea passage, but being a large hole in the mud against a steep shore it is not very attractive. There is a club with a bar on an old lightship, but it is a long walk to the nearest village. If going all the way to Ipswich it is possible to lock in to the wet dock there and lie alongside the quay near the old Custom House. It puts you in the middle of the town and probably in the company of at least one sailing barge, but it is not worth the trouble unless you are staying over a few days. It is more convenient then to put in to the little marina at Fox of Ipswich boatyard opposite the power station and beside the A137 road bridge over the Belstead Brook. They can supply every service that you might need and across the road is the Ostrich, a good pub, parts of which date back to about 1600. You usually have to book a table for dinner, which is a measure of the quality of the food. A half-hourly bus service runs from outside the marina the 1¾ miles into the centre of Ipswich. For a week during June the marina becomes the 'Boat Afloat' section of the East Coast Boat Show so you would only get a mooring in the river instead of a berth alongside a pontoon.

Ipswich was the home town of Cardinal Wolsey, but there is little left to remember him by other than the red-brick gateway of the great college which he intended founding. Even the site of his grave is unknown, and the magnificent tomb he had built for himself is now in St Paul's Cathedral and contains the mortal remains of Lord Nelson. For instant sightseeing make for the junction of the Buttermarket, Dial Lane and St Stephen's Lane where there is a group of timber-framed buildings, the most famous and extraordinary of which is the Ancient House, or Sparrowe's House as it was originally called. Built over 500 years ago as a hall, it was later divided into living accommodation by the Sparrowe family about 1670. They adorned the façade with pargetted plaster work which remains as one of the prime examples of this form of decoration in the country. Massive oak pillars, black with age, are carved with a riot of fruit and flowers. Elaborately carved bay windows divide the plaster work illustrating the four continents (Australia had yet to be discovered) and the figure of Atlas supporting the globe. The centre device is the coat of arms of Charles II. Inside there is a wealth of carved oak, panelling, decorated ceilings and a hammer-beam

The Ancient House at Ipswich, built as a hall over 500 years ago and now divided into shops (including one of the best bookshops in East Anglia), is one of the country's finest examples of pargetted plasterwork

room. Now that it is a bookshop browsing around is no problem. An architectural wonder of a different kind is the great dark glass-clad Willis Faber and Dumas building which acts as a giant mirror for the surrounding buildings, especially the parish church of St Nicholas. When it was completed in 1975 it was the largest open-plan office in the world with 1,300 people working on 5 floors. The reporter Charles Dickens visited Ipswich to cover an election and as a result of his visit wrote *The Pickwick Papers*; it was in a bedroom in the Great White Horse Hotel that Mr Pickwick had his embarrassing encounter with the lady in yellow curling papers. The present lounge with its glass roof was the original courtyard of Dickens's time. Some of the bedrooms still have four-poster beds. Christchurch Mansion and its park a few minutes' walk from the centre of the town are certainly worth a visit. The 65-acre park full of trees and up-and-down paths is a peaceful haven after the bustle of the town. In the house, built in 1548, you walk through history from elegant room to elegant room, each one period furnished from Tudor to Victorian, and see how life was lived in a large English country house over the centuries. After the elegance comes the functional reality of the servants' wing with its huge kitchen fully equipped with roasting spits, copper pans and a large collection of cooking utensils. Down by the docks around the Custom House the scene has changed very little from photographs taken at

the turn of the century, apart from parked cars and lorries. The lock gates and the
dock as we see them today were opened on 7 July 1881, the same day as the
library and the Post Office. In Fore Street which runs parallel with the quay is the
Nelson public house which I recommend for local colour. It is used by crews and
charter parties off sailing barges when they are in port, a few old men who sailed
them when they were trading and seafaring men off the commercial ships in the
port. You are safe from tourists and coach parties in the Nelson.

Returning to Harwich Harbour we turned west for the 11-mile trip up the
River Stour to look at the old Malt Houses at Mistley. Then we went ashore and
took a taxi to East Bergholt where Constable was born in 1776 and of which he
wrote: 'I even love every stile and stump, and every lane in the village'. Then we
drove by a circuitous route of one-way lanes in a queue of coaches to Willy Lot's
Cottage and Flatford Mill by an arm of the non-tidal Stour. They are both very
much tidied up but basically unaltered since Constable's day. Like all such places
it needs much concentration to ignore the large car park, the souvenir-cum-tea
shop and the crowds of sightseers in summer in order to visualise the scene as
painted. Since then I have discovered a better way of going to Flatford Mill – by
boat. Anchor in the channel opposite Mistley (beware of a 4-knot tide running on
the ebb) or take the ground against the quay, then go by tender across the river to
the north sluice above Cattawade bridge. There are rollers to help you port the
tender up to the fresh water on the other side. From there the river, now more a
stream through water meadows, can be navigated to Flatford Mill. It is a
winding course of a little over a mile which you will almost certainly have to

The head of the Stour estuary. The north sluice gate, where you can drag your tender into the
river that flows gently down from Flatford Mill, is beyond the bridge, far left

yourself. The River Stour was made navigable by Act of Parliament in 1705 and is passable by small boats, porting round derelict locks, at least from Sudbury to the sea. The River Stour Trust has renovated Flatford Lock and made several improvements to enable the public to enjoy the right of navigation. Some years ago the Rev Peter Elvy circumnavigated the diocese of Chelmsford which is bounded by the Stour on the north side, the North Sea on the east, the Thames on the south and the Lee and Stort navigation on the west. He used a Wayfarer dinghy for the rivers and a Drascombe Long Boat for the sea passage and Thames estuary. The waters do not quite connect up so he had a total of 12 miles' portage. It took him a week to complete the circuit. Manningtree is an attractive small town to walk about with many old houses and shops, some with roof beams many centuries old. It was in Manningtree that Matthew Hopkins, who assumed the style and title of 'Witchfinder Generall', pursued his profession of witch hunter being paid 20 shillings for each witch he found. He grew very rich before suffering the same fate as his witches – being 'swum'. Unfortunately he floated which proved him guilty, and so he was hanged and is buried at Mistley.

Back to sea again and our next destination was to be Maldon up the River Blackwater by-passing both Walton Backwaters and the River Colne from Brightlingsea up to Colchester. Even in a motor cruiser it is not possible to put in to every interesting place on the East Coast in a week and we still had a lot of ground to cover before we got to London. More recently I have been to Walton Backwaters during a weekend out of Pin Mill on board a lovely old Itchen Ferry, a vessel ideally suited in character, if less so in draught, to visit this network of islands, creeks and saltings. They were the inspiration and setting for *The Snow Goose* and Arthur Ransome's *Secret Water*. They are less secret than they used to be with dozens of local yachts seeking peace and quiet in Walton Channel and Hamford Water during the summer, but compared with the Broads, to which they are sometimes likened, they are relatively uncrowded and there are no hire cruisers. The comparison is a poor one. The Backwaters cover only a fraction of the area of the Broads and the developer's hand has not touched one square foot of them. Apart from a farm on Horsey Island, no one lives in the Backwaters, and there are precious few buildings to be seen near the shores. Of course there is plenty of mud at low water, but when you cannot move there is a lot of bird life to watch. Skipper's Island on the west side is used by the Essex Naturalists Trust who have erected a bird-observation tower. There are no strong tides away from the entrance at the end of Pye Sand so it is ideal for children to potter around in dinghies. Finally it has plenty of completely tranquil and safe anchorages with good clay holding ground everywhere. It is also a haven in strong winds. The ditch-crawling pilotage of this fascinating world is amply explained in the *East Coast Rivers Pilot Book*, and when the water runs out for cruising boats there is still mileage left for exploring in the tender although much of it may be along narrow gutways. The quay in the south-east corner alongside the Walton and Frinton Yacht Club can be reached at high water, or by tender from ½ mile away at any time except for 1 hour either side of low water. The club is most hospitable to visitors. Nearby is a boatyard and chandlers, and it is only a few minutes' walk into Walton-on-the-Naze, which has everything you expect of a small seaside resort including a nondescript pier. A nature trail has been marked out along the Naze itself. Boats can be launched at the Walton town hard and beside it is a most charming little marina. Well, not quite a marina, rather a basin in the saltings looking very much as if nature had made it. Six feet of water is held in the basin by a gate which is let down to lie flat on the ground when the tide is high enough. It is the home of a fine collection of old gaffers and wooden boats with bowsprits. If you wish to stay a day or two afloat in the basin contact Ron Wyatt at the chandlers hut (Frinton 5873) who runs the marina on behalf of the local Yacht Trust who own the land. There is another yacht basin with dry landing but no facilities among the saltings on the south bank of the Twizzle, but from there it is a long walk to the town.

The next river going south is the Colne with Mersea Island and Brightlingsea at its mouth. It is navigable by coasters right up to The Hythe on the outskirts of Colchester. Not so many years ago Brightlingsea was famous for oysters, sprats and yachts in that order, the oysters being the Colchester Natives or 'Pyefleets' considered by some connoisseurs to be the most succulent in the world. In the harsh winter of 1962/3 millions of them died when the creeks froze solid and I wonder, as I write this in the winter of 1981/2, if they have suffered a similar fate.

The yacht basin at Walton-on-the-Naze. The retaining gates are lowered at high water to give direct access to Walton Backwaters

Certainly the industry is not what it was, and all along the foreshore of West Mersea are the derelict remains of oyster pits. Today most people think of Brightlingsea only as an active yachting centre with its creeks filled with moored yachts and the excellent facility of the 300ft floating jetty of the Brightlingsea Yacht Club. The Jacobes Hall in the High Street where you can eat is one of the oldest timbered buildings built before 1400. The best sea mark for miles around is All Saints church on a hill 1½ miles outside the town. The 100ft tower rises out of a clump of pine trees, and inside the church there are over 200 memorial plaques bearing the names of Brightlingsea men who have lost their lives at sea. The first were placed there in the last century by the vicar, Arthur Pertwee, who used to go up to the top of the tower in stormy weather and wave a lantern to guide the fishermen home.

A short expedition in the tender 2 miles up Brightlingsea Creek and St Osyth Creek will take you to the road bridge just outside St Osyth Priory. The building dates back to the eleventh century, and the later massive gateway is considered one of the finest of its type in Europe with its elaborate flint-and-stone panels. In the grounds which are open to the public there are red deer and peacocks, smooth lawns, lovely flower beds, fish ponds and good examples of the topiarist's art. The priory was, until the Dissolution in 1539, an abbey but is still wrongly called a priory because it was built on the site of a nunnery founded by St Osyth, the daughter of a Christian King of Mercia, in 653. She was married to Sighere, King of Essex, but at the wedding feast he deserted his bride to join a party to follow a stag that had been sighted. In a fit of pique his bride ran away and took the veil. Her husband took it in good part and gave the village of Chich to his virgin bride when she founded her priory and became its abbess. Chich is now called St Osyth (the 'O' pronounced as in rose), but the locals call it 'Toosey'. Soon after St Osyth founded the priory the Danes arrived and cut off her head. Do not bother to walk down the road signposted 'St Osyth Beach' or you will find yourself in a caravan conurbation 'with shops, pubs, entertainments galore and "all the fun of the fair"' as a Tendring District tourist publication gleefully describes it. However, to the west of the beach past the chalets at Lee-over-Sands is the Colne Point Nature Reserve managed by the Essex Naturalists Trust. It is an important site with a shingle ridge nearly two miles in extent enclosing 400 acres of saltings where over 200 species of birds have been identified. The area is patrolled by volunteer wardens during the breeding season. The reserve is also the home of many varieties of plant which have been killed off elsewhere by seaside and leisure developments, especially the blue-flowered sea holly. There is another nature reserve run by the same trust on the west side of the Colne at Fingringhoe with a nature trail. The exact location is OS 168.0419. It can be reached from a boat, landing by tender at an old loading jetty at the site of a Roman fort on the west bank just before the opening of Alresford Creek. The greater part of the reserve, comprising disused gravel workings and saltings, is open only to trust members.

Wivenhoe, birthplace of Beau Brummell, is a pretty place where yachts lie alongside the gardens and jetties of the riverside houses. At the Nottage Institute, an adult-education centre on the quayside, students hand-build pulling boats and dinghies during winter evenings. They have to find their own wood, are only allowed to work with hand tools, and no synthetic materials of any sort may be used. A man may spend 3 years building an 18ft clinker boat at the institute, and much of the final winter will be devoted to applying and rubbing down coat after coat of varnish. It is a sanctuary of amateur craftsmanship, a temple to perfection. All boats dry out at Wivenhoe for half of every tide, and there is little room for visitors except alongside a pier by the shipyard.

That is as far as I have been up the Colne, and the last time was on board the sailing barge *Xylonite*, one of the two remaining iron hulls. But it is quite possible to go a further 4 miles to The Hythe at Colchester. There you will dry out in glutinous mud below a 15ft-high quayside sandwiched between coasters. Colchester has much to offer those with time to stop over a tide. As every schoolboy will know, it was the first Roman town in Britain. It is rich in remains from that era, including much of the original wall – the finest of its kind in the country – and the town museum has a big collection as well as models of the Roman town. Subsequent generations including the Saxons and Normans put Roman bricks to good use by incorporating them in their own buildings. Colchester (Camulodunum to the Romans) was prosperous when St Paul was writing his Letters to the Corinthians. It was here that Boadicea rode in her chariot to do battle with Nero's colonial garrison. The castle was built in the last years of the eleventh century and the walls in some places are 31ft-thick solid masonry. It has the most massive Great Tower in Britain, similar in design to the Tower of London's White Tower, but bigger. You can eat well in the town for it is an affluent place.

Mersea Island separates the entrance to the Colne from the entrance to the Blackwater and cannot be circumnavigated because it is joined to the mainland by a causeway carrying the B1025 from Colchester. West Mersea on the southern shore of the island is another of those places where the ancient and modern of yachting are all mixed up together with fishing boats, houseboats and mud. On entering the Mersea Quarters moorings stretch as far as the eye can see and beyond up the Salcott, Ray and Strood Channels. On the hard in front of the town boats sit high and dry while gumbooted owners and friends scrub and paint seemingly whatever the season. On the foreshore there are some interesting old boats converted to houseboats including *Marguerita*, a once-splendid 19-metre. In season oysters are on sale on the beach. I often wondered how accurate was the saying that you should only eat oysters when there is an R in the month. A long time ago I enjoyed a half dozen at West Mersea early in May and suffered a nasty attack of food poisoning, since when I have never been able to look an oyster in the face. The rest of the crew was similarly affected. The Victory Inn is the most-used local, there are two clubs – the West Mersea Yacht Club and the Dabchicks Sailing Club – and two yards with slipways. There is not much to see on the island, but while at West Mersea do walk to the north end of the foreshore and look for the little lane leading steeply up from the water. A short way up is a row of the prettiest tumbly cottages you could find anywhere. Once oystermen's humble homes, they are now all brightly painted and awash with flowers. West Mersea is very crowded indeed and you will normally have to rely on anchoring, which means that if it is blowing from the east it is not a good spot to stay the night.

Next door to Mersea Quarters is Tollesbury, a handful of five creeks, considered an area of outstanding natural interest where time has stood still. At the heads of the creeks lie the decaying remains of wharves where barges and small coasters brought coal, timber, bricks and manure and took away grain and stacks of hay and straw from the surrounding farms. At low water only the smallest boat can keep moving along the narrow gutways separated from anything like solid ground by many yards of sloping glistening mud. Eventually there is not enough water to run the outboard and you have to row, at which point it is time to turn back or you will spend hours marooned. From deep inside the saltings spinneys of masts can be seen. As the flood comes and the creeks fill they slowly rise to reveal their hulls set free from their gooey waterless holes. Eventually the creeks become wide channels, the saltings develop a myriad of little waterways and everywhere there are boats afloat again. Some are of recent vintage, the majority are old-timers and a few are narrow-gutted motor yachts now serving a useful purpose as weekend houseboats. Then there is *Memory*, an ex-Thames sailing barge which will never sail again. She can be reached by a footpath across the saltings or by dinghy at high water. *Memory* is now the floating hostel of Fellowship Afloat, a trust which combines the proclamation of the Gospel with dinghy sailing, RYA Dayboat Courses, wild-life studies, fishing and music. It caters for groups of children from schools, colleges, churches and clubs, but individuals are also welcomed as are volunteer staff with the right experience. Life on board is a sharing of chores, no radios or cassette players are allowed, and lighting is by Tilley lamps. An atmosphere is maintained in keeping with the natural environment. On board the most common occupation is bird watching; they have Brent geese in the winter and in the summer terns, buntings and warblers. Resident birds include oyster catchers, shelduck, redshank and cormorants. The children are introduced to the specialised plant life of the saltings: sea purslane, sea aster, thrift and sea lavender which can tolerate an occasional spring-tide inundation, and marsh samphire and cord grass which thrive on salt water every tide. Special nets are used to collect samples of plankton, and sea-bed creatures are dredged up for examination such as the filter-feeding oyster and the slipper limpet with its odd sex life, crab and starfish.

What can interest children can interest older visitors to these waters. A lot of nature information on the area can be gleaned from a talk with the Warden of the Fellowship who has his office in one of the wooden sail lofts which stand on stone stilts beside the quay at the head of Woodrolfe Creek. These sail lofts were

These sail lofts at Tollesbury were built some eighty years ago by the owners of J-Class and 12-metre yachts which were wintered there

Mud berths in the saltings off Woodrolfe Creek, Tollesbury. The boating scene here has not changed these past fifty years

built between 1902 and 1904 to store the sails and gear of the J-Class and 12-metres which wintered at Tollesbury. There is now a marina at the head of Woodrolfe Creek, and a tide gauge at the entrance to the creek gives the amount of water over the sill. Although the marina has pontoons, a yard and a slipway it hardly brings Tollesbury Creek into the 1980s. It is a large hole dredged in the mud which will take 200 boats from which you can walk ashore dry shod. The village, a mile from the quay, has a delightful square surrounded by cottages with plaster-and-brick fronts of various ages and the church with its thick squat fourteenth-century flint tower stands on a rubble foundation of Saxon origin. Inside there is a font acquired in 1718 for the sum of £5 which was extracted from a John Norman who came drunk to church and cursed and talked during the service. An inscription on it warns you not to behave as he did.

Across the Blackwater estuary from Mersea Quarters is Bradwell Creek and Marina. There is enough water at all states of the tide for most boats to get in (provided the owners can keep dredging every year) and a visitors' berth at the end of the first pontoon. Facilities include water, fuel, shipwrights, an engineer, chandlery and Bradwell Quay Yacht Club. For whatever reason you may put in to Bradwell, leave yourself time for a 3-mile walk and back first to the village, Bradwell-on-Sea (Bradwell-juxta-Mare), and then to the Chapel of St Peter-on-the-Wall. Bradwell Waterside, a few houses beside the marina, has a pub called The Green Man and a shop. It is then a mile to the village itself, which is fortunate in being at the end of a road which leads nowhere but to the marshes overlooking the estuary and the atomic power station. So it has been left more undisturbed than many villages which are on through roads. There is still a village lock-up, a minute brick building with pointed tiled roof and a grill in its door. Up until 1840 every village was required by law to maintain a lock-up for the temporary accommodation of law-breakers. The one at Bradwell is so small that it would have been overcrowded with three people in it. Beside the door are iron-hinged wrist irons which presumably were used either to secure prisoners for whipping or as a form of punishment in itself, a variation on the stocks. At the church gate a flight of six stone steps surmounted by an iron post provided a variable height mounting block for those coming to church on horseback. The church is fourteenth century with a Georgian tower, and the cottages around are long, low and plastered. Bradwell Lodge, a timbered building once the rectory but now a private house, was built in 1520. Gainsborough worked at the Lodge, and Erskine Childers lived there while he was writing *The Riddle of the Sands*. From the village it is a 2-mile walk to St Peter-on-the-Wall. The way is along a Roman road which runs straight as a die past a pub and four farms across a dead-flat landscape. What you see at the end of the road, the last part of it really a broad footpath, is almost certainly the oldest church in Britain still used for worship. It looks like a tall substantially built barn which, for several hundred years, is what it was. Built some time shortly after 653 by Bishop Cedde as one of several Anglo-Celtic churches in the kingdom of the East Saxons, it has since stood as a landmark to seafarers on the bleak shore overlooking the approaches to the Colne and Blackwater. But before there was a church there the Romans had built a much bigger landmark on the same site, the Fort of Othona, one of a ring of forts from the Wash to the Isle of Wight known as the Forts of the Saxon Shore. They are thought to have been largely the work of Carausius, the first of the Counts of the Saxon Shore appointed by Rome at the end of the third century to defend the then-troubled Empire against Saxon and Frankish barbarians who roved as pirates in the narrow seas – the North Sea and English Channel.

Othona, if that was its true Roman name and there is some doubt about it, was originally a square enclosure of about six acres with walls 12ft thick. Half of that area is now under the sea, as also is the quay which would have served the fort. Today only a small section of the Roman wall is visible above ground. After the Romans had gone a Saxon settlement established itself on the site attracted, no doubt, by the landing place and the Roman road which led inland. When Bishop Cedde arrived he had his church built of rubble from the fort and set square across the foundations of the main entrance, a decision which has enabled the building to stand for 1,300 years without even showing a crack in its walls. There is little doubt that a religious community developed around the church, and the Domesday Book records fishing and salt pans. But in 1099 there was a disastrous tide which destroyed whatever else was there other than, miraculously, the church. After a new church was built in Bradwell village St Peter's became its chapel-of-ease, and in 1142 a report from the local clergy to the Bishop of London said that no one knew when it was built or by whom. Some time in the seventeenth century it ceased to be used, the chancel was pulled down and the nave became a barn. It was not until 1920 that its then owner, Mr C. W. Parker, gave it to the Provost and Chapter of Chelmsford and it was re-consecrated. Much sympathetic restoration work has been done since then, and it has become the place of an annual pilgrimage which is one of the big events of the diocesan calendar. It is almost bare inside; a crucifix above a simple altar and a few chairs are all it contains. One bright summer day when the light was flooding through the west door I had the place to myself and became absorbed in photographing the interior. As I was putting the tripod away I turned round to see a small group of people standing patiently inside the doorway waiting for me to finish. They were members of the Othona Community come to hold their daily service, which they do from July to September. They were of several nationalities and denominations, and none of them was ordained; for musical accompaniment they had brought a guitar. They live as a changing community in a building nearby but out of sight in a hollow. Beside the church is a 200-year-old cottage which once housed a coastguard and his family. It is now leased to bird watchers, and nearer the sea they have an observation tower from which they get a clear view across the North Sea, the same commanding view that the Romans had.

The Blackwater is the big river of the East Coast flowing 17 miles up to

Thames barges preparing for action at Maldon on the Blackwater

Maldon, wide and unconfined by hills. The wind blows free across flat land making it a good sailing ground except at low water, and even then there is width enough to tack all the way up to Osea Island and into Collier's Reach for Heybridge Basin to wait for the tide to take you into Maldon. Coming in from the sea along the south shore, where the water is deepest, there is no stopping place after Bradwell until The Stone where landing is possible on a shingle beach in St Lawrence Bay where many yachts are moored and the small village behind has a few shops. The Stone Sailing Club provides the start line for the annual Maldon Barge Match. Further upstream is the Marconi Sailing Club – the company started life and is still based in Chelmsford, 10 miles west of Maldon. On the next point opposite the eastern end of Osea Island stand the ruins of

Stansgate Abbey, from which Lord Stansgate took his title, and Stansgate Abbey Farm now the country seat of his son, Tony Benn.

Osea Island provides a good anchorage a little way out of the strong tide on its south side. Two green lights at the end of the pier help the night sailor find the island and the anchorage, but the pier is not for landing by ordinary folk. Osea was many years back a retreat for alcoholics, and their cure was often prolonged by the well-meaning local boatmen who, for a generous tip, smuggled drink onto the island at night and hid the bottles under bushes. It is a private island now owned and farmed by Cambridge University. The farm is entirely arable, covering 200 acres of highly productive silty loam on London clay. In all, Osea extends to about 320 acres, of which 70 are saltings which are the undisturbed habitat of numerous wildfowl. The university, through its estate manager on the island, lets three houses for self-catering holidays throughout the year. The farm is out-of-bounds to all visitors, but a perimeter track allows them to watch the activities and various breeds of rare sheep and pigs on the permanent pasture. Neither are shooting, speedboating or waterskiing allowed from or on the island; the house-letting arrangements are intended to appeal to those wanting rest and peace. However, fishing and sailing are encouraged, and visitors are welcome to bring their own boats and launch them by the pier. It is an ideal holiday location for the family with a small cruising boat or dinghy who want to combine day sailing with domestic comfort at night. Access is by a mile-long causeway, originally built by the Romans, from the north shore of the Blackwater to West Point on the island. It remains open for cars for about two hours either side of low water.

The channel into Maldon runs round the north side of Northey Island, which has a farm on it and is in part run as a nature reserve by the Essex Naturalists Trust. There is a sea wall which you can walk round, but if you sit in your boat with binoculars you will probably see more, particularly at low water when the birds are busier feeding. A boat anchored near the shore is a wonderful hide; if you mind your own business birds will mind theirs. The island is connected to the south shore at low water by a short causeway which leads directly to South House Farm and the site of the Battle of Maldon in 991. After looting Ipswich the Danes sailed up the Blackwater and established themselves on Northey Island. At low tide they crossed the causeway and attacked the Saxons led by the great Earl Brithnoth. All went well for the Saxons until their leader fell, when they were put to flight and the Danes occupied Maldon. This was at the time of Ethelred the Unready who spent the Saxon wealth paying Danegeld instead of fighting them. Brithnoth was a patriot who thought otherwise. Off the north tip of Northey is Heybridge Basin, a shallow anchorage with mud berths, and the Jolly Sailor, a nice pub when it is not crowded. If you have a 3ft draught you will be able to stay afloat in the basin for about four hours; beyond that you must expect to take the mud. After a drink at the Jolly Sailor or the Ship, take a walk along the towpath of the willow-lined canal, a fresh-water haven of locked-in

Clinker hulls and bowsprits. A typical scene at Maldon

boats of every shape and size, state of conservation and decay. There are grand yachts of Edwardian vintage which may never move again, barges Thames and Dutch, weekend chalets on floating hulls, a very few modern boats and lots of small old wooden yachts. I have always thought that the two sides of this section of the canal are lined with dreams, dreams of putting some impractical bargain back into commission and sailing away for ever and a day.

From Heybridge the river twists its way round to Maldon whose Hythe Quay is usually crowded with sailing barges, old gaffers and a number of other veterans, among them the ex-Admiralty Harbour Service launch *Puffin*, 52ft 6in, built in 1919 and still in steam and *Brent*, a 54-ton steam tug which, surprisingly, was built as late as 1946. She is probably the most expensive-to-run pleasure craft on the East Coast. In 1976 I followed the Oyster Smack Race up the Thames to Billingsgate on board *Puffin* while *Brent* acted as tail-end-Charlie to the fleet of old gaffers. Her master, Bill Hall, told me that his coal bill for the round trip from Maldon was £100. It is easier for the tourists who throng the Hythe Quay at Maldon to stare in wonder at the barges and steam boats to find a parking space for their cars (and they have some difficulty) than it is for a visiting yacht to find a berth. There is a visitors' section of the quay, 150ft long, between the Queen's Head and the Maldon Little Ship Club crane, but a 10ft space must be left clear in front of the club. You may berth there free of charge providing you do not obstruct any vessel which is paying wharfage and leave on the same tide as you arrive and do not dry out. The alternative is to berth alongside pontoons near the slip at Dan Webb & Feesey's yard and settle into the mud when the water leaves. Walter Cook & Son at the end of the quay are still doing barge-repair work, and somehow from somewhere still get some oak to do it with. Beyond Cook's yard a hard sloping beach is used by the local open fishing boats and it is from along that beach, with the fishing boats in the foreground, that one gets the best view of Maldon rising up from the water or mud, depending on the state of the tide.

St Mary's Church with its square tower and small steeple stands above the quay and for centuries has been a landmark for mariners coming up the Blackwater. At one time it had a beacon on its tower. These days it often appears, from the water, to be sited amongst a copse of branchless trees – the masts of sailing barges, old gaffers and other boats which lie rafted against the quay below. Up in the town All Saints Church has a stained-glass window, a gift in 1922 from Maldon's American namesake founded by Essex immigrants 300 years ago, depicting the landing of Columbus, the arrival of the Pilgrim Fathers and George Washington taking the oath on becoming president. It is an interesting coincidence that Christopher Jones, the captain of the *Mayflower*, was christened in this church. On the south wall well-wrought figures of Maldon's six famous men stand in niches: Brithnoth clad in mail, Bishop Cedde, Archbishop Mellitus, Robert Mantell who founded the priory, Sir Robert Darcy, and Thomas Plume who founded a school and the famous Plume Library which is housed in the building that used to be St Peter's Church. Its medieval tower still remains. The library contains some 6,000 books published between two and three centuries ago. The ancient register records the death of Lawrence Washington (now buried in the churchyard of All Saints), a parson who had been ejected from his living at the rectory at Purleigh, after which both his sons emigrated to America; one of them, John, was the great-grandfather of George Washington. The town has many medieval, Tudor and Georgian corners if you wander around the narrow streets leading down to the river, and a fifteenth-century moot hall which is now the Town Hall. The Blue Boar at the top of the hill opposite St Peter's has a modern front, a THF sign outside and their regime inside, but behind the façade are old timbered buildings of the fourteenth and fifteenth centuries surrounding a courtyard with overhanging storeys. One could call it an hotel of great archaeological interest. The A414 road bridge over the River Chelmer in the town marks the effective head of navigation. The Blackwater takes its leave of Maldon before the bridge, going inland as it were to join the canal in Heybridge village. But for those who enjoy a little trip in the tender it is possible to go under the bridge and on to a lock about a mile further upstream where you will find a rare sight in Essex – a waterfall. It is at this point that the Blackwater and the Chelmer are joined by locks, and there is a navigation via the Chelmer & Blackwater Navigation all the way to Chelmsford.

A point of interest in All Saints Church, Maldon, is the stained-glass window, a gift from Maldon's American namesake, depicting the landing of Columbus, the arrival of the Pilgrim Fathers and George Washington taking the oath on becoming president. The latter's great-great-grandfather lies buried in the churchyard

Out of the Blackwater we made through the Ray Sand Channel on the flood using the power and speed of the engine to make sure of getting through with ample time to spare, and so entered the Crouch just off Foulness Point. The first 4 miles of the river up to Burnham are very boring with almost no view at all above the sea walls except at high tide, and then it is very flat featureless land. At half tide and below you pass between high wide banks of mud. The river is ruled by the Crouch Harbour Authority who charge visitors mooring or anchoring there. With the Royal Corinthian Yacht Club, Royal Burnham Yacht Club, Crouch Yacht Club and Burnham Sailing Club, two sailmakers, several shipwrights and engineers along the waterfront, hundreds of boats permanently moored alongside the fairway and its own Week in September, Burnham-on-Crouch is an élitest yachting centre, a carbon-copy Cowes of the East Coast. From the water the front looks good with its red-brick Georgian buildings, but it gets a bit crowded during the season with both boating folk and trippers. In the church a mile from the river there is a tablet to the memory of Dr Alexander Scott, the Vicar of Southminster, 2 miles north of Burnham. He was the chaplain on HMS *Victory* who must have heard Nelson's dying words: 'Thank God I have done my duty'. When he was paid off along with the ship he took with him a souvenir – the chart table Nelson had used. If you go to Southminster and look

in the vestry you will see a rather plain table on which wedding couples sign the register; that is the chart table. There is a bureau and a mirror there too, also taken off *Victory*.

Further up the Crouch the scenery improves as the countryside forms gentle slopes down to the marshes and saltings edging the river. While Burnham is mostly associated with racing, North Fambridge is a cruising man's place where boats in mud berths must wait for the tide. It was at North Fambridge that I caught the boat-bug way back in the 1950s. I was then writing about cottages for *Ideal Home*, and had the heretical idea that boats might be used as weekend cottages. The editor liked the idea, and North Fambridge was where I first went looking for them. In those days it was at the end of nowhere where everybody did their own work and helped each other. Boats lived in mud holes below the sea wall, and the only professional installation was a wood-and-tar shed standing on stilts in the mud. I forget the name of the man who did everything including lending his tools, but he was full of information about boats and the river. He took me along a wobbly plank on board a boat where we sat below in a snug cabin with a coal-stove burning. He brewed a pot of tea on a gimballed paraffin stove and told me that in a week or two she would be ready to float on a spring tide and sail off to some faraway place. I had found a weekend cottage from the windows of which its owner could, should he so wish, have a different view every morning. It seemed quite simple then. After a few drinks in the Ferry Boat, a pub built of ships' timbers which lies 10ft below the river level and has often been flooded, I had decided to buy a boat myself! Not very long after that Mr Prior at Burnham sold me a clinker-built 21ft two-berth cabin cruiser with a Vedette petrol engine. It was a narrow-gutted pre-war boat with a very high coachroof for its beam and it rolled like a pig. Today North Fambridge is a bit changed. There are dozens of boats on moorings along both sides of the fairway, and inland below the sea wall a large yard has been developed where boats are laid up on hard standing and people build reinforced concrete hulls. Half a mile further upstream Stow Creek, a quiet drying backwater perfect for a night with nature when I first knew it, is now a marina with pontoons and a yard. Brandy Hole, a half-tide drying anchorage near Hullbridge, has a large caravan site nearby and is not as remote as it used to be.

The office at Paper Mill Lock, Little Beddow, of the Chelmer & Blackwater Navigation which connects Heybridge, by Maldon, with Chelmsford

Boats of the local Troy class sailing in Fowey
Harbour, a 'splendid deep-water anchorage at
the mouth of an extremely beautiful river'
(*Harry & Billie Graeme*)

# 10 Westcountry Rivers

With a boat you can always get away from people which makes it the ideal vehicle in which to travel to the Westcountry where for much of the summer, and certainly during the school holidays, the roads are clogged with coaches, caravans and cars and everywhere ashore is unbearably overcrowded. In July and August, and sometimes even early in September, it would have to be some very urgent matter that would persuade me to travel by road to anywhere on the south coast of Devon or Cornwall. It is understandable that people want to go to these coasts for they are amazingly beautiful, but throughout the long holiday season the discriminating traveller can find little pleasure there unless he travels by the only clear road – the sea.

Apart from being a lovely coastline, sometimes gentle, sometimes dramatic, it is an easy one to cruise. There are no offlying dangers except those like the Eddystone and Wolf Rocks, which are all too obvious. There are no shoals, no rocks other than those so close to the shore that they do not constitute passage hazards. The tides are very moderate, rarely being much more than one knot even at springs, and the main harbours, all reasonably easy to get into, are regularly spaced an easy day's sailing apart. The weather is normally as good as, if not better than, elsewhere around the British Isles – not that one can be careless about listening to the forecasts. We must never forget the Fastnet Race of August 1979. The scenery is not as awe-inspiring as Western Scotland or the coasts of Snowdonia, but at least there will more often be good visibility to see it. When the sun shines the colours – the Indian red of the soil and the lush greens of wood and pasture – are almost tropical in their vibrance. The coastline is neither flat nor straight, much of it is cliffs topped by rolling hills and heavily indented with bays, many of them horned with rocky headlands and when sailing reasonably close in one sees it as a succession of cycloramas. It lacks only those offlying islands which make cruising in other parts so interesting, but in compensation it has its rias, or sunken valleys, which provide hundreds of square miles of sheltered-water sailing deep into the countryside. Most of the estuaries and rivers of these valleys have extensive networks of creeks and tributaries with shores that are never seen by the motorist and in many stretches cannot even be reached on foot. They lead to villages sufficiently out of the way to have remained unspoilt, and en route there is everywhere an abundance of changing scenery and bird life. When you have gone as far as the tide and your keel will allow, the tender will take you on beyond the normal limits of navigation to even remoter corners of the countryside.

This option of being able to cruise deep inland as well as along the coast is one which only a minority take up. Perhaps they are uncertain of what water is navigable and what is not and think it not worth the risk of going aground and having to sit out a tide. Certainly cruising tidal rivers and creeks requires as much homework and pilotage as making your way around the coast. It does not deserve the derogatory term 'ditch crawling'. There are of course many people who cruise more for the sailing than the scenery and to whom time in harbour or

The Globe in Lympstone has a reputation for its lobster suppers

estuary, except perhaps overnight, is time wasted. On the other hand I know a man who has not only cruised the whole of the south coast of England many times, but has been to the head of navigation of every river between the Thames and the Helford with one exception, the Exe. He makes full use of his inflatable dinghy as a little boat in its own right, although not without coming up against a few difficulties for, as he says: 'The average jelly dinghy does not take kindly to running aground on abandoned bicycles and other metallic objects on the river bed. It is also very uncomfortable to use after it has been parked under a sewage outfall. When visiting towns at the heads of rivers there is frequently a problem in finding somewhere to park the dinghy away from vandals.'

The Exe is not always an easy river to enter and should not be attempted in strong onshore winds when the ebb has started to run. There is a strong tidal stream in the entrance and the sands are liable to shift, so very careful attention must be paid to the buoyage and no corners cut. The stream also runs fast past the entrance to Exmouth Dock which is narrow and spanned by a bridge which has to be opened by arrangement with the Harbour Master. Inside the basin partially dries and has to be shared with coasters. There has long been talk of constructing a marina off Point to the north of the dock, and for all I know it may happen. Although one wonders what it will cost to keep it dredged because it would be sited at just the right place to capture all the silt coming down river.

If it ever is built it could mean the end of the village of between-the-wars shanty bungalows, each one with a few square feet of garden fronting the water which makes Point something of a curiosity. To go up the river you have to follow a dog-leg channel south-west and then north between Great Bull Hill sandbank and the hooked spit of Dawlish Warren which blocks three-quarters of the river mouth. The Warren would make a perfect bird sanctuary, but has long since been taken over by man as a golf course, caravan site and park for 2,000 cars.

The Exe is about a mile wide up to Topsham and the land low-lying on both sides so the wind is free. It is, therefore, a good river for sailing although only at high water. At other times it dries out high on both sides of the channel, which is well marked. Lympstone on the east bank is a delightful waterside village which was an important fishing port until around 1800. There is now no more than 5ft of water at its quay at high-water springs, but if you can get alongside of an evening do so for a lobster supper at The Globe. Work out the tides and book early in the day. It is worth the trouble. On the west shore just before coming up to Topsham is the Turf Hotel, a pub on the point of what looks like an island but is the end of the outer embankment of the Exeter Canal. It is a watering hole which cannot be reached by car. There are no other buildings in sight and anybody approaching from water or land would be seen long before he arrived. I am not sure what opening hours the landlord keeps, but he is also the canal lock keeper. There is no longer any commercial traffic up the 5 miles of canal to Exeter and the city council have been toying with the idea of leasing or selling it for a marina. Meanwhile it is used by boats which winter in the basin on the edge of the city. In the sixteenth century small ships could sail with the tide up the river to the walls of Exeter, but the Countess of Devon who owned Topsham had a weir built so that ships had to stop at Topsham. The city fathers responded by building a canal – the first pound-locked canal in Britain – which bypassed the Countess Wear, as it is called. When the canal was opened in 1566 it was 16ft wide and only 3ft deep so could only have been used by fishing boats and lighters. Over the centuries it has been enlarged and lengthened and is now 50ft wide and 10½ft deep. Further work to improve the canal and locks was started at the end of 1982. The building of the M5 viaduct over the canal means that only craft with a mast height under 35ft can get to Exeter without unstepping their mast. With the pub at Turf's Lock and another at Double Locks (so called because it will take two ships side by side) the towpath makes a pleasant walk leading to the Exeter Maritime Museum with its historic boats afloat by the town quay and others in the old riverside warehouses. The trip can be made by boat, but it is rather expensive to lock in and out of the canal; a tender and outboard would be more practical.

The Maritime Museum is a prime tourist attraction and, for the cruising man, a very legitimate one. There are more than eighty craft on display: coracles, a Venetian gondola, a sampan, several Arab dhows, a Tagus lighter, a steam tug and a reed boat from Lake Titicaca in the Andes are a random sample. For steam

*Sotero*, a Tagus lighter, one of the many craft on view at the Exeter Maritime Museum

buffs there is Brunel's dredger *Bertha* built in 1844, which is the oldest working steam vessel in the world; she is put in steam annually. There is also a film set constructed for the *Onedin Line* which includes a triple-expansion marine steam engine. Launch trips on the river, rowing boats for hire, tearooms and a maritime shop are additional attractions. The museum is run by the International Sailing Craft Association established in 1964. The initials ISCA are appropriate as the Roman name for Exeter was Isca Dumnoniorum.

(*Above*) A disused quay at Topsham has become a riverside garden but the wall still serves yachts for scrubbing; (*opposite*) the seaward view from Bayards Cove, Dartmouth (*Peter Allen*)

Topsham is an ancient and beautiful small town which was a seaport second only to London in medieval days, and even at the time of the Napoleonic Wars there were twenty-seven men o' war based on the port. Now, although there is a large town quay to which a few coasters still come, almost all signs of maritime activity – shipyards, warehouses, ropewalk, docks and lime kilns – have gone. Much of the waterfront has been filled in and become gardens to the houses which front the river. The streets are narrow so some impossible situations arise when visiting cars drive down Ferry Road and the Strand and come to a dead end with no room to turn. Many of the houses have Dutch-style façades, and the sixteenth-century Shell House on the Strand has a Grinling Gibbons ceiling suspended by chains. On evening high-water springs the river is decorated by boats of the Topsham Sailing Club, their sails translucent against the lowering sun shining across the water. It was along the east banks of the Exe that Turner painted several of his sunsets.

The Dart is almost every yachtsman's dream of what a sailing river should be. It has no bar and the 12 miles to Totnes are considered by many to be the most beautiful stretch of river in England. You enter between two historic castles, Dartmouth and Kingswear, but it is not always easy to do so without using the engine. There are high cliffs on both sides which make it very fluky; then, as you pass the castles, the wind can drop even when it is blowing a gale outside. To sail in you need to have the tide with you. After that the river opens into an ideal anchorage with two marinas, Dart Haven and Dart Marina. The mooring buoys on the Dartmouth side are not particularly easy to pick up and it is better to go for one of the moorings on the Kingswear side or into a marina. That leaves you with a longish row over to Dartmouth, but there are so many harbour launches running about that it is easy to get a lift or you can take the ferry. Fuel from a small tanker anchored in the river is cheaper than in marinas.

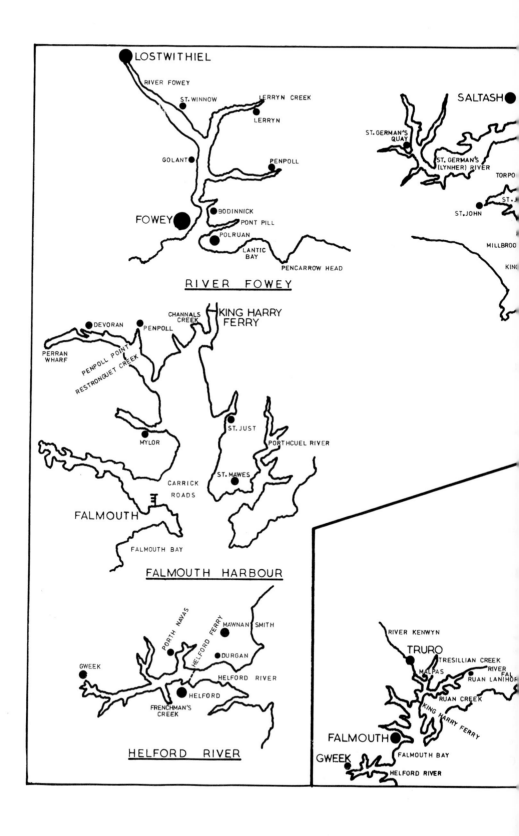

LOSTWITHIEL

RIVER FOWEY

ST. WINNOW

LERRYN CREEK

LERRYN

GOLANT

PENPOLL

FOWEY

BODINNICK

PONT PILL

POLRUAN

LANTIC BAY

PENCARROW HEAD

RIVER FOWEY

SALTASH

ST. GERMAN'S QUAY

ST. GERMAN'S (LYNHER) RIVER

TORPO

ST. J

ST. JOHN

MILLBROO

KIN

DEVORAN

PENPOLL

CHANNALS CREEK

KING HARRY FERRY

PERRAN WHARF

PENPOLL POINT

RESTRONGUET CREEK

MYLOR

ST. JUST

PORTHCUEL RIVER

ST. MAWES

CARRICK ROADS

FALMOUTH

FALMOUTH BAY

FALMOUTH HARBOUR

PORTH NAVAS

HELFORD FERRY

MAWNAN SMITH

DURGAN

GWEEK

HELFORD RIVER

HELFORD

FRENCHMAN'S CREEK

HELFORD RIVER

RIVER KENWYN

TRURO

TRESILLIAN CREEK

MALPAS

RIVER FAL

RUAN LANIHOR

RUAN CREEK

KING HARRY FERRY

FALMOUTH

GWEEK

FALMOUTH BAY

HELFORD RIVER

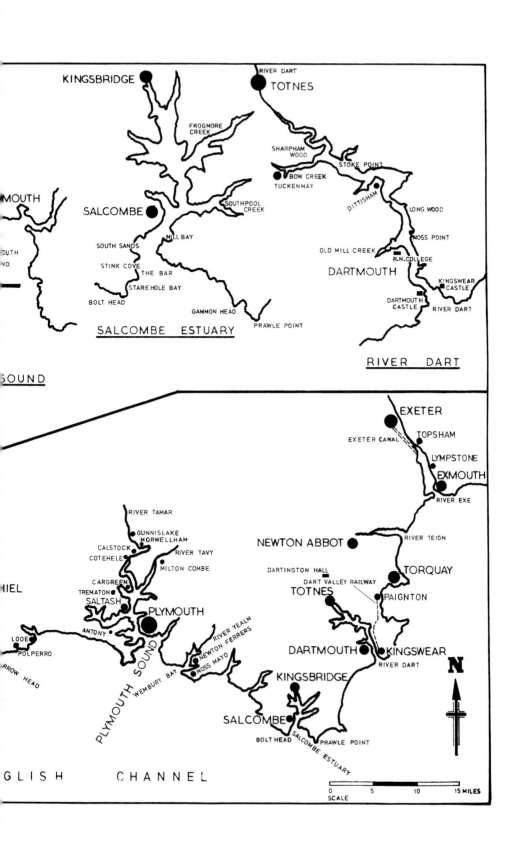

KINGSBRIDGE

RIVER DART
TOTNES

FROGMORE
CREEK

SHARPHAM
WOOD
STOKE POINT

BOW CREEK
TUCKENHAY

SOUTHPOOL
CREEK

SALCOMBE

DITTISHAM
LONG WOOD

MILL BAY

NOSS POINT

SOUTH SANDS
OLD MILL CREEK
R.N. COLLEGE

STINK COVE
DARTMOUTH
KINGSWEAR
CASTLE

THE BAR
STAREHOLE BAY

BOLT HEAD
DARTMOUTH
CASTLE
RIVER DART

GAMMON HEAD
PRAWLE POINT

SALCOMBE ESTUARY

RIVER DART

SOUND

EXETER
TOPSHAM

EXETER CANAL
LYMPSTONE

EXMOUTH

RIVER EXE

RIVER TAMAR

GUNNISLAKE
MORWELLHAM
NEWTON ABBOT
RIVER TEIGN

CALSTOCK
COTEHELE
RIVER TAVY

MILTON COMBE

TORQUAY

DARTINGTON HALL

CARGREEN
DART VALLEY RAILWAY
TOTNES
PAIGNTON

TREMATON
SALTASH

PLYMOUTH

HIEL

RIVER YEALM

ANTONY
NEWTON FERRERS

DARTMOUTH
KINGSWEAR

LOOE
NOSS MAYO
RIVER DART

POLPERRO

KINGSBRIDGE

RROW HEAD
WEMBURY BAY

SALCOMBE

N

BOLT HEAD
SALCOMBE ESTUARY
PRAWLE POINT

GLISH CHANNEL

0   5   10   15 MILES
SCALE

Dartmouth Castle is the oldest surviving fort that was specially built by Henry VIII to take cannons. With Kingswear Castle on the opposite bank and a chain which could be slung across the river mouth, Dartmouth was an impregnable harbour. Dartmouth Castle is now open to the public and contains a good collection of weaponry from the Civil War. The cannon ports appear to be unusually low down, the reason being that the early guns of the fifteenth and sixteenth centuries were mounted on heavy timbers laid on the ground, not on wheeled carriages. In the town the Butterwalk has a fine row of timbered houses, their upper storeys overhanging the sidewalk and supported by stone columns. One of them is now a very good maritime museum, and nearby is Thomas Newcomen's Memorial Engine – the first commercially used steam engine which he built in 1712. He was born in Dartmouth in 1663, and his invention came nearly 60 years before James Watt's improved design, by which time at least 200 Newcomen engines were in service pumping water out of the mines. The one now on display was working as a canal pumping engine until 1913 and, apparently, could be made to work again today.

Bayards Cove at the southern end of the river quay is the most complete section of the old river front. It was used by the BBC to represent the port of Liverpool in its series the *Onedin Line* and was one of the several embarkation points for the passengers on their way to America aboard the *Mayflower*. The ship had suffered damage on her stormy passage down the English Channel from the east coast and put into Dartmouth and then Plymouth for repairs and revictualling before her comparatively easy passage across the Atlantic. The oldest part of the town is along Higher Street, now well inland from the river, which in Elizabethan times ran parallel to the harbour on a bank about ten feet above high-water mark. Here and there can be seen remains of the close-packed dwellings of Tudor times with one outstanding example of an even earlier period, The Cherub, a restored half-timbered wool-merchant's house dating from about 1380. It is now a splendid pub which prides itself on its traditional English cooking both in the bar and in its elegant dining room. In 1958 the building was utterly derelict and ripe for demolition. It was completely restored by Mr Cresswell Mullet and opened as a free house and restaurant in 1972. It was then named The Cherub after a type of boat built locally for carrying wool. In the dining room there is a rare collection of Madeira dating from 1792 and one of the world's oldest drinkable wines, a Tokay of 1740. English wines are a feature of their cellar to go with their locally caught fish – bass and brill caught on the Skerries Banks, River Dart cockles, Dover sole from Dartmouth, crab (Dartmouth is England's largest crabbing port), salmon from the river and blue shark in August and September.

For a day's expedition away from Dartmouth to keep the children amused there is the privately owned Dart Valley Railway whose steam trains run alongside the river from Dartmouth Ferry on the Kingswear side for several miles before turning inland for Paignton, part of a sprawling seaside conurbation but with very excellent zoological and botanical gardens. Alternatively, an open-top-bus ride can be taken all the way to Babbacombe beyond Torquay to visit Kent's Cavern, one of Britain's oldest pre-historic sites where man lived and hunted cave bear, mammoth and sabre-toothed tiger 200,000 years ago.

If anyone has any doubts about the possibility of navigating the Dart up to Totnes suffice it to say that at spring tides coasters of about 1,000 tons, up to 240ft LOA and drawing 12½ft go up the river to Baltic Wharf which is half a mile below Totnes Bridge. Small boats can certainly make the passage at any tide except for 1½ hours either side of low water in the upper reaches of the last 2 miles before Totnes. Dartmouth Harbour is overlooked by the massive red-brick-and-stone bulk of Britannia Royal Naval College built between 1899 and 1905 to replace the hulks of two wooden warships, the *Britannia* and the *Hindustan*, which were moored in the river and had housed the college since 1863. Round the corner above the college is Old Mill Creek, a narrow waterway which comes to a point surrounded by trees. At the mouth of the creek are rows of small naval craft, pinnaces, whalers and more sporty sailing boats belonging to the college. At low water it is nearly all mud, but if you can take the ground there is a little lane which goes from the head of the creek up to Fire Beacon Hill, about two miles away, the summit of which gives a grand view of the Dart, particularly the middle reaches above and below Dittisham.

The Dittisham pedestrian-ferry landing stage. Fairly clean landings can be made on the shore from tenders

(*Left*) The very steep street in Dittisham which ends on the foreshore and the Ferry Inn. A pedestrian ferry works regularly to Greenway Quay seen across the water; (*above*) There are several small, narrow creeks off the Dart. Dittisham Creek is a typical one

Further up river beyond Noss Point, Philip's Yard and Noss Marina on the east shore is Long Wood, now National Trust property. Its sturdy oaks were used by shipwrights for grown shapes and charcoal burners gathered the small stuff for metal smelting. In the reach to Dittisham Ferry the river narrows to form a bottle-neck partly stoppered by the Anchor Stone which is awash at high water but has a stake on it and is guarded by a port-hand buoy. It is also called Scold Stone because, local legend has it, nagging wives were put on the rock at the beginning of the flood and only taken off after promising to mend their ways. The twin villages of Higher and Lower Dittisham have steep narrow streets going down to the water on both sides of Gurrow Point. They still have a small ration of thatched cottages, and the church contains a unique example of a Devon wine-glass pulpit with carved and painted saints around it. Dittisham is quite famous for its damsons which were originally brought from Germany, and in the autumn they are to be had in great quantity.

Stoke Gabriel at the top of the middle reaches on the east side of the river is in an idyllic setting at the end of a short creek, its houses climbing up a hillslope above a mill pool. Unfortunately most of the white-painted houses which spread well back and along the hill and are all too visible were built in the last 30 years and spoil the picture. However, the old core of the village is largely undamaged although it is not much seen from the water except for the tapering church tower rising above the trees which grow thick along the banks. For a thousand years or more Stoke Gabriel has been the centre of the Dart salmon-fishing industry, and

The twelfth-century Church House Inn at Stoke Gabriel. It has some interesting features such as a priest's hole and a back oven which may have been built originally to bake all the village bread

there was a church there to serve the spiritual needs of the fishing community long before the Norman Conquest. In the Exeter registers of 1300 there is reference to the dilapidations of the old church at Stoke Gabriel; the present one is largely a fifteenth-century re-build. The church registers are complete from the year 1539 with the entry that year of the baptism of John Davis who sailed to the Arctic in a 10-ton pinnace in 1587 and discovered the strait which connects Baffin's Bay with the Atlantic and now commemorates his name. In 1592 he discovered the Falkland Islands, whoever else may have subsequently claimed to have done the same. The most intriguing thing about the church is its yew tree, the low twisting branches of which spread a canopy over a large area of the graveyard, spanning two paths and several garden seats. There is no documentary evidence of its age, but expert opinions have given it as between 1,000 and 1,500 years. It was possibly some hundreds of years old at the time of the Norman Conquest.

The Church House Inn at the foot of a cobbled walk leading down from the church dates back to the twelfth century with markings incised in one beam giving the date 1111. It has quite the biggest inglenook I have seen, and in which a whole pig was roasted over a wood fire as recently as New Year's Eve 1982. There are many other features in this old pub to interest the antiquarian including a priest's hole and a back oven which was large enough at one time to bake all the village bread. Like several other Church House Inns in Devon, it is thought that it was originally built to house and feed the stonemasons during the time it took them to build the church. The centre of the village is now a conservation area and there are several houses and cottages worthy of the camera and everywhere there are apple trees, survivors of the time when Stoke Gabriel was a cider-making village and there were fewer houses and all the land between them was given over to orchards. But one stretch of orchard running from Church Walk down to the mill pool has been preserved and is now owned by the village. The apples go to make cider as of old, but with paths and seats among the trees it doubles as a park.

Down by the creek there is a large flat foreshore where the fishermen used to spread their nets; it is now a car park with a lawn and flowering trees. The old tidal mill at the end of the dam has long since gone and more recently been replaced by a spick-and-span cafe which sells yachtsmen's packed lunches. You can lie alongside the quay paying a small fee to the cafe owners. There is also a catwalk out across the mud which can be approached in a tender soon after low water. Salmon netting still thrives on a part-time basis during the season from 15 March to 15 August, five days a week from 6am Monday to 6am Saturday. Rowing boats are used with a crew of four; one to hold one end of the net at the water's edge, two to pay it out and the fourth to row the boat in a circle to enclose the area where a salmon has been spotted 'vowling'. All four then draw the net into the shore, heavy or light, depending on what may be in it.

If you have the time and the water under you to take a midday or evening trip up Bow Creek opposite Stoke Gabriel it is worth going the 1½ miles to Tuckenhay and the Maltster's Arms. From the road it is a white-painted stone inn with a low doorway, and looks old and cosy. The back of the building facing the creek has been unsympathetically developed to provide a picture-windowed lounge and restaurant. Unexpectedly there is a large wide quay between the pub and the water, a leftover from the time when Tuckenhay was a small industrial centre with a paper mill, corn mill and a gasworks which gave this little village gaslight in 1806, the same year that it was introduced in London. Now the creek is only used by yachtsmen, salmon netters and shelducks who have just enough water at low water to keep afloat. Among the old warehouses on the quayside is Giuseppe Cannizzaro's Winery in an old cider store. A sign says 'Pepe & Son'; the son is still a schoolboy, and his father comes from Sicily where his elder brother tends 60 acres of vines. It is from there that Pepe gets the raw material for his wines. He makes about 7,000 gallons a year of red, white and rosé, also Marsala, mead and apple and cherry wines. Visitors are automatically pressed to a tasting before there is any suggestion that they should buy. To sail up a Devon Creek to taste wine with a Sicilian is something quite out of the ordinary, but unhappily Pepe may not be there for much longer. The proprietors of the Maltster's Arms have told him that they want their cider store back when his lease runs out. They were not sure what they would do with it when I was last there, but thought it might make an amusing restaurant or that they might turn it into a miniature brewery and sell their own home-made beer. With all that quayside for cars they are looking to extend their family tripper trade. Tuckenhay will then be another car-filled destination and Bow Creek will not be so worth going up any more. But Pepe has his escape route planned – he is going to start his own vineyard among the sub-tropical fields of Torbay. He will import the hardy vines from his brother's vineyard to produce English wines.

After Bow Creek the Dart narrows between Sharpham Wood and Ham Copse through two S-bends before straightening out for the 2-mile run into Totnes. If navigating those bends around high-water springs watch out for the masts of a big coaster showing above the trees coming round the bend in front of or behind you, and on no account anchor anywhere near the channel. At Totnes you can lie alongside the wall in front of the Steam Packet Inn but not over a tide as the ground is uneven and stony. For an overnight or over-tide stop go further up the left arm of the river called the Mill Tail where there is mud on top of sand. The moorings in the right arm, which continues under the bridge to the weir, belong to the Totnes Boating Association which has a clubhouse on the bank. A non-drying mooring there may sometimes be had by arrangement.

The salt-water limit which can be reached in a tender or dinghy is at the weir 2 miles upstream, above which the fresh water flows peat-coloured off the moors. Totnes has a castle with a fourteenth-century shell keep and well-preserved

The head of navigation on the Dart at Totnes. The Mill Tail, mud on sand for overnight stops, extends from the Steam Packet Inn, the white building on the left

battlements. But the most interesting building is Dartington Hall, 3 miles to the north off the A384. It is a medieval courtyard house built between 1388 and 1400. The tilt yard has raised grass terraces for spectators, and the house is surrounded by a beautiful garden of flowers and Spanish chestnuts, in the midst of which is a swan pool. The house is still lived in, but the banqueting hall and gardens are open to visitors.

Salcombe Harbour and Kingsbridge estuary compare favourably with the Dart in many respects, but are topographically very different. Instead of one long, relatively narrow river, in parts running through wooded gorges, it is an open splodge of water surrounded by low hills with several broad creeks on both sides. The whole area dries far more than the Dart, but all the creeks can be entered at half flood by a cruising boat and very much sooner by tender or launch. The bar can be pretty vicious and is a hazard at low water without local knowledge, and is liable to be dangerous at any state of the tide in strong southerlies or south-easterlies or if there is a heavy swell running from the south-west. Even the harbour itself can be untenable in southerly storms when hundreds of boats at their moorings have to be moved up the estuary into The Bag. Because the estuary is wide and the surrounding hills low, movement by tender can sometimes be a wet and uncomfortable journey. But for most of the season it is a delightful place with plenty to explore without going out over the bar.

A very short waterborne expedition can be made from the harbour to South Sands either by tender or the half-hourly ferry from Whitestrand Quay in Salcombe. Apart from the wide popular beach which is sheltered from the prevailing south-westerlies and ideal for children, there is the Tides Reach Hotel, very modern and equipped with all the three-star facilities of heated swimming pool, sauna, hydro spa, squash court and secluded gardens. The South Sands Hotel, right on the beach, is handy if you are just going ashore for a drink or a coffee, and a little way up the hill is the Bolt Head Hotel which, I am reliably told by locals, has the best cuisine in Devon. Less than half-a-mile's walk from South Sands is Sharpitor Garden with its 6 acres of rare plants and shrubs and a spectacular view over the bar and entrance to Salcombe Harbour. In the garden is the Overbecks Museum devoted to ships and shipbuilding, with a collection of shipwrights' tools. It also houses some local natural-history exhibits as well as a children's room with dolls and toys. Sharpitor is National Trust property and leads directly to one of the most dramatic sections of the South Devon coastal path along the cliffs to Bolt Head. The cliff rock is mica schist, a hard material which has weathered into strange shapes, at the foot of which on a windy day the sea breaks with a regular boom and sends up fans of spray. At one point the path has been cut through the outcrop of Sharp Tor, little more than a goat track with the sea below, and the rock face of the tor hanging above. The views back past Stink Cove to the Salcombe bar and east across the bay to the sharp craggy ridge of Gammon Head and Prawle Point are bonuses on a walk which is itself exciting.

The Bag, Salcombe, where you have to moor in bad conditions, or also because there may be no room opposite the town

Starehole Bay between Sharp Tor and Mew Stone is a nice bay for landing from a tender, sheltered from the prevailing winds and with a small beach when the tide is out. There is nothing else there, but a short climb up the surrounding cliffs will take you on to the coast path to Bolt Head. Starehole Bay is the place to wait for water over the bar in south-westerlies. The coastal path continues eastwards round Prawle Point starting at Mill Bay on the east side of the harbour. Mill Bay is an enticing beach and much used by bilge keelers between tides. Along the coast from there all the way to Prawle Point there is a succession of tempting coves, several with virgin sand. They are best left that way. It is not advisable to land from a small boat anywhere on that bit of coast which is wide open to the prevailing wind and swell. From Limebury Point east to Prawle Point should be regarded as a lee shore and avoided unless you want to get your boat swamped. Even Sunny Cove, which is well inside the bar and appears to be protected by Blackstone, can get very treacherous when there is anything of a swell running, and there is a beacon which warns of the danger of landing.

Salcombe is built in the lee of high ground which runs south towards Bolt Head, a magnificent stretch of real estate with many villas half hidden among the trees, each with its own garden and prized view over the river mouth and harbour. On a sunny day the scene from the water is almost Mediterranean. The town has little to show of architectural interest, but it does have waterside charm with narrow lanes leading to jetties and slipways. The corner with most appeal to the yachtsman is Island Street which is full of little yards and workshops lining the shore of Shadycombe Creek. There you can find chandlery and repair shops, engineering works, life-raft repairers and firms building dinghies, fitting out GRP hulls and one man hand-building the traditional Salcombe yawl. Among the cafés, chip shops and crêperies is the Creep In up a little alley among antique shops, which tries hard to be much better. Food is served in a room with black decor by ladies in black and you are expected to wait and study the menu at the upstairs bar. It is not a cheap place, but appreciated after feeding on board for a day or two.

Having one of the best climates in the country and exceedingly scenic country around it, Salcombe is very much a holiday resort and tourist attraction so in high season the narrow streets become very crowded, but boating people still seem to be in the majority, particularly of a summer's evening when crews come ashore. For a drink with locals, fishermen and other yachtsmen go to either The Victoria, known as Bernard's, or The Shipwright. The Island Cruising Club, so called because it is based in that part of the town known as the Island because it once was an island, is a unique establishment run for its members by its members to provide big-boat cruising and day sailing in jointly owned craft. There is a very convivial clubhouse in Island Street where visiting yachtsmen are received as guests. The HQ ship, *Egremont*, an ex-Mersey ferry, is permanently moored in a part of the river known as The Bag where members can stay and sail the fifty dinghies and eight keelboats also owned by the club. The more romantic side of the ICC is its fleet of venerable cruising yachts which take members on voyages along the West Country coast, to the Isles of Scilly, the Channel Isles and the Brittany coast. Cruises are also run to Ushant, Spain, Southern Ireland, Scotland and the Hebrides. Occasionally passages are made in stages to the Baltic, Portugal or Madeira and the biggest boats also compete in the Tall Ships Races. There are very few people today who could afford to own, maintain or find crews for boats of the size and character of those owned by the ICC. The largest is *Hoshi*, a 72ft gaff schooner, a classic gentleman's yacht of the Edwardian era. *Provident*, a 70ft former Brixham sailing trawler built in 1924, is maintained by the Maritime Trust and chartered to the club. She takes a crew of sixteen and, like all fishing boats of her type, is quite capable of weathering Atlantic storms, Channel gales and the Arctic conditions of the Icelandic fishing grounds. *Lucretia*, a 56ft ketch built in Amsterdam in 1927, has elegance and comfort with a fine panelled saloon. *Irina*, built in Scotland in 1935, is a 54ft Bermudan ketch and a good example of a pre-war performance cruising yacht. Membership is open to all, with or without experience.

Moored just upstream of *Egremont* is *Blue Arcadia*, a former dumb barge built in 1911 for carrying ammunition. It is now the floating hostel of Blue Water Sailing, a mixture of sailing school and sailing-holiday organisation. They have berths for sixteen in comfortable cabins, a bar and a restaurant. They hire sailing dinghies by the day or the week, and are open to non-residents. Visiting yachtsmen are welcome aboard to use their bar, showers, drying room, battery-charging service and restaurant where a Cordon Bleu cook provides meals as good as most you will find ashore. This is a useful service for boats moored or anchored in that part of the river and saves a long trip in the tender to Salcombe although they run a ferry service with their own launches. *Blue Arcadia* also provides a 'hide' from which to watch sixteen pairs of herons which nest in a line of trees on the shore about 100 yards off. So if you go on board for a drink take your binoculars with you. You can call *Blue Arcadia* on channel 37(M) or telephone 0548 3605.

The passage up the estuary to Kingsbridge can be made in all but the very largest cruising boats from half flood onwards allowing about two hours to lie alongside the quay by the Crab Shell, a pub that is a mixture of old and new. With a small boat the trip can be started at least half an hour earlier. The channel above Gerston Point, three-quarters of the way there, is very narrow and needs to be followed exactly, but it is well marked with frequent red-and-white-striped port-hand beacons. At low water the channel virtually dries out so if you stay too long at Kingsbridge you will be trapped for at least another 5 hours.

Frogmore Creek or Lake, also well marked with port-hand beacons, is a popular 2½-mile backwater with a channel all the way to Frogmore village and the Globe, a pub with a restaurant. On neaps you can start up at half flood and have a little more than an hour ashore for lunch, but on springs you can start up just before opening time in the evening and, in a tender, you might be able to stay until closing time if you do a bit of rowing. Similar time scales apply to Southpool Lake but because it is only about one-and-a-half miles long, you can get more time at the village and the Mill Pool pub which serves wonderful crab and beef sandwiches and salads. The beef comes from a local farmer at Chillington up the road. Apart from being a very charming old-world pub, even though there is a little too much horse brass in the bar, it has a minute garden at the back where you can sit and watch a family of six white ducks which live in the stream that feeds the creek 50 yards away. They are very partial to potato crisps. There is a bit of a beach about a quarter of a mile before the pub where you can land without having to get your feet wet, but with a little effort it is possible to row an inflatable all the way to the stepping stones which cross the top of the creek and you are then only a minute away from the Mill Pool. If you do that take your wellies because, when you come out, you will probably have to tow your tender over the mud to find enough water to float it. Southpool channel is not marked and is not really suitable for visiting cruising boats, but in a launch or tender you have about four hours of water. If you go up to Southpool on a bright night to visit the pub and come back down again in the dark the sense of adventure is just enough to start the adrenalin running. When you turn the last bend still among tall trees you know that you have made it as you suddenly see the shapes of boats moored in the deep water of the entrance to the creek silhouetted against the bright lights of Salcombe across the estuary.

The head of Frogmore Creek. Clearly you have to work the tides if you wish to visit the Globe in the village, but it can be done

With good timing of the tides and a fair wind the passage from Salcombe to Plymouth can be made in about five-and-a-half hours, but it may take much longer. The most tedious part can be the long drag from the Great Mew Stone to the breakwater and then the final 2 miles across the Sound. If you are making along the coast in either direction and have no desire to put into a city, the River Yealm is as nice a spot to stop as any and shortens the passage. Again it is a ria, but a miniature one with scenery not unlike the Dart. Coming from Salcombe you turn east into Wembury Bay instead of carrying on into the Sound and save yourself up to 2 hours on passage. Entry into the Yealm can be a little scary in strong onshore winds but otherwise, unless you are trying to do it at low water, it is no great problem and many dozens of yachts sail over there from Plymouth during summer weekends. The anchorage is in the pool west of Warren Point. Newton Ferrers rises steeply in tiers of villas and hotels set among the trees and, with a big stretch of the imagination, one might be in Portofino as it was up to the 1950s. You may need to use two anchors to restrict your swing because it is a very small place and usually crowded. The Yealm runs due north past Newton Ferrers Creek and is navigable at high water for about three miles through the steeply sloping Wembury Wood where the trees come right down to the water. Very pretty, but it leads nowhere unless you want to take the ground and walk a couple of miles into Plymstock, a not very attractive suburb

Noss Mayo across the water from Newton Ferrers

of Plymouth. The main arm turns east halfway up and goes into Yealmpton, just before which is Kitley Cave which you can get to in a tender. It is another cave where remains of bear, mammoth and rhino have been found. Nearby lived Old Mother Hubbard about whom the nursery rhyme was written in 1805.

Entrance can be made into Plymouth Sound in even the worst possible conditions provided the western entrance, between the breakwater and the Cornwall shore, is used. With the wind in the west there is a good anchorage in Cawsand Bay without going as far as the breakwater. The twin villages of Cawsand and Kingsand climb up the hill overlooking the bay, and some of the houses are perched on rock actually overhanging the sea. Some years ago I was coming ashore in my inflatable and saw a man open a large window of one of the houses and launch a clinker dinghy by lowering it on a rope down the rock face straight into the water. Although the villages are a bit off the beaten track as far as the motorist is concerned – it takes a good half hour through winding lanes to

reach them from the ferry at Torpoint – they are invaded every summer's day by boatloads of day-trippers from Plymouth. The biggest development in the bay is the Plymouth Sound Boatel, an old house set on a rock by the water which has been converted into two-room, self-catering flatlets with a small restaurant and club bar open to visiting yachtsmen. They have sailing dinghies for hire too. When it is blowing southerly or easterly avoid Cawsand Bay like the plague; the swell is sick-making, and it is impossible to get a boat off the beach without swamping.

Plymouth breakwater, nearly a mile long and 2 miles from the shore, was completed in 1841. It was built by the simple process of quarrying limestone at Oreston near the Cattewater opposite the Barbican, loading it into specially built barges with trap doors in their bottoms, and dumping it in the sea. The Sound, which it protects from southerly gales, encompasses about 1,200 acres in which 1,000 vessels or more could anchor. Originally the insignificant little River Plym was the harbour, and Plymouth town grew up around the mouth of its creek, now known as Sutton Harbour and the Barbican. The streets are narrow and lead to a cobbled quay still used by quite a large fishing fleet. Unfortunately modernised pubs and too much neon and fluorescent lighting have largely spoilt the Tudor atmosphere. It was at the Barbican that the pilgrims embarked on their way to the shrine of St James of Compostella in Spain in the fourteenth and fifteenth centuries. Weymouth, Dartmouth and Exeter were also 'licensed' to handle this pilgrim trade. Francis Drake left from there in 1577 to circumnavigate the world, taking 2 years and 10 months to do it. In 1966/7 Francis Chichester made his single-handed circumnavigation from Plymouth taking a little more than a third of Drake's time in a purpose-built yacht. In 1620 the Pilgrim Fathers finally sailed on the *Mayflower* from the Barbican after a punishing passage from the East Coast; Boston in Lincolnshire was almost certainly the place from which they originally sailed. Plymouth is still the main starting-off point for circum-navigations and Atlantic crossings, and hosts a number of marathon-type sailing events.

I have sailed in and out of Plymouth on a variety of boats and followed the start of many big races but always, when my work was done, I would escape from the yacht club and racing scene, from the city and its teeming holidaymakers, to seek the peace and emptiness of the Tamar river. It is a great river which rises far to the north near Bude on the Atlantic coast and forms the boundary between Devon and Cornwall, almost succeeding in making the latter an island. It is navigable, but only just, for almost twenty miles. To cruise the Tamar and its tributaries and lakes, as the creeks are called, explore the furthest shallows in a dinghy, and see all there is to see on the Devon and Cornwall shores could

In Plymouth Sound, when the wind is in the west, Cawsand is a pleasant anchorage without going in as far as the breakwater

A good small-boat picnic spot in Plymouth Sound

profitably occupy a week. The first anchorage is just past the Cremyll Ferry landing point round the corner above the Edgcumbe Arms Hotel. You are then off the Cornwall shore, but in full view of Mount Wise and Stonehouse in Plymouth. It is a sheltered spot from all but a north-westerly, when you will get a bit wet rowing to and from the shore. Mashford's nearby, a family boatyard of several generations, may look a little old fashioned but it has a superb reputation. Most trans-Atlantic and round-the-world sailors have been to Mashford's at one time or another for a major or last-minute job to be done. If you like to talk about traditional boats and boat building find a Mashford's shipwright and buy him a pint. It is a short walk up from the ferry to Mount Edgcumbe Country Park at the eastern end of the South Cornwall Coast Path. The sixteenth-century house was burnt out during the last war, but has been largely restored and is open to the public, as are the grounds with their English, French and Italian gardens and deer park. From the wooded slopes of the park you get a fine view of the Sound on one side and Millbrook Lake on the other. From Cremyll you can explore the lake, but you need to go up on a rising tide and come back soon after the ebb starts. At Foss Point on the north side of Millbrook Lake there is an old stone quay once used by a long-since demolished brickyard. It is now the 'harbour' for a large colony of multihulls which have adopted the lake as their home. They are the only craft that can happily tolerate sitting on the mud for more than 12 hours in every 24. Their home is a quiet place with woods on the south slopes out of which deer sometimes emerge in the early morning and evening. They are within walking distance of Millbrook at the head of the creek for shopping and, when the tide comes in, they are only 15 minutes from Plymouth by outboard or a ½-hour's sail to the breakwater and the open sea. Immediately above Millbrook Lake is the much bigger St John's Lake which also dries out all over. If you go to the head of this lake you come to the pretty village of St John beside a stream in a hollow. Old cottages hide behind high hedges through which can be glimpsed some lovely little gardens. This is orchard country, and in the spring the lanes are carpeted with fallen apple blossom. The north bank of the lake is the built-up area of Torpoint and its adjacent naval barracks.

Going up through the Hamoaze past Devonport, the once-great naval dockyard now looks rather run down. The St Germans or Lynher river which strikes inland to the west above Torpoint is navigable with the tide up to St Germans Quay. Church fanciers will find enough to occupy them, until the tide starts to ebb, in the Norman church which stands on the site of the cathedral of Cornwall in Saxon times. At the entrance to the river on the south bank is Antony House, one of the great houses of Cornwall now owned by the National Trust. It is built of silver-grey Pentewan stone shipped by water from near Mevagissey. Sixty-three acres of parkland lead down to the water where there is a jetty. On wild ground near the river is the Bath Pond House, built about 1790, which consists of a bath partly roofed over in the manner of a Roman atrium. It is filled with salt water from the river through a sluice. Opposite Antony House on the other side of the river is Antony Passage, a ½-mile creek leading to St Stephens which is a small village on a hill at the backdoor of Saltash. Trematon Castle, now a roofless Norman keep and gate tower thickly covered in ivy, is a few minutes' walk from the water. A 200-year-old house built inside the remnants of the walls is surrounded by terraced lawns and flower gardens. The castle gate house at the end of the gardens has a portcullis and a dungeon. From the gallery at the top of the keep you get marvellous views of the river and surrounding countryside. Altogether well worth walking to.

After passing under the rail and road bridges at Saltash – which was a borough before Plymouth was thought of – the Tamar widens where it is joined by its tributary, the Tavy, coming down through forest gorges from its source below Fur Tor on Dartmoor. There is a winding channel, navigable after half flood, up almost as far as Lopwell Dam from where it is about a half-hour's walk through the woods to Milton Combe and the Who'd Have Thought It, a pub with the character to go with its name in a hideaway village squeezed between the close-set contour lines around it. The entrance to the Tavy is spanned by high-tension cables (36ft clearance) and a railway bridge, but is navigable on the flood by dinghies and low-masted shallow-draught boats. Most people cruising up the

Tamar go no further than Cargreen on the west bank a mile above the entrance to the Tavy. Here there is over 12ft of water, but beyond the channel narrows, is unmarked and needs local knowledge to find the way between the mud shoals. The Spaniards Inn at Cargreen has done much to encourage yachtsmen, having built a pontoon and laid visitors' moorings. It is a much tidied-up old-world pub which offers food and showers and the great convenience of an overnight deep-water mooring. Cargreen used to be a ferry point, but today the village street ends abruptly at a quay with stone bollards. A mile south of the village is Landulph Church, unremarkable from the outside but inside is a tablet recording the death of Therodoro Palaeologus, 'descended from ye imperial line of ye last Christian Emperor of Greece'. The last known descendant of the Byzantine emperors, he died in the parish in 1636.

Although quite large boats do make it up as far as Calstock, and at one time trading schooners went even further to Morwellham below Gunnislake, the river here on is very silted and the stranger would do better to explore by dinghy or tender, or play really safe and take the 5-hour cruise on the river boat from Phoenix Wharf, Plymouth. These tripper boats have bars and buffets and, when the tide is right, go to the uttermost limit of navigation – Weir Head on the outskirts of Gunnislake. After 2 more miles the river, becoming very narrow, takes a loop back on itself round marshes on the Devon side and overhanging woods on the Cornwall side to Halton Quay which still has a rusting hand crane

The River Tamar at Morwellham is not generally considered navigable but even in a sea-going boat it is possible to make this wooded reach at the top of the tide

The Devon Great Consols dock at Morwellham on the River Tamar was once capable of accommodating ships of 300 tons

but is quite unused. In the last century it served sailing barges loading copper ore and arsenic. Cotehele Quay below Cotehele Woods is of much more interest and has been taken over by the National Trust. The restored sailing barge *Shamrock* lies against the quay whose mellow stone warehouses now house a maritime museum. A short walk up the valley leads to the manorial water mill which has been put back in working order. Cotehele House, built between 1486 and 1539 in grey granite, is a perfect example of an early Tudor manor house. It is open to the public and contains some original furniture, armour and tapestries and is surrounded by a garden on several layers overlooking the river. From the quay a woodland walk along the river bank takes you to Calstock which has a station on the panoramic Plymouth to Gunnislake line. Calstock has long been famous for its Boot Inn and its food, for which you are advised to book a table weeks rather than days in advance. The ownership changed a year or two ago, but when I was there early in 1982 there was no chance of a casual table and the menu looked as good as ever. Although there is water to float a boat for half a tide at Calstock, the problem is getting ashore and back on board. After about half ebb a barrier of deep glutinous mud cuts off all access to and from the shore. The truly adventurous might risk getting stuck in the mud and go up on a spring flood to Morwellham Quay, 2 miles below Gunnislake on the Devon bank, from which the richest copper lode in Europe mined at Wheal Friendship (Mary Tavy) and Devon Great Consols was shipped off in Tamar barges in the eighteenth and nineteenth centuries. The place is now a tourist enterprise run by the Dartington Hall Trust, a charitable venture. The partially restored remains can be seen of the inclined railway planes, docks, quays, waterwheels and lime kilns, and the vestiges of the Tavistock Canal which started 200ft above the port. A tramway takes visitors underground into the disused George and Charlotte copper mine which was last worked in 1868. The complex includes a port museum and nineteenth-century-life museum together with the mandatory picnic sites, adventure playground and souvenir shop. It would, of course, be impossible to digest all this before the water ran out from under your boat, even an inflatable.

For cruising people the next comfortable port of call after Plymouth is Fowey. Looe and Polperro both dry out and tend to be very crowded in the summer season and although you can drop anchor in the outside harbour at Mevagissey (west of Fowey) it too is jam-packed in the summer. Fowey, however, is a splendid deep-water anchorage at the mouth of an extremely beautiful river and well sheltered in all but the worst of south-westerly gales. Local yachtsmen say it is best to enter midway between St Catherine's Point and Punch Rocks; once clear of the entrance keep over to the Polruan side and you are well placed for the harbour. This is a commercial port as well as a yachting centre, exporting china clay in vessels of up to 10,000 tons, but the clay jetties are tucked away beyond the town, strung along the west bank of the river northwards from Caffamill Pill. The Royal Fowey Yacht Club has visitors' moorings on the east side; they are, however, in almost constant demand and you will probably have to anchor there or pick up a vacant mooring.

It is possible to moor a dinghy at the jetty beneath the RFYC and climb up to the clubhouse where you can be sure of a welcome, a shower and a good plain meal at moderate prices. Alternatively, tie up your dinghy at either the Town Quay or Albert Quay (next to the Custom House with its brightly painted royal coat of arms) and explore the town from there. It is a real delight, with the older part squashed in at the bottom of a hill and wrapped around a long and twisting narrow main street that wanders along parallel to the river, intersected here and there by even narrower streets and alleys.

There is a wide choice of restaurants and pubs in the town. The Cordon Bleu on the Esplanade provides *haute cuisine* but it is, inevitably, expensive; Stanton's, likewise on the Esplanade, and Food For Thought on the Town Quay also have excellent kitchens. Further up the river, on the east side at Bodinnick Ferry, The Old Ferry Inn was in the *Good Food Guide* years ago and still maintains high standards. As for pubs, the Ship Inn in Trafalgar Square, the Safe Harbour in Lostwithiel Street and the Lugger in Fore Street are all popular with locals and have good atmospheres. If you are in a St Austell house and want something a little stronger than the palatable Tinners draught try a pint or two of HSD bitter. This officially stands for Hicks Special Draught but is colloquially known as 'High Speed Death'; as a local warned me, 'It's lovely beer but mind your oars.'

There are two chandlers in Fowey, the Troy Chandlery in Lostwithiel Street

and the Upper Deck Marine Centre in Passage Street but, rather surprisingly, more major marine facilities are only available at Polruan, the lovely village on the other side of the harbour. A to-and-fro passenger ferry operates between Whitehouse Quay, just down from the Esplanade, and the Town Quay in Polruan, where you can moor a dinghy at any state of the tide. The Winklepicker (open seven days a week, May–September), on the quay, is an essential shop since it supplies diesel fuel – as far as I can ascertain the only source in the harbour – and water as well as marine paints, fishing tackle and so on. Just upriver from the quay is Toms Yard, belonging to C. Toms & Son Ltd, and they will carry out any repairs and are able to slip a 60ft boat. There is also a good basic fisherman's chandlery on the premises. The lower part of Fore Street boasts a small supermarket and off-licence, a butcher's shop, a post office, a greengrocery and a bakery, while back on the quay the Lugger Inn is snug and hospitable.

Polruan is attractive in its own right, accessible only by water or a minor road, but it is also a particularly good place from which to explore the neighbouring cliffs and countryside, much of it in National Trust hands and consequently unspoiled. A marvellous way to see Fowey and the river from the surrounding wooded slopes is to take the Hall Walk from Polruan to Bodinnick and thence by ferry to Fowey. The path climbs up out of Polruan and follows the south shore of Pont Pill to the head of the creek where the National Trust has restored quays once visited by sailing coasters. Before continuing any further it is worth making a diversion up to the beautiful and isolated Lanteglos Church, the centre for this scattered rural parish. Hall Walk continues high along the north side of Pont Pill and then swings round to follow the main river to Bodinnick. At Penleath Point is a granite memorial to Sir Arthur Quiller-Couch ('Q'), the now-neglected writer who celebrated Fowey in his Troy Town novels.

The river is tidal as far as Lostwithiel and a visit to Fowey should not pass without at least one dinghy trip to enjoy the beauty of the upper reaches. It is obviously best to go up and return with the tide; when the water is low hazards to look out for are the large sandbank opposite Golant – where there is a jetty and the Cormorant Restaurant, mentioned in Egon Ronay – and the mudbank just below St Winnow Church. Lerryn Creek is particularly lovely, with the deeper water under the steeper bank. Lerryn itself is another tiny village that schooners used to trade to, bringing coal and lime in return for local produce. There is a good riverside walk from Lerryn to St Winnow, passing through Ethy Wood.

The ten rivers and creeks which wiggle inland from Falmouth Harbour and the Carrick Roads look deceptively wide and blue on the Ordnance Survey map – an essential 'chart' if you are at all interested in what you see on land and have any

Noah's Ark, part of it dating from before 1500, is believed to be the oldest house in Fowey. There is now a shop and folk museum on the premises (*Harry & Billie Graeme*)

intention of making selective expeditions ashore, and that goes for all inland
cruising by big or small boats. Admiralty Chart No 23 is more revealing; even so
I thought that in one Bank Holiday weekend, using a Westerly Griffin as a base
boat and a small inflatable for going up creeks, I could cover most of the area. In
the event time spent ashore meeting interesting people, extreme spring tides and
very high pressure made a nonsense of my ambitions and I only covered about a
quarter of the area. Far more time was spent waiting for mud to cover than had
been estimated from the tide tables. That frustration is freshest in my memory for
it was the last exploration I made, but the same can apply when planning any
sojourn in tidal estuaries and rivers, particularly at times of high pressure and
after a long dry spell.

My first call was at Mylor Yacht Harbour whose large floating pontoon is a
boon for those with gear to load and wanting to land in good clothes in the
evening. Their swinging moorings are but a short row from the pontoon or the
slip. They do everything except build boats, and of great value to 'touring'
yachtsmen is their trailer-sailer park with the use of the slipway. A chandlery,
brokerage office, electronics firm and clothing shop, 24-hour public loos and
shower, yacht chartering, a sailing school, restaurant, and a number of holiday
flatlets all located in a compact group of stone buildings by the quay, make Mylor
an eminently practical place on which to base a holiday on the Fal and Truro
rivers. From 1806 until the 1930s Mylor was the smallest naval dockyard in
Britain, and was the berth of the training ship HMS *Ganges* from 1866 to 1899
when she moved to Shotley opposite Harwich harbour. The naval living quarters
with their stowage arches below now make nice little two-room flatlets much

(*Opposite*) The ancient graveyard at Mylor beside Carrick Roads. The moorings and pontoons are Mylor Yacht Harbour; (*above*) there is nothing new about graffiti: a stone on the outside wall of St Mylor's Church

The granite cross at St Mylor's Church is thought to be pre-Christian with Christian markings added later

Devenish
VICTORY
INN
1792
VICTORY
Devenish
Devenish
Devenish
SANDWICHES
PLOUGHMANS
LUNCHES
HOT PASTIES
COFFEE
VICTORY
INN
RESIDENTIAL
HOT SNACKS
Devenish
FOOD
AND
NO
PARKING
OUTSIDE
THIS DOOR

patronised by dinghy-sailing families. The Ganges Restaurant on the quay, formerly the small naval hospital or sick bay, specialises in fish, most of which comes from Newlyn although their Dover sole comes from Flushing round the corner. The graveyard of the parish church of St Mylor which comes right down to the quayside provides a peaceful retreat along flower-bordered paths which wander among ancient tombstones under the spreading branches of old trees. The Holy Well of St Mylor burbles away in one corner, and the detached bell tower houses a tiny parish shop where home-made jams and such like can be bought on the honour basis – you put the money in a box. The church itself is full of interest for those with an historical and architectural bent, much of it Norman with other parts thirteenth and fifteenth century. Most impressive is the massive 17ft 6in granite cross of St Mylor. It is thought to be far older than the church, even perhaps pre-Christian with the Christian markings added later. It stands 10ft 6in high beside the south porch, 7ft of it being in the ground. St Mylor was the local Celtic saint, and his church goes back 1,500 years to when he sailed from Brittany to the Carrick Roads about AD 411 and built a simple wattle church and a wooden monastery on the site of the existing building.

There are no village shops by the quay, but it is a pleasant walk of just over half a mile along the creek to Mylor Bridge where most supplies can be had. Or you can take your boat up there 1 hour either side of high water and, either way, a visit should be made to Terry Heard's yard on the south shore near the head of the creek. He trades as Gaffers & Luggers, which title describes precisely what he builds. He took over the site in 1960 when it was a broken-down farm with hayricks on the foreshore. Tregatreath, the official name of his place, means 'dwelling by the shore' in Cornish. His forte is the Falmouth Oyster Dredger (or Work Boat as they are simply called locally), in both 28ft and 23ft lengths. Every Saturday during the season these gaff cutters with their 14ft bowsprits and jack-yard topsails set can be seen racing in Carrick Roads and after Falmouth Week, which follows Cowes, they passage race to Fowey for their 'Week'. For oyster dredging, which takes place in the winter only, tackles are used; but for racing or cruising there are two winches – the one to leeward for the staysail and the other to windward for the backstay. The nearest they get to series production at the Tregatreath yard is their 18ft 6in Tosher, the original mould of which was taken off a craft over 100 years old which was used for sailing to the pollack and bass grounds off the Manacle Rocks.

St Mawes on the other side of Carrick Roads is supposed to be a delightful anchorage and very sheltered up the Percuil river behind the town, but the place does not appeal to me. The village is almost totally tourist-orientated, although it does have some delightful corners if you wander around early in the morning before visitors are abroad. In the Victory Inn there is a collection of eighteenth-

St Mawes may be a typical Cornish tourist resort but when the local regatta takes place during Falmouth Week the town goes *en fête*

**There** are several good walks from St Mawes, including one about a mile along the coastal path to St Mawes Castle (dating from 1542) and then on to St Just Church

century prints of the area, and photographs of the Work Boats and local regattas going back to the early part of this century. They are well worth looking at, but otherwise the place no longer has any Cornish character – even the stonework is printed wallpaper now. The harbour dries, but there is plenty of water for mooring or anchoring within rowing distance of the beach and there are several good walks starting from St Mawes. The most obvious one is about a mile along the coastal path to St Mawes Castle (dating from 1542) and then on to St Just Church, a further 2 miles. As this follows the coastline of the Carrick Roads it is particularly interesting on days when yachts and Work Boats are racing.

At low tide the water coming out of Restronguet Creek on the west side of Carrick Roads above Mylor is a deep rich rust colour, a very visible sign that stream washings and spillage of tin, copper and arsenic from the mines up the Carnon Valley have, over the centuries, made it the most heavily heavy-metal polluted water in Great Britain. Waste deposits from mine workings further inland have silted up the creek so that it is no longer easily navigated beyond the Pandora Inn. Although the village of Devoran at the head of the creek can be reached during the 2 hours either side of high water by small cruisers, it needs a spring tide before the average 30ft or bigger boat can get there and then only during 1 hour either side of high water, with the result that few cruising yachts venture up it. However, there is high water twice a day on springs – you can go up in the morning and back in the evening. For anybody with the slightest curiosity about industrial archaeology it is an exciting creek to explore by tender with a small outboard when, with care, you would have nearly five hours of usable water under you in the channels. The Pandora Inn just inside the creek was so named by Captain Edwards who was commissioned to bring back the *Bounty* mutineers to face justice. His ship foundered on the Great Barrier Reef, he was dismissed the service and retired to Cornwall where he bought the inn which he renamed after his last command. Parts of the building go back to the thirteenth century, most of it is fifteenth century and not at all spoilt. The cold buffet lunches and restaurant dinners are really excellent. The very convenient and almost absurdly large floating pontoon at the end of the pub pier was designed to provide space for tables and chairs for pub customers, but the idea was vetoed by the planning authority. On the opposite shore at the end of a north-pointing arm of the creek is Penpol Boat Yard, a traditional lay-up yard established just after the last war, where they build the Penpol 27, a long-keel family cruiser of traditional design with five berths and standing headroom. The yard can be reached by boats drawing 2ft at neaps and up to 5ft 6in at springs, and they can slip boats up to 40ft length. Moorings off the yard dry for about two hours. Going upstream from Penpol opposite Point there are two withies guarding a pile of stones which are almost covered at high water. They are the

The Pandora Inn, Restronguet, was so named by Captain Edwards whose ship of that name foundered when he was on his way to bring back the *Bounty* mutineers. He was dismissed the service, retired to Cornwall and bought this inn

remains of an island formed by a spoil dump of a tin mine which was worked under the river. The shaft was at Point, and further up on the north bank at Chycoose the remains of an engine house can be seen on a beach where a collection of local boats are drawn up. The mine operated from 1822 to 1871, but the owners were greedy and when they dug too near the surface to get at the rich alluvial tin, gases from the mud entered the mine. It was the only tin mine to be gassed. A single withy marks a pile of stones, covered 2ft at high water, which are the remains of a ventilation shaft for the mine.

At this point the creek divides into two arms or rivers. The north one leads to the old docks and railway sidings at Devoran although it takes a keen eye to recognise them as such if you are unaware of the industrial history of the place. From 1820 up until World War I this now-sleepy backwater was a busy trading port with schooners bringing in coal from Wales for the mine engines and taking away tin. Up until 1850, when a steam railway was built from Chacewater to Devoran, transport to and from the mines was by pack horse. All but one of the docks have long since been filled in and now form the gardens of the creekside houses, but all along the water's edge are stone pillars, some still erect, which were the bollards; and the ruined walls of railway sidings and sheds now provide shelter for people working on their boats. One dock has been renovated and is the miniature yacht basin of LBC Flotilla Holidays who have a large fleet of boats which cruise the Devon and Cornwall coasts in company. The southern arm, the Kennall river, is very narrow but can be navigated for a further 2 miles in a rowing boat at low water or in a launch at high water – but in nothing longer than 20ft because it would be impossible to turn round at the end of the navigation at Perran Wharf. This rust-coloured little river meanders through saltings and water meadows and then into woods where it suddenly becomes a stream. It stretches the imagination to believe that this waterlogged rural scene was, in the last century, an industrial complex with foundries, mill shops, forges and other engineering works all worked by water power, supplied by a network of tailraces connected to the Kennall river off which were docks and timber ponds.

The main tourist site on the Fal river is Trelissick House on the left bank at the top of the Carrick Roads. The orthodox way to visit this National Trust property from the water is to anchor below King Harry Ferry, walk up the road and enter the grounds the same way as the cars and coaches do. But you can anchor in Channels Creek immediately south of Trelissick House and go ashore on the beach in the tender. It costs £1 to go round the gardens unless you are a member of the National Trust and, according to the staff, it takes 2 hours to do it properly, which I can believe. The trees were laid out between 1790 and 1832, and the older exotics were planted between 1844 and 1913. Much of the present garden was started in 1937 when it was largely a shrubbery of rhododendron, laurel and other shade-bearing shrubs. Since then many species have come from North Africa, the Far East, South America, South Africa, Australia and New

You can anchor below Trelissick House in Channels Creek and visit the gardens of this National Trust property

Zealand. The signposted paths lead to several high viewpoints of the Carrick Roads and the Fal. Plants can be bought in the garden shop and there is a restaurant. The Georgian porticoed house itself is not open to the public. Around the periphery of the farm and parkland is a woodland walk of about four miles which, for the most part, is also a waterside walk along the south bank of Lamouth Creek, the Fal shore past King Harry Passage and round Channels Creek. A very popular stopping place is Smuggler's Cottage on the right bank in the narrows above King Harry Ferry. The cottage is in part 500 years old and until 1832 was a pub serving a ferry, after which it became a private dwelling. But for the last 120 years it has served cream teas to pleasure-steamer passengers. It now has a licence and serves lunches, cream teas and suppers, with barbecues on the beach on fine summer evenings. It is not a pub so it is no good stopping there just for a drink, but if it is a meal you want there is always a minimum of 6ft of water off the end of its floating jetty and 60ft of water midstream. In times of recession in the shipping industry the otherwise beautiful view is blanked out by the towering hulls of merchant ships laid up in the river. There were nine of them moored from below King Harry Ferry to above Tolverne in the summer of 1982. Although the cottage has a good road to it (built by the Americans during the last war when the foreshore was concreted over to provide a launch site for D-Day landing craft), it relies on a well for water. In mid-summer there is barely sufficient for their catering needs, and any yachtsman taking a can ashore for water is liable to get a polite refusal. They have ten red-buoyed moorings available for overnight stops. Just beyond the cottage the Fal bends sharply east past a string of wartime concrete barges and enters Ruan Creek which is supposedly navigable at high water for boats drawing up to 3ft as far as Ruan L'anihorne. I had no time to wait for water in the creek, but I am told that it is very beautiful with heavily wooded banks and extensive mud flats which are the

There is always 6ft of water at the end of the floating jetty below Smuggler's Cottage if you want a meal there

haunt of hundreds of waders. There is still an old quay at Ruan L'anihorne, a reminder of the days in the last century when ships sailed up these creeks. If you take a small boat up Ruan Creek you can have Cornish pasties and beer in the garden of the King's Head under the watchful eye of a peacock. From the entrance to Ruan Creek the river, which carries the deep-water channel up to Malpas and then on to Truro, is called Truro river.

Malpas, where the Tresillian joins the Truro, is the highest point in the river where you can remain afloat at all states of the tide and there is landing at a slipway beside the private floating jetty used by pleasure boats. The problem with the slipway is that it dries a long way out. The local pub is the Heron which caters for the pleasure-boat passengers who stop there when there is no water up to Truro. It is the only pub in the area which serves lunches and suppers 7 days a week. At the west end of the village an old coal barge on the beach is the workshop of Malpas Boatyard and Engineering run by Bernard Yendall who specialises in traditional wooden repair work. It seems a strange place for a yard with the only access to the beach a steep path from the road above, but large fishing boats were built there for many generations in the past. Bernard Yendall and his wife live in a smart two-storey wooden house above the yard, a distinctive and very different landmark from the coal barge on the beach. The house was originally built several hundred yards nearer the village as the office of what was a coal wharf. In 1940 it was trundled round the corner on rollers drawn by horses to its present site. At the other end of the village just up the Tresillian river is Bar Creek Yacht Station which combines building a variety of boats, mostly in wood, with running a group of holiday flats, hiring out rowing boats and yacht chartering. The Yacht Station has a half-tide floating jetty and deep-water moorings in the river which are available on a nightly basis and are popular with French and German yachts. The river is navigable at the top of the tide for 2½ miles to the bridge at Tresillian, but there is an awful lot of mud and it is a question of going up no sooner than 90 minutes before high water, staying no more than half an hour and then coming straight back. The channel is not marked, and it takes a lot of concentration or luck to make it there and back without going aground, as many boats do every year. At high water it is possible to navigate the narrow buoyed channel into the heart of the cathedral city of Truro and lie against the quay, but it would have to be a brief visit to get back down the channel on the same tide. At low water you can wade down it. If you go up in your tender you can stay for just over an hour either side of high water.

No visit to Falmouth Bay would be complete without sailing up the Helford River, that beautiful inlet from the sea that runs westwards a good five miles inland. The first anchorage is Durgan on the north side which is exposed to

Out-of-work big ships lining the deep channel of the River Fal

The anchorage at Durgan on the Helford; the surrounding land is owned by the National Trust

south-easterly winds which can bring in a big swell, but you can anchor in deep water and make an easy landing on a hard beach. There is a footpath eastwards above the cliff to Mawnan Smith church with a magnificent view across the Channel from its peaceful graveyard right on the edge of the cliff. Alternatively, take a path in the other direction to Glendurgan, a small National Trust house with a fine garden which includes a miniature maze. No facilities.

The usual anchorage is further up the river, off Helford Village in 5–14m between mud banks, but you can normally make a dry landing at all tides. There is a good general store with a wide variety of foods and a post office. The shop keeps open surprisingly long hours to accommodate yachtsmen and the Shipwright's Arms provides good bar meals and a sophisticated variety of drinks. The Helford Sailing Club is on the left as you row up the little drying creek to the village. It has a fine clubhouse with showers and a bar, and good plain food. In the village the Riverside restaurant cooks top-class meals at matching prices, but it is open in the season only. At Helford Passage, on the other side of the river, the Ferry Boat Inn has good beer and bar snacks.

Just past Helford Village, Porth Navas Creek on the north side is a pretty, quiet anchorage but room is very limited and you must choose your spot carefully and not too far up because it becomes very shallow soon after high water. You can reach the quay by dinghy at least three hours either side of high water and there is another good general store ten-minutes' walk away. The headquarters of the Duchy of Cornwall Oyster Farm is at Porth Navas and anchoring above Helford Village must be done with care for it is prohibited over the oyster beds which extend from the creek to the junction of the river where it divides into two channels towards Constantine and Gweek.

Daphne du Maurier has made Frenchman's Creek so famous it is wellnigh obligatory to poke your nose up it at high tide. It turns south one mile up from Helford Village. Working the tides you can, with care, continue up to Gweek but, to be free of anxiety, you are well advised to make that part of the trip by tender. The experience is well worth the effort. The banks are densely wooded mostly with stunted oak and there are useful granite quays said to have been specially built for Queen Victoria's convenience when she visited Helford in the royal yacht. Be circumspect about landing though for all the land is private, albeit wild! At Gweek itself there is a substantial boatyard which can handle most repairs and the seal sanctuary with its large pools of seals which have been, or are being, given medical care are a tourist attraction but children will not mind that.

I have kept to the last my visit to St Just on the east side of Carrick Roads opposite Mylor Creek. I know it is one of those beauty spots endowed with entries in all the guide books and probably known to every holidaymaker who has stayed in the area. But it is still a jewel, and going by the back door of the sea you have the advantage over those who must find their way there through narrow lanes choked with slow-moving cars and coaches. And you see it all the better

The Helford River: Polgwidden Cove is a pleasant, easy landing place but Durgan, left of centre in the distance, is a better anchorage if you do not wish to go up to Helford Village

'I would like to know if there is in the whole of England a churchyard more beautiful than this' –
H. V. Morton on St Just-in-Roseland

from the water. I anchored in the entrance to the creek and went ashore on the beach alongside Pasco & Son's yard. From there it is a 5-minute walk up a hill to the lychgate of St Just-in-Roseland Church, from which you look down on the tower of this old church set in a hollow among trees on the water's edge. I cannot improve on what H. V. Morton wrote in 1920: 'I would like to know if there is in the whole of England a churchyard more beautiful than this.' It is, as he said, a Garden of Eden, a green amphitheatre of trees, flowers and tombstones with hardly a level yard anywhere. The church dates back to AD 550, but the present building was dedicated in 1261. There is a legend that Joseph of Arimathea was a tin merchant and brought the boy Jesus with him to St Just. Many people believe that it could have happened. I have also often been told by locals that Joseph planted a tree which still grows in the churchyard. But on my visit I talked with one of the church wardens who roundly dismissed that as a complete myth. Among the shrubs around the church are strawberry trees, Chilean myrtle, bamboos, rhododendrons, azaleas, magnolias, camellias, fan palms and many, many others. Even those who are not normally given to visiting churches when they go ashore should try to visit this place, or at least go up the creek on a summer's evening on a spring tide when the low sun bathes the church and its garden in a warm glow with the scene faithfully reflected in the still water of the pool.

# Index

*Italic numbers refer to illustrations*